THE STOIC, THE WEAL & THE MALCONTENT
Malcontentedness on the Elizabethan
& Jacobean Stage

The Stoic, the Weal
& the Malcontent

*Malcontentedness
on the Elizabethan &
Jacobean Stage*

Julia Lacey Brooke

RICHMOND · TIGER OF THE STRIPE

First published in 2013 by
Tiger of the Stripe
50 Albert Road
Richmond
Surrey TW10 6DP
United Kingdom

ISBN 978-1-904799-59-7

Typeset in the UK by
Tiger of the Stripe

FOR ALEXANDER TETTENBORN

to 'Nigel' from 'Aunt Beryl' with love

CONTENTS

ACKNOWLEDGEMENTS

I owe some considerable debts of gratitude for this book. Many of these are somewhat historic and long overdue: this book began life as a post-graduate thesis in the middle-and-off 90s, and to Dr Martin Wiggins and to fellow members and contributors of the Renaissance Drama Research Group c 1995–7 I remain immensely grateful for much support and many seeds of inspiration. I cannot thank Dr Wiggins adequately for his continued help. *British Drama, 1533–1642: A Catalogue* is now a unique, on-going resource running into several volumes and invaluable. In 1995–8, Kate Welch and the Library staff at the Shakespeare Institute in Stratford-upon-Avon bore with my silly technical questions with friendly forbearance, as did Sue Cousins and her colleagues at Chippenham College library. I also thank, with many fond memories, those students of my own who bore with me so patiently and with enthusiasm as I ran ideas by them and who helped me more than they know. To my dear friend Barbara Lloyd-Evans I am forever indebted for her Latin translations and for her unstinting kind hospitality.

More historic still is the debt I owe to two truly great and remarkable teachers: Professor Robert Ashton, whose brilliance and sheer energy – which amounted to a kind of genius – has informed not only this book and my sense of Jacobean moral politics, but all my classroom teaching ever after. The other is the late and much missed Professor Nicholas Brooke, to whom I owe an even greater debt, for his unswervingly honest encouragement of my writing, and the almost constant dialogue we exchanged during a remarkable marriage 'of true minds', minds which revelled in laughter of the horrid, Jacobean kind. This book could never have existed without his inspiration and guidance.

But this book almost never existed as such at all. Buried and almost forgotten on an antiquated floppy disk and shoved to languish at the back of a drawer through many moves including my last to Italy twelve years ago, I have plundered its substance for lectures but scarcely given it a thought qua book for many years, the last few of which have been dedicated almost entirely to fiction. Now it remains for me to thank Peter Danckwerts of Tiger of the Stripe, a publisher of rare sympathy and learning who, during a long conversation concerned mostly with fiction, urged me to send the text of *The Stoic, The Weal & The Malcontent* for his consideration. I dug it out finally, after a long search, and panicked – and thus more thanks are due indeed to Giulio and Mario, the young techno-experts here in Tuscany who rescued the floppy disk and enabled me to work on the text. I sent it to Peter. Here it is...

JLB
Wiltshire, London, Siracusa and Arezzo

FOREWORD

This study was prompted about twenty-five years ago by John Marston's *The Malcontent,* a satirical comedy-drama (first performed in c. 1603 and entered onto the Stationers' Register 1604) which I was obliged to teach, at very short notice, to a group of A Level college students who were a third of the way through the play. They, and I, needed to find an explanation of Marston's 'joke': Who was this 'Malcontent' figure whom Marston had turned into a comic hero, in a play full of in-jokes about other plays? Satire is notoriously contemporary: jokes, lampoons and parodies have a very short shelf-life. I needed to know about the first idea in order to explain the second.

Although the English Renaissance drama had been an undergraduate passion, my head filled with such unanswerable questions as 'How mad is Hamlet?' and the persuasive conundrum of Iago's 'motiveless motivations of malignity', I realised that I knew next to nothing about Malcontents as such. Marston had apparently taken what was evidently a 'stock' figure, of sorts, from popular tragedy – think Iago, *King Lear's* Edmund, Vindice from *The Revenger's Tragedy,* among many others: cynical, devious, disruptive and essentially secondary characters in plays where flawed heroes famously die along with almost everybody else, heaped up on the stage at the end of Act Five. Marston's eponymous 'Malcontent' is the hero of a play he styled 'tragicomedy' – a play in which *nobody* dies – and all ends well. A familiar genre was being sent up

I began trawling the libraries for references to Malcontents. There were, dismayingly, very few. I found vast resources in respect of villains, a great many references to 'melancholy' – a state of mind associated with what we would probably now call anti-social maladjustment; to Machiavelli, and the Machiavel figure on the English Renaissance stage. Of 'Malcontents' specifically, there was very little. I was also intrigued by Marston's hero's continual attacks on Stoicism, and in particular his impertinent tilts aimed at the great Roman tragedian and Stoic philosopher Seneca. Perhaps there were other plays which did the same? There are; and I had embarked on a series of discoveries.

Perhaps many studies begin like this: I ended by attempting to write the book I couldn't find.

INTRODUCTION: WHAT IS A
MALCONTENT?

i

This study has primarily to do with the theatre: with the plays
written and presented on the public and private stage in England roughly between 1580 and 1625. This was an especially fer-
tile period for playwrights – one of those periods in history in
which a particular art form, experimental, revolutionary even,
makes its permanent mark.

Contemporary literature records the 'Malcontent' as a familiar social phenomenon from the late 1500s on, a figure that became a legend in his own time. The dramatist Robert Greene
and such luminaries as Thomas Nashe, Joseph Hall, Sir Thomas Overbury, Robert Burton, and Francis Bacon all describe an
over-educated (usually) young man, deeply discontented with
his lot, who seems to have been fictionalised on the stage almost at once, partly as a result of their observations. However,
surprisingly few modern commentators have concerned themselves with a discussion of the Malcontent figure in the classic
drama of the late sixteenth and early seventeenth centuries. This
is despite the obvious presence of such a figure in many plays
and, perhaps more surprisingly still, the fact that a 'Malcontent'
is the eponymous character of what has long been regarded as
a pivotal play of the era. The very word 'malcontent', when it
does not refer directly to Marston's play, is notably absent from
indexes, whereas 'melancholy' – a related condition – of course
frequently does, as do a great many references to Machiavelli
and 'Machiavels'. This in itself is not especially odd, since melancholy was once a term frequently applied to explain a state of
maladjustment, and the most famous work of Machiavelli had

[1]

been translated into English and captured the imagination of a small but significant reading public.

Material concerning Malcontents is remarkably scarce. E. E. Stoll's paper 'Shakspere, Marston and the Malcontent Type' which appeared in *Modern Philology* in 1906 is, disappointingly, less an exploration of 'the malcontent type' than an argument for the dramatic and historical relationship between Jaques, Malevole and Hamlet (each of whom Stoll defines emphatically as 'Malcontents') predicated on now largely discredited assumptions concerning the dating of *The Malcontent* and the authorship (by Thomas Kyd, he suggests, although this is uncertain) of the so-called 'Ur-Hamlet'.[1] Other commentators were more helpful; there is Theodore Spencer's essay, 'The Elizabethan Malcontent' (1948), which provides a persuasive discussion of melancholy and its characterization on the stage, arguing that the presence of such figures, and such a mood, is a case of cause and effect: a reflection of the troubled times in which both dramatists and their audiences lived, the Malcontent's presence on the stage reflecting a state of turbulence and imbalance off it.[2] Lawrence Babb offers the fullest discussion of the subject that I was able to find, in his chapter 'The Malcontent Types' in *The Elizabethan Malady* (1951), a work which offers a very full and thorough account of the Renaissance perception and portrayal of various forms of melancholy. Like Spencer, Babb identifies five separate species of melancholy, of which the 'malcontent type' is one. Since Babb's work, there have been but scant references in works largely concerned with other things.[3] This apparently

---

1 Stoll, Elmer Edgar, 'Shakespere, Marston and the Malcontent Type', *MP* 3, (1905–6) 281–3.

2 Spencer, Theodore, 'The Elizabethan Malcontent' in J.G.McManaway, G.E.Dawson and E.E.Willoughby (eds.), Joseph Quincy Adams Memorial Studies (Washington DC, 1948), collected in Selected Essays,(New Brunswick,NJ, 1966).

3 Babb, Lawrence, The Elizabethan Malady, A Study of Melancholia in English Literature from 1580 to 1642 (Michigan, 1951).

general omission presents problems, since 'malcontent' is a term often used non-specifically, one which appears to take the condition for granted without offering explanation. Conversely, it is a term which is used elsewhere to purport a 'stock' figure on the Elizabethan and Stuart stage, provided with a dress-code and a language which will distinguish him.

When one considers such diverse figures as Hamlet, Malevole and Jaques, undoubtedly the Malcontent *is* a recognizable dramatic phenomenon, identifiable more by mood and language than by his costume, and a figure that defies 'stock' stereotyping: a loose set of characteristics, merely. Common to them all, however, is 'abstraction or alienation from society; they are characters on the fringes who do not partake of or contribute to human intercourse or the body-politic' and thus we can recognize him in his 'surly preoccupation, taciturnity, and unsociability; folded arms and hat pulled low; negligent disorder in dress; his sense of superiority; his tendency to rail enviously at an unappreciative world; inclination towards treachery and sedition.'[4] Philip J. Finkelpearl identifies: 'a man of some parts, developed by education and foreign travel, he was poor, usually unemployed, and obsessed by a sense of unrewarded merit; often he was melancholic. Thus he was a prime source of danger to the kingdom, since he was readily available for schemes against the established order.'[5] These modern delineations echo contemporary Jacobean ones. Joseph Hall's character book, *Characters of Virtues and Vices* (1608), describes the 'Malcontent' thus: 'What he hath he seeth not. His eyes are so taken up with what he wants; and what he sees he cares not for because he cares so much for that which is not. When his friend carves him the best morsel, he murmurs that it is a happy feast wherein each one may cut for himself.

---

4   See Martin Wiggins, *Journeymen in Murder : The Assassin in English Renaissance Drama* (Oxford, 1991), p. 152.

5   'The Malcontent: Virtuous Machiavellianism' by Philip J. Finkelpearl in *John Marston of the Middle Temple: an Elizabethan Dramatist in his Social Setting* (Harvard, 1969).

[3]

When a present is sent him, he asks, *"Is this all?" and "What, no better?"*[6]

His placement in 'opposition to the established order' is all-important to the figure portrayed on the stage, where he acquires the role of cynical commentator and judge of a society to which he patently does not entirely belong, as well as, in some cases, that of rogue disruptor, one who is not only prepared to question but to damage anything and everything that comes within his compass. Some plays provide a back-story which offers some explanation for the Malcontent's disaffection; others do not. Whatever, he is a potent force in most plays, whether represented by the relatively mild, harmless railings of Jaques in *As You Like It* or the wilful malignity of *Othello*'s Iago.

Mere villainy is a different matter, and needs to be distinguished from the outset from the state of malcontent, although there are often shared characteristics and a Malcontent may, perforce, be a villain also. Yet a typical stage villain is not usually a Malcontent as such; for while a villain is almost certainly power-crazed, egotistical and treacherous, he is not necessarily harmful to any but his enemies, or in any general way to the world. Nor, most importantly, is he (or she) set against that sense of obedient general order over which he seeks to triumph by villainous means; so that while it is possible to identify superficially malcontent facets in many a stage villain, there are legion villains who do not share the malcontented view: Claudius apparently believes in the 'order' of which he has murderously designed to be top, as do Macbeth, Lussurioso and Mendoza, among many others. The stage villain's view is usually short-sighted and probably doomed, but it is significant that, in the wider moral context of a play, 'order' is probably paramount, and there may be considerable emphasis on such a figure precisely because he serves this very point. The villain's eventual defeat therefore enforces the moral status quo – ie, that evil, and evil-doing, cannot 'win'.

---

6   Hall, Joseph, *Characters of Virtues and Vices* (London, 1608).

[4]

Some villains are ambiguous. Sometimes there is an obvious moral dilemma at work. In Claudius we see mordant hints of a 'conscience'; and a conscience-struggle is something developed dramatically between Macbeth and his Lady. These internal struggles indicate not simply the villain's awareness of moral wrong-doing but of his desire to be very much part of the 'body-politic' as such, to be a successful 'insider', one might put it, however illicitly or treacherously this is to be achieved. Malcontents, on the other hand, would seem to rejoice in being on the *outside;* and while ostensibly some may seek retribution for wrongs, nevertheless they seem prepared to disrupt anything and everything, even their own interests, in an ultimate contempt for the world order; and even if, like Edmund in *King Lear*, ambition seems to have been the original impetus. It is as if the Malcontent, with his grudge against mankind in general, cannot escape the logic which must include himself as detestable. A 'Malcontent' would seem to be, primarily, possessed of a state of mind whereby a villainous intent to profit or, as in the case of the revenger, to reconstruct the machinery of justice according to his own lights is largely superseded by a will to disrupt for its own sake.

Outsider he may be, yet this 'outside' mentality possibly permits him a truer judgement of the world, and to be more acutely tuned to the moral status quo than other, more 'engaged' individuals, so that there is often, oddly, a marked contrast between the self-serving hypocrisy of the mere villain whose personal interests are at stake, one who is prepared to risk damnation in their service, and the overtly 'moral' tone frequently adopted by the Malcontent. However jaded, disillusioned and faithless a Malcontent may be, he seems to be able to put his finger on the sickness of mankind because he himself suffers from the same disease. Compare the villainous language of the Cardinal (and, indeed Ferdinand) with the moral measuring of Bosola in Webster's *The Duchess of Malfi*, or the insistence upon an almost tortuous moral rectitude on the part of Vindice in *The Revenger's*

Tragedy in apposition to the villainous arrogance of the Duke and his sons, and it becomes clear that it is as if the Malcontent has judged the so-called morality of his society, found it deplorably wanting and sets out deliberately upon a regime which will expose its limits and failings. This is not to say the Malcontent's motives have much, if anything, to do with reform. He has nothing better to put in place of the corruption he judges and condemns. The will to destroy, damage, or disrupt can be therefore oddly un-self-centred in its nihilistic purpose.

Not all Malcontents are as extreme as this, and the degree of effectiveness perpetrated by these 'outsiders' varies as greatly as the Malcontent roles do themselves. Relatively 'harmless' Jaques belongs in a comedy, villainous Iago in a tragedy. Leaving aside for the moment the problems of such rigid genre-definition, and the growing popularity of so-called 'tragi-comedy' in the early seventeenth century, the Malcontent role would appear to be able to lend itself to either. This adaptability could be said to be true of other 'humour' types also, as is obvious with such 'stock' roles as the villain, the bombast and the parasite. The Malcontent can be without doubt cast as a 'type', especially where the play is concerned with this kind of stock-figure representation, as in, for instance, Shakespeare's *Much Ado About Nothing*. Here, the Malcontent Don John, a bastard who makes mischief in the court of his prince brother, is just another humour-type alongside many others in a light comedy, his role is of a piece with a play that is not especially philosophically 'deep' or as suggestive as some of Shakespeare's other comedies; and Don John, although he is indeed a maliciously-intentioned destroyer, is not ultimately effective in his destruction. Typically, though, his malice is largely impersonal: he seeks to wreck the trust between the lovers, Hero and Claudio, not because he hates them, but because as carefree courtly lovers, they make an amusing target for malevolence.

Another factor is the focus of the Malcontent within the play. Jaques, Feste and Thersites, though differing greatly in terms of 'weight', both tragic and comic – and thus in the commensurate amount of trouble they can provoke – are largely 'choric' figures, on the margins of a main plot where the 'action' is centred on others. At the opposite extreme, Iago directly affects the tragic action of *Othello* without (arguably) being a tragic character himself, while De Flores, Bosola and Flamineo, while morally marginalized, are not only directly concerned in their plays' action but to a greater or lesser extent accrue to themselves an emotional and moral depth which can be seen as individually tragic. Hamlet and Vindice, in their very different ways, combine being both tragic heroes, placed at the centre of the action, with being Malcontents also. Timon is not perhaps, strictly speaking, a tragic hero, but the play is the story of how a man becomes a Malcontent, and therefore *Timon of Athens* is 'tragic' in its charting of such alienation and despair, while Ben Jonson's *Every Man Out of His Humour* shows Macilente acquiring the Malcontent's mantle in a bitterly comic mode. Malevole, in Marston's *The Malcontent*, is, to all intents and purposes, a hero in a Malcontent's disguise (but both of his personae are problematic, as I shall show) while Richard of Gloucester is the villain-hero whose villainy is prompted and nurtured by his bitterly malcontented nature.

All of these figures, and the many other bastards, younger brothers, Jews and social outcasts that form the Malcontent tribe fulfil the Malcontent prescription, and their 'loose set of characteristics' is, despite a manifest diversity, nevertheless identifiable. We have to presume that these Malcontents were entirely recognizable as such to their original audiences for two reasons: first, because their common ancestry from allegorical stage archetypes like the medieval Vice is frequently apparent and often directly stated, but secondly because they came to represent a more contemporary *social* archetype: alienated, destructive, anarchic, a character-type with a real-life model which belonged in context to plays which had more to do with the exploration of attitudes and ideas in keeping with the tenor of Renaissance questioning of these things, than with characters or personalities as such. 'Stock' characteristics existed where necessary, of course, and sometimes these were flagged up by such obvious theatrical devices as the melancholic's typical black or dowdy costume, or by some physical deformity. Frequently it was more subtle than just this, however, and it was the moral and spiritual deformity of the role that was revealed and became itself the 'characteristic' malcontented humour.

The stage Malcontent frequently declares himself with no explanation or apology, something that is sometimes difficult to understand through a post-Freudian lens. It is only comparatively recently that we have been constrained by a need to think in terms of full psychological explanations for behaviour, or to demand that the drama give such a psychological account. The writers for the Elizabethan and Jacobean stage, under no such constraint or compulsion, often allowed the reasons lying behind a character's humour to remain partially or, in some cases, entirely, obscure. However, the presence or absence of such an explanation can be seen to have had a considerable dramatic significance. The malcontented nature might be presented, in the fashion of humours generally, as the result of an unexplained but accepted quirk of 'nature', something innate and unchangeable, or presented as the result of outside influences, an individual's response to slights and sufferings which have had the power to distort his outlook and demeanour. More usually, the answer is seen to lie, probably uncomfortably, between the two, and for the balance to be seen to shift as the play progresses: it is part of the Malcontent nature to make himself detestable, which in turn prompts further slights and ostracism from his society.

From a dramatic point of view, the impact of 'external' influences and the resultant character-alteration is powerful theatre; grief, thwarted attempts to invoke justice, and subsequent loss of credibility causes a gentle and balanced figure like Hieronimo to turn revenger, for instance; or rejection by others causes the patron Timon to turn misanthrope; or anger and grief bends the happy lover, Antonio, to destroy a trusting child, and it is upon these 'turns' that much of those plays rest. The distinction between the Malcontent 'born' (that is, one making his first appearance on the stage as unquestionably malcontented by nature) and the Malcontent 'made' so by external forces during the course of the play, is therefore important for this narrative reason. Frequently, however, dramatic tension is achieved by keeping this distinction between the innate and the externally-caused deliberately ambiguous. Known causes cannot in themselves hold our attention unless they are accompanied by the dramatic immediacy of action, or at least predicate the emotional tension on the stage. Our sympathies and perceptions are thus manipulated by the *play* – as opposed to the character – which might allow us small but significant glimpses into the essential humanity of the 'alien' humour, while paradoxically allowing the quality of alienation to remain, and without necessarily providing a convenient reason for this condition.

Perhaps the most significant factor unifying Malcontents of all kinds is their role as satiric spokesmen and censors of their society. For this purpose the Malcontent needs must be on the outside in some sense, literally or metaphorically, and to be imbued with circumstances, internal and external, that dictate this condition. This would seem to apply equally to those Malcontents appearing in the overtly tragic drama as much as the predominantly comic, and as much to those directly involved in the dramatic action of the play as to those with a more obviously 'choric' function. Here, the judgemental, but uninvolved (and therefore, literally, ineffective) role of the Chorus of ancient drama is important, partly because it lends to Renaissance drama a certain Classical authority. To take again those useful polarities, Jaques and Iago: Jaques' railings are 'harmless' precisely because he does not possess a 'hidden brief', as it were, to affect the central action directly in an adverse way, whereas Iago does, and his utterances concerning, say, the vile unaccountability of women, are anything but 'harmless' in terms of the effects they

intentionally produce. On the face of it, Jaques, choric and disinterested, can mock and even expose, but cannot affect; Iago,
involved and interested, also mocks and exposes, but for the express purpose of interfering in and confusing the central action.
A subtle but important variation of this polarity is evident in the
twin personalities of Malevole, whose apparently disinterested
railings and mockery are in fact a cloak for his determination to
involve himself definitively in the central action: apparently random hits which act as cover for direct aims at a specific target.

The paradigmatic world of the play is, through the themes
and ideas developed in it, necessarily a re-creation of a 'real'
world beyond, and it is from this point of view that we may see
that the satiric thrust of the Malcontent figure, regardless of his
relationship to the plot, action and outcome, is invested with
considerable moral and political force when considered in the
light of the drama's relationship to the world outside the theatre. John Marston's *The Malcontent*, because of the dual role of
Malevole/Altofront which both is and is not divisible, explores
and exposes this structural illusion very thoroughly through its
intense theatricality. This play, with the detachment necessary
to satire, explores both the nature of the 'Malcontent' as a figure,
at the same time as offering, in a satirical send-up, an exploration of the nature of the malcontented drama. In other words,
The Malcontent, as well as being a thoroughly entertaining and
stageable play, shows us the workings, as it were, from the inside.

ii

While Malcontents, as such, seem to have been rather left out of
count in modern criticism of the Jacobean drama, the impact of
what I have chosen to call the 'malcontented stage' has frequently occupied much critical debate. The proposition that, while the
Malcontent may be a caricature of the disaffected individual, his
presence, and the disturbing ambience of such a figure in and of
the play, is not only a reflection of such disturbance in real life,
but a positive prompt to rebellion of thought, even of action, is

a persuasive argument for a potent 'malcontented theatre', but one would then have to accept the idea of such a theatre as a pro-active political machine. On the other hand, and probably equally persuasive, is the argument which asserts the impotence of the theatre to affect anyone or anything very much: that it was, by dint of the 'escape clause' offered by 'Art', a concept made 'functionally ambiguous'.[7] Not surprisingly, there remain deep divisions of opinion as to the political potency of this theatre, not least because so many contemporary commentators, supporters and detractors alike, were convinced of its power, but did not necessarily have a very realistic grasp of what that power consisted of. Perhaps, especially when the tone of the detractors became especially hysterical, this is not unlike a similar reaction in our own age to violent computer games, films which tend to glorify war and destruction, and our fear of their influence on the young and impressionable. If we have to have a modern post-twentieth-century model, however, we must turn to those rigid, draconian ideological regimes (Cold War Russia; Putin's Russia still? Extremist Islam? The creationist debate?) in which true democracy and freedom of speech and the press remains a dream for some, to be suppressed at all costs for others in order to 'keep the faith' of whatever colour; regimes still in fear of and in the business of putting down artistic expression. It is these that best mirror the politically turbulent times of post-Reformation England.

Satire is, and always was, insidious. So is public performance, potentially. Both can reach an audience that mere polemic cannot. The aspect of the ephemeral, the sense that public entertainment can be dismissed as mere frivolity, allows the drama some latitude (a condition dramatists used over and over) but many critics and polemicists perceived a certain serious menace. The contemporary arguments of, say, Stubbes on the one hand, and Nashe on the other, who, from either side of a very tall fence at least agreed that the theatre *mattered*; that is, made a difference

---

7   See Paul Yachnin's essay, 'The Powerless Theatre', *ELR* 21 (1991) 49–74.

to the way people thought and behaved and considered their political governors. They may have exaggerated the position for the purpose of polemic, but that they took it very seriously indeed is well documented. One could argue that behind every panicky Mary Whitehouse there exists a serious debate regarding censorship and public morals.

Another more moderate argument concerning theatrical satire might run along the lines that 'ambiguity' causes people to laugh and then to puzzle. This is not to suggest that it produces a serious effect, either on morals or upon political practice – let alone revolution, but – think Monty Python, for example – it might prompt a fashion of mind, cause a quiet cultural revolution rather than outright civil war. But these were different times. To have a joke against the 'sacred', and here I mean partly kingship, the Lord's Anointed, and all the machinery of government and an obeisant society which upheld it, could only have been regarded as heretical, a prompt to revolt.

As for what I have termed the 'malcontented stage', the nihilistic view propounded by such plays might produce a state of despair sooner than prompt revolution. It is not, as I remarked earlier, the Malcontent's job to reform. The moral (as opposed to the political) position of the later Elizabethan and Jacobean drama is in any case problematic, since it adumbrates Christian theodicy and Classical authority, and seems to have existed in the theatre as a result of what might be seen as a mood of challenge to both.

Renaissance intellectual culture tended to embrace Classical authority, something which lent so much weight to the modernising of more obviously old-fashioned, medieval Christian ideals. Stoicism, with its central ideas of acceptance of an ideal destiny and the subordination of the individual will to the greater universal Good, sits relatively comfortably with Christian notions of placid behaviour and faith in the Divine Will of God. Superstition, on the other hand, notoriously overlaps religion of all kinds, and must also account partially for a wider acceptance of both the Classical and the Christian concept of Fortune. Both pagan and Christian doctrines would have it that mere mortals are at the mercy and dictate of Something: and that 'something' – other, bigger, more mysterious than other human beings, even Kings, princes and priests – be it the gods, or God, or Fate in general, rules the lives of men. It was as much this as much as anything which the Humanists challenged in their striving for human determinism.

The concept of Fortune as a fickle goddess who played wantonly with the lives of men, or as the great universal Wheel which bore up the individual to a peak from which, inevitably, he began to fall, is an image that recurs in the drama of the Elizabethans and early Stuarts again and again. For the Stoic, and for the Christian, (and therefore for the neo-Stoic-Christian) Fortune was rationalized as Providence or Fate: the workings of a divine or at least extra-human Will, which ordained the fates of ordinary individuals and princes alike. This applied equally to station in life: to one's position in the Order of things and to the vicissitudes of personal fortune, and which, again in accord with both Stoic and Christian doctrine, must be borne in faith and serenity. Humanist thought in the Renaissance tended towards a reclaiming of responsibility for personal (and therefore civil) fortune, without, necessarily, disclaiming either Divine faith or the authority of the great Classical philosophies. Simply put, Renaissance Humanism sought to harmonize everything: superstition with theodicy, pagan with Christian, Classical with modern. Of necessity, as Lawrence Babb drily remarks, it failed.[8] Its impact, however, was overwhelming, and the drama of this period, possibly more than that of any other, reflects the troubling effect of modern thought upon modern man. The 'wheel' of fortune has become reclaimed in terms of the 'weal' of Man's civil inheritance; mankind looks at himself and his society in both moral and political terms, and there cannot be any easy

---

8   L.Babb, op. cit., 73 ff.

answers, either in terms of pragmatic politics or ethical supposition.

The fixture of 'Degree' in which man's place in a world-picture which placed God at the top, anointing a Prince to rule in His name over Divinely defined orders of humanity, in a metaphorical model of rigidly ordained hierarchy becomes something to be challenged in a world of increasing social mobility. These contemporary plays exposed the sacred office of royalty as having a fallible human being as its bearer; the 'saws of books' are but the thoughts of men, to be challenged, and men – and women – are ultimately frail. God must exist (atheism was punishable by death) but He does not necessarily favour the just and the good. Rather, in much of the greatest drama of this period, there is an evident rejection of the idea of justice and goodness as attainable states, and not, as Seneca's drama so often portrays it, because the gods themselves are unjust and 'play' with man, but in a view of the ethical concepts of Christian virtue and justice as being ideas which are, in themselves, ultimately jejune. Man, it is implied, is at the mercy of other men, who frequently are seen to show only erratic and self-interested mercy; and mankind's existence in the real and temporal world is viewed with a cynicism, even a sadness which tends to negate, rather than reaffirm, man's ability to manage his moral, and therefore political, affairs for himself. But he has at the same time negotiated himself out of the 'wheel', and taken on the 'weal': responsibility, for good or ill, for his own fate. God, and fate, have been marginalized in the sense that man has become his own master. It is man's position as being mastered by other men which is therefore revealed as pressingly important at one and the same time as utterly transitory, and dictated, not so much by a question of 'degree', but by his own ability and strength to challenge that position in the immediate temporal world. It is no wonder therefore, that such ideas appealed as alarming, even abhorrent, frightening, to those in the business of maintaining the old status quo.

The Malcontent's role, therefore, is undoubtedly one of focusing, one way or another – often licenced-Fool fashion – man's fallibility to himself. Like the Fool, because he is made to stand outside his society, the role is essentially a politically contentious one. For one thing, the Malcontent has a provenance in the late-Elizabethan cum early-Stuart world as a visible presence in the real milieu, and plenty of discontented (and the term was more or less interchangeable with 'malcontented') literate, politically educated and verbally adroit young men were seen to be a menace to an unstable society. That such figures were seen frequently as also rather ridiculous, as *poseurs* and intellectual snobs, of course inspired mockery off the stage as well as on it but, contained in the mockery, was an acknowledgement of their potential threat. On the stage, the Malcontent is almost never a mere figure of fun; he gives a comedy its bitter edge, while in the tragedy he picks open the seeming-smooth complexion of the heroic ideal and leaves it ragged and gaping for all to see. In this sense, it is the theatre itself which can be seen to adopt the 'malcontented' role: on the margin of society and commenting bitterly upon it. It is this function of exposure, not just by the malcontent character in the play, but as part of the function of the play that this book will explore.

PART ONE

THE MALCONTENT ON
THE STAGE

CHAPTER ONE

THE VICE, THE FOOL AND THE MELANCHOLY MAN

i

The Malcontent is emphatically a 'modern' figure of the late Renaissance stage. He is the product of a social phenomenon which became legendary in its own time, partly as a result of the fascination with Machiavelli, with Italy and all things Italian, and from which dramatic fictional representations followed almost immediately. At the same time, he is a coalescence of several familiar archetypes of the popular theatre in England which, at a point of radical change on the English stage, were reworked into representations of a Renaissance 'real life' myth. It was the popular theatre which provided the most obvious dramatic models, for while the Classical drama of the ancient Romans had enormous bearing on plays and play-making in the Renaissance, it provided no specific, obvious source for the Malcontent role, except perhaps where we can occasionally discern a glimmer in the 'Parasite' figure from the Roman comedies. Moreover, while ancient dramas were an important academic study in schools, these were probably never performed in public and were thus to a much lesser extent part of any wider public consciousness. A scholarly figure, however, came to be identified as malcontented, a figure which to a large extent emanated from the universities and the myths and suspicions surrounding learning.

In short, it is impossible to impose a linear history on the stage Malcontent, but it is possible to identify three clear and recognizable archetypes in the English malcontent's theatrical ancestry: the Vice, the Fool, and the Melancholic. The first belongs to the world of medieval dramatic entertainment; the second is a social, as well as a theatrical phenomenon; the third was a later 'adoption' from popular medical-cum-psychological lore.

From the medieval Vice, the Malcontent inherits his function – that of arch-disruptor of established virtue who switches allegiances as the fancy takes him. From the Fool, he inherits status: the license, granted or assumed, to get away with verbal abuse of his bosses and betters that in others would be illegal or treasonable. His malcontent nature he derives at least partly from the Melancholic, who is understood, by dint of his peculiar balance of the humours, to be a 'natural' outsider. The Malcontent can and frequently does claim direct ancestry from the Vice of the earlier medieval and sixteenth-century stage (witness Richard of Gloucester's identification with the Vice in Act III) and he has a collateral ancestor in the Fool, who persists onto the Jacobean stage in his own right, and indeed in the medieval Devil, who unlike the Vice was seldom a comic character, but was sometimes presented (often as the butt of the Vice's satire) as a Fool.[9]

The Vice, originally a type of clown, was the comic scoundrel, the sardonic humorist and notorious double-crosser of the medieval Morality plays and Interludes. He was bent on the mocking destruction of accepted virtues, a trait which is particularly discernible in the 'modern' Malcontent of Shakespeare's time. One can trace a direct lineage between the two, and see that the late-Elizabethan cum Jacobean Malcontent is, amongst other things, a 're-invention' of the Vice, at once a recognizable traditional figure and a modern adaptation, re-worked to the requirements of the modern drama. The Morality Vice is a singularly welcome figure on the stage whenever Virtue threatens to become tediously sanctimonious and oppressive, but one in whom the audience's delight is coupled with a necessary condemnation. Nowadays, pantomime villains enjoy the same status. In a more serious way, this ambivalent response is also demanded by

9 The Devil as Fool is an ancient idea, and the title of Ben Jonson's play *The Devil is an Ass*, first acted 1616, for instance, uses a metaphor that preceded the mediaeval drama by centuries.

the Malcontent, and one of the Malcontent's functions, like that of the Vice, is to bring mischief to the stage as a sort of comic relief. In this sense, by manipulating the response of the audience, by making them laugh, the Vice-function acts as a temporary perverter of public morals, by making them laugh at things which they ought to condemn. Here, arguably, is the nub of the intrinsically ambiguous nature of the Malcontent, if not theatre itself.

ii

Overt political challenge gained more primacy in the theatre in the early sixteenth century. The later Morality plays, such as John Skelton's *Magnificence* (c. 1520) and John Bale's more innovatively political *King John* (c. pre-1540) illustrate a development away from the older, more generalized themes of the medieval Moralities towards political and theological propaganda, whilst retaining many of the stereotypes of the older form. However, this older form continued to exert influence on the more sophisticated Elizabethan drama long after the Moralities had ceased to be regularly performed, and the character-stereotypes, especially those of Vice and Virtue, reappear in the plays of Marlowe, Kyd, Dekker, Jonson, Shakespeare and others. The Vice reappears in Robert Greene's *Friar Bacon and Friar Bungay* (c. 1588) as the servant Miles who rides the Devil's back, and as Wagner in Marlowe's *Dr Faustus* (1588). Elsewhere in *Dr Faustus*, the old Morality influence is felt very directly in the debates between the Good Angel and the Bad Angel and in the Devil's presentation of the seven deadly sins. In both parts of Shakespeare's *Henry IV* (c. 1597), Falstaff's Vice-like qualities are obvious (although it is equally obvious that Falstaff is no Malcontent for all his mischief).

Shakespeare's *Richard III* (c.1592-3) borrows a great deal from this older form. Richard of Gloucester is of particular interest to this study for several reasons, not least of which is, once he attains his ultimate position as king, as king-Malcontent he is placed in the extraordinary and paradoxical position of existing at the core *and* on the periphery of his world simultaneously. During the course of the play, we witness his winning of the crown, but always he has, like the Vice, effectively been 'king' of the play, a relationship which he directly claims:

> Thus like the formal vice, Iniquity,
> I moralize two meanings in one word.   (III, i, 82–3)

The Vice, whose characteristics Richard adopts, has a special relationship with the audience, a kind of sly ironic confidence insinuated between us and the other players, as though we share a joke. Richard, typically of the Vice, and of many Elizabethan and Jacobean Malcontents, attempts to draw the audience's anarchic sympathy away from the perceptibly ordered world, a sympathy which he then goes on to betray. Some Malcontents achieve this by drawing attention to the unsatisfactory nature of the behaviour of others, in which respect they are very similar in function to the Vice. The 'betrayal' comes when, having got us to recognize the irony of our own fundamentally fallible condition and feel a kinship with him, we are shown a vileness (whether of word or deed - and of course in Richard's case we are speaking very much of deeds) and a cynical disregard for almost everything, in a way which turns out to be morally beyond us. Ultimately, we cannot approve.[10]

Richard has his own particular variant on this. Obviously he is too overtly ambitious in his declaration of a superior evil to make the claim that the other characters are as bad, if not worse, than he is. On the other hand, his cleverness and conniving are mightily impressive: wicked, intended to shock; but because this is underpinned by the dramatic device of the morality Vice address – he speaks to us directly in a way none of the other characters do – Vice-Richard develops a direct relationship with

---

10   See Nicholas Brooke, *Shakespeare's Early Tragedies*, (London, 1968), pp. 48–80.

the audience. By the time we (good Tudors all, nurtured on anti-Richard propaganda) realise we cannot support this villain any longer, it is as if we have been dumped by a confrere.[11]

Many of the later Malcontents combine the Vice's functions in the drama - those of presenter and arch-disruptor - at the same time as possessing the status of their other great archetypal ancestor, the Fool: one licensed to do what in others would be impossible, punishable. Whereas the Vice is an exclusively theatrical figure, however, the Fool, though a standard theatrical archetype, was a social phenomenon - the private entertainer – which predates his appearance on any public medieval and Renaissance stage. A type of domestic servant in the homes of many medieval and Renaissance aristocrats, Fools or jesters were regarded more or less as pets or mascots, and they served not simply to entertain or amuse, but to criticize their powerful masters and mistresses and their important guests. Their purpose seems to have been twofold, and it must have been an uncomfortably precarious dual role. Professional entertainment was certainly part of a Fool's brief (as can be seen in Shakespeare's *Twelfth Night* when Malvolio encourages Olivia to have Feste the jester sacked for not being funny enough), but it was the Fool's special licence to observe and criticize the follies of his betters,a role which constituted at one and the same time a decadent kind of entertainment, and which served, functionally, as an antidote to the sin of Pride in the great and powerful.[12]

In *King Lear,* as in numerous other plays, the monarch evinces disgust at the flattery of courtiers:

---

11   In Christopher Marlowe's *The Jew of Malta, The Revenger's Tragedy* and Ben Jonson's *Volpone*, the knavish heroes each serve as the introductory 'presenter' and primary contriver of the play. See Robert Jones, *Engagement with Knavery* (Durham NC, Duke 1986)

12   For a very full discussion of The Fool, see Enid Welsford's classic study *The Fool: His Social and Literary History* (London, 1935), and William Willeford's *The Fool and His Sceptre – A Study in Clowns and Jesters and their Audience* (London, 1969).

They flattered me like a dog and told me I had the white hairs in my beard ere the black ones were there. To say 'ay' and 'no' to everything that I said 'ay' and 'no' to was no good divinity... Go to, they are not men o' their words. They told me I was everything; 'tis a lie...'   (*KL*, IV, v, 94–101)

A Fool was the only one in such a household who could be relied on not to tell lies or flatter, and thus his position in a royal or noble household was unique, if uniquely equivocal. His power was supreme, in one way, since he was licensed above the laws which applied to others and could say what he liked; but, ambiguously, being somehow less (or more) than ordinarily human, he was denied promotion in any ordinary sense, and, having typically the status of a valued slave wholly owned by his master, had no power at all. Either way, he was at his master's mercy; he might be whipped for his excesses, as Lear's Fool is threatened; Queen Elizabeth, on the other hand, is reputed to have rebuked one of her fools for not being severe enough with her.

Fools were obviously 'outsiders'. They might be mentally deficient or physically deformed or both – they were 'exceptional' in almost every respect – and their powerful patrons at least offered protection from the humiliation and abuse they were likely to meet with in the outside world. While distinctions were made between the 'natural' Fool and the 'artificial' or professional Fool (who was probably more akin to the actor-comedian in private practice) it was the 'natural' Fool who carried a special mystique. In lore, it is the 'natural' Fool's gifts which account for his privileged status in royal or noble houses; for while his folly could be seen as the ravings of a madman, it could also be seen as divinely inspired. The natural Fool was 'touched' by God, and regarded, superstitiously, as being beyond the laws of men, and his outspoken criticisms as containing the seeds of Divine judgement. The distinctions overlap, inevitably. The Fool in *King Lear* bears many characteristics which suggest he is a 'natural' Fool, and not an 'artificial' one, even though his perception and wit show that he is far from being an idiot or moron, however 'touched' he may otherwise be.

The popularity of the Fool or jester on the stage increased after Robert Armin replaced Will Kempe (who had specialized in clowns, or country bumpkins) among the players of the King's Men and made a speciality of Fools. He successfully undertook the roles of Touchstone, Feste, and Lavatch in Shakespeare's comedies, of Carlo Buffone in Ben Jonson's *Every Man Out of His Humour* and Passarello in John Webster's additions to John Marston's *The Malcontent*. It is possible that he also played Lear's Fool. Such popularity of Fool-roles is partly explained by the presence of such illustrious comic specialists to play them but, in turn, the popularity of such Fool-actors indicates the contemporary significance of such an old-fashioned staple to the Renaissance stage.[13] This progression, from the medieval tradition to the experimental stage suggests two things: that the Fool continued to hold a particular relevance for contemporary audiences, one probably grounded in sentiment for a theatrical tradition; but that now the role had been significantly refocused, and the Fool's condition (of slavery, and even possessing a political agenda on this account if we consider Feste) was directed to a more sophisticated audience. In itself, the role had apparently altered little: all the usual signs were there: the profanity, prob-

---

13   See William A. Ringler, Jr, 'Shakespeare and his actors: some remarks on King Lear' in *Shakespeare's Art*, ed. Aycock, pp. 187–93, who argues that Armin probably played Edgar, since Armin was adept at shifting roles within a single play, and that the boy actor who played Cordelia doubled the role of the Fool. There are problems: Jay L. Halio in his Introduction to *King Lear*, ed. The New Cambridge Shakespeare (Cambridge, 1992) points out that Armin was a small man, and may not have been suited to the role of Edgar, especially as the champion against Edmund in V, iii. Moreover, there is surely a doubt as to a boy actor's having sufficient experience to carry off the Fool role. The parallel between the roles is important, as is the ambiguity of the line 'My poor Fool is hanged' (V, iii, 279). Significant doubling for effect was a familiar device to Shakespeare and those before him. See Giorgio Melchiori's essay, 'Peter, Balthasar, and Shakespeare's art of doubling', *Modern Language Review* 1983.

ably the cap and bells, the outlandish cod-piece; above all, the double-talk and the mockery. The most successful of the Renaissance Fools, however, were those which had acquired a voice.

Lear's Fool is deliberately placed as the wise foil for his increasingly mad master; Feste in *Twelfth Night* is highly vocal as both slave and anarchist, and occupies a central role in the play, claiming not to be Olivia's Fool, but 'my lady's corrupter of words' and possesses a wit and talent none of the other characters do. Arguably, in *Lear,* since the role is still little more than emblematic in a highly emblematic play, we perhaps do not perceive the Fool as a human being until Lear himself does, during the storm: '... How dost, my boy? Art cold? | I am cold myself.' (*KL,* III, ii, 67–7). In the role of Feste, however, we have an emblematic figure (a Fool cannot help being this) which becomes a strikingly 'human' being, as we see when he begins to succumb to an all-too-human resentment of his position and to make, in the process, a political point.

Feste, as I shall be discussing a little later, combines the role of the Fool with that of the Malcontent; he is, as far as I know, unique in this. Mostly, Fools seem to have survived onto the Renaissance stage alongside the much more modern development of the malcontent role, even (as is the case with the public version of Marston's *The Malcontent*) to have been inserted partly as a sop to a sentimental tradition for such a figure (Passarello is a minor role in every sense.) However tempting it is to regard the Malcontent as a sort of hybrid of Vice and Fool, with the germ of political awareness and activism thrown in, this is too simplistic. The Malcontent is 'new', in terms of a specific figure on the stage, albeit he has 'borrowed' essential features from both of these traditional roles. While the Vice more or less disappeared and was subsumed into the modern Malcontent, the Fool continued, for a while, anyway, in his own right. His renewed reign on the English Renaissance stage was brief, however; and the literal disappearance of Lear's Fool toward the end of Act III, giving way as he does to the more complex characters of Edgar (as

Poor Tom) and Edmund as the genuine Malcontent, indicates a theatrical significance. No Fool said much afterwards; and after 1606 or thereabouts, the Fool is redundant as far as significant roles are concerned. Armin himself died c. 1611, and no other actor replaced him in his prominence in such roles.

Like the Fool, the Malcontent, in his assumed 'professional' garb of cynicism and licence, holds a privileged position in relation to the other characters, and this seems to be the assumption common to all stage Malcontents. Both Malevole and Jaques, for instance, hold the traditional Fool's relationship to their master-Dukes as semi-official mockers; when Jaques asks to have such liberty as a jester has 'To blow on whom I please' (*AYLI*, II, vii, 49), the request seems unnecessary, for he takes such liberty already. Perhaps not oddly, in *The Malcontent* and in *As You Like It*, the Malcontents seem to be on excellent terms with the licensed Fools, revelling in their grotesque wisdom and flinging it in the face of the more (in the other sense) foolish world. In most cases, however, the Malcontent is significantly different from either the Fool or the Vice, in the respect that he would appear to embrace more immediately human and therefore political motivation. Even in those Malcontents most obviously associated with a theatrical concern for emblems, those which have a more obviously 'choric' role - for instance, Thersites in *Troilus & Cressida* – we can see that they are nevertheless imbued with human feeling and, often, all- too-human resentments. That Shakespeare wrote the Feste role to combine these two disparate factors indicates a shift of emphasis. We cannot afford the anachronistic word 'psychological', but a Renaissance perception of the melancholy temperament and its dramatic potential perhaps partly explains the gradual disappearance of the largely emblematic Fool.

There is another factor, however, which is much more insistently and immediately 'sociological'. Chapter 3 discusses the emergence of the real-life phenomenon of the malcontented and melancholic intellectual. However, it is in William Stevenson's *Gammer Gurton's Needle* (written c. 1553, but possibly earlier) that we first encounter a figure who, while still primarily a Vice, and licensed, Fool-fashion, to beg from whom he chooses, also incorporates a distinctly 'modern' aspect of the drama, for there is an element of social-cum-psychological realism in Diccon who, while displaying little that is truly melancholic, derives his nature instead from the social influences and pressures that both condemn and free him. The play, which importantly combines elements of Latin comedy and old Morality play with a realistic portrayal of English rural life, has at its centre a very precisely-drawn figure: the licensed beggar from the madhouse Bedlam. As such, Diccon has a distinct and identifiable place in (or rather on the fringes of) the society of the time. His disruptive mischief-making belongs not only to the old, recognizable allegorical stereotype of the Vice, but also to a recognizable social phenomenon: the insane outcast, in effect the Fool without a post. Diccon is blatantly delinquent; he steals, he lies, he begs; he refuses to kneel and repent of his crimes whilst making play of doing so – this refusal is in fact the crowning moment of the comedy, when instead of kneeling and swearing an oath on the servant Hodge's breeches, he whacks Hodge on the bottom and thus finds the missing Needle – and all these things he does because he has nothing whatever to lose. His status as madman is paradoxical: while he is barred from the normal social construct as represented by the eponymous old widow, her servants, the tavern-keeper and the constable, his 'official' madness frees him to do and be almost anything on the periphery of a society which has ordered his alienation. His madness condemns him to belonging 'elsewhere' – the asylum – but excuses him from any reasonable – that is, sane and responsible – behaviour or speech. *Gammer Gurton's Needle* is of course a good-natured comic farce, one which ends with the whole company, and Diccon as the hero of the hour, celebrating the finding of the Needle in the tavern. Diccon undergoes no final banishment; his madness in terms of personal torment remains unexplored (and obviously, this would be inappropriate in the context of such a play). Rather, it is an accepted fact upon which much is played.

However, in Diccon, and to a lesser extent in Matthew Merrygreek, from Nicholas Udall's *Ralph Roister-Doister* (c. 1553) and Ambidexter from Thomas Preston's *Cambises* (? before 1569), we probably have other 'missing-link' ancestors of the Jacobean stage Malcontent, just as these early plays are recent ancestors of the later drama. Merrygreek derives partly from the 'Parasite' staple of Roman comedy, combined with which his role more than suggests the Vice, with his continual switching of allegiances and his trouble-making, but he lacks the topical satiric thrust of the outcast Diccon's role. Ambidexter is more overtly treacherous, affecting the action closely, and more 'allegorical', in that the play places the blame for the moral corruption of its hero firmly upon Ambidexter (whose name means 'plays with both hands') as the personification of Treachery at its conclusion. In *Cambises,* a medley of classical influences, crude farce, allegory and abstract characters from the Moralities, social realism is more or less beside the point, but is interesting for the theatrical reason of being a play which, at a highly transitory stage of development of Elizabethan tragedy, combines obviously 'Senecan' (and therefore intellectual) elements with recognizable allegorical abstractions from the medieval popular drama. But it is Diccon's role, on the other hand, which has been imbued with a social realism that forms part of the dramatic explanation for the way he is, and the play deploys a realistic figure with a realistic social background. It is this realistic social background which begins to distinguish the later Malcontents from their allegorical ancestors.

iii

The third major factor in the Malcontent's make-up is Melancholy. Literally meaning 'black bile', melancholy was understood as a physical 'humour' of the body among four principal humours (sanguine, phlegmatic, choleric, melancholic) which in unique balance compounded the physical and chemical conditions which dictated a person's individual nature. An understanding of the four humours provided whatever explanations existed for the Renaissance notion of complex psychology. The doctrine of the Four Humours, present in Hippocratic writing, but which derives principally from the writings of Galen (AD c. 130–c. 200) had long since passed into popular psycho-medical lore, and figured prominently in contemporary attempts to explain the various behavioural characteristics or personal temperaments that so obviously existed among individuals. Each humour which an individual possessed in unique balance, could become sick or 'adusted', that is, too hot and dry – a state that could lead to forms of madness, or at least eccentric or disturbed behaviour. A malcontented nature, therefore, was one likely to have been produced by an imbalance of the melancholy humour. One of the principal topics of Robert Burton's *Anatomie of Melancholy* is the particular seriousness of such imbalance in the choleric and melancholy humours, one that was likely to produce 'melancholy madness', together with its possible causes and cures.[14]

In the drama, the association of melancholy humour with criminal violence and intrigue occurs frequently. In *Titus Andronicus*, for example, Aaron is plotting iniquities. Saturn, the ruling planet of Melancholy, he says, 'is dominator over' his desires.

> What signifies my deadly-standing eye,
> My silence and my cloudy melancholy...? (*TA* II, iii,31-33)

Shakespeare's King John, on the point of instructing Hubert to murder Young Arthur, makes a show of hesitation. He tells Hubert that he would speak plainly, however, 'if that surly spirit,

---

14 Timothy Bright's *Treatise on Melancholie* (1586) is said to have prompted the much more widely known *Anatomie of Melancholy* by Robert Burton (printed 1621, reprinted in five later editions.) Another important contemporary analysis is in Sir Thomas Overbury's character writings: *A Wife: Now the Widow of Sir Thomas Overbury* (published posthumously in 1614).

melancholy | Had bak'd thy blood and made it heavy-thick.' (*KJ*, III, iii, 42–43). Lady Macbeth calls upon supernatural powers to 'make thick my blood' (I, v, 44) in order to murder Duncan: 'thick' blood is melancholic blood. The hero of Chettle's *The Tragedy of Hoffman* (probably written 1602, printed 1631) living as a disaffected savage, nurses his hatred and devises his bloody schemes of revenge permeated by 'clouds of melancholy'.

Melancholy is a problematic state of mind, at once forgiveable, even lovable – which, at the same time, since it can tip so easily into mania, is treated with suspicion and fear. It is not so strange, therefore, that the state of melancholy as a precondition of malcontentedness would seem to bifurcate in the drama, in one direction towards a dangerously amoral villain like, say, Bosola from John Webster's *The Duchess of Malfi*, whose dissatisfaction with the world leads him on to perpetrate all kinds of inhumanities without remorse for much of the play, and in the other direction towards a much gentler type of malcontented cynic, such as Jaques, who is regarded with tolerant amusement rather than with contempt or fear. Since he is on the borderline of sanity, he is granted the licence which is naturally given to irresponsible persons. He has privileges somewhat like those of the court jester or Fool. He may be as sour and surly, as acidly satiric, even as offensive, as he pleases. Those about him often question him, prod him, in order to induce his satire, just as one might provoke an animal to make it show its tricks. The Duke says of Jaques:

I love to cope him in these sullen fits,
For the he's full of matter   (II, i, 67-6)

'Matter' means interesting stuff, ideas, even learning, and is important, potentially inspiring. Similarly, Duke Pietro indulges the disguised Altofront in Marston's *The Malcontent*, assuming an attitude of amused patronization toward him and questioning him indulgently to elicit his snarling satire. It is as if Pietro is in possession of an exotic exhibit, made all the more exciting because of its dangerous potential. Malevole is, according to Pietro, 'rather a monster' than a man,

> more discontented than Lucifer... his speech is halter-worthy at all hours: I like him 'faith, he gives good intelligence to my spirit, makes me understand those weaknesses which others' flattery palliates... he is as free as air: he blows over every man.' (I, iii, 17–30).

Such ambivalent responses to Melancholy in the drama tend to bear out an ancient paradox. On the one hand, most medical works in the tradition of Galen describe melancholy men as

> sluggish, dull and blockish... fearful and sorrowful without apparent cause and... subject to the most terrifying and ridiculous hallucinations... wretched creatures who have fallen to the level of brutes...

On the other hand, there is the clear perception of the Melancholy Man as

> of all others... most witty, [and their melancholy] causeth many times divine ravishment, and a kind of enthusiasmus... which stirreth them up to be excellent Philosophers, Poets, Prophets...

This ambivalence to Melancholy is rooted in a classical conundrum. Renaissance scholars were greatly interested by a problem of Aristotle's, which begins with the question: 'Why is it that all those who have become eminent in philosophy or politics or poetry or the arts are clearly of an atrabilious temperament...?' Many of the ancient Greek heroes, according to Aristotle, were melancholy, and he cites Heracles, Ajax, and Bellerophon, all of whom went mad. The great thinkers Empedocles, Socrates and Plato also were 'atrabilious' - that is, tending to produce black bile and thus be melancholy. In addressing this question, Aristotle first propounds and answers another: why does black bile, like wine, have such diverse effects upon behaviour? This humour, he says, may become either very hot or very cold and therefore produces, in one instance or another, all the various traits of personality which arise from internal heat and cold. Cold melancholy causes torpidity and despondency; hot melancholy sometimes causes insanity.

> Many too, if this heat approaches the region of the intellect, are affected by diseases of frenzy and possession; and this is the origin of Sybils and soothsayers and all inspired persons, when they are affected not by disease but by natural temperament. Maracus, the Syracusan, was actually a better poet when he was out of his mind. Those in whom the excessive heat dies down to a mean temperature are atrabilious, but they are cleverer and less eccentric and in many respects superior to others either in mental accomplishments or in the arts or in public life.[15]

Nowadays, we would probably diagnose bi-polar disorder. Aristotle suggests that while black bile has detrimental effects when it is very hot, very cold, or very abundant, atrabilious men whose melancholy is moderate in temperature and quantity - those who 'possess a mixed temperament' – are likely to be 'men of genius'. The works of other ancient writers tended to confirm for Renaissance scholars the veracity of Aristotle's assertions, especially in the matter of poetic creation. Both Democritus and Plato assert that the true poet is touched with a divine madness, and although neither of them specifically mentions melancholy, Renaissance authorities assumed that, like Aristotle, they attribute poetic inspiration to black bile. Marsilio Ficino, the Florentine humanist, philosopher, and physician, who was the first significant commentator on the Aristotelian conception of melancholy,

---

15   Problemata, XXX, i. in Vol. VII of *The Works of Aristotle*, W. D. Ross, ed. E. S. Forster, trans. (Oxford 1908–31). L. Babb (op. cit) points out that while there is now considerable doubt concerning the authenticity of the Problemata, in classical times the passage in question was considered definitely to be Aristotle's.

has much to say concerning the relation between melancholy and the mental faculties in *De Studiosorum Sanitate Tuenda*, the first book of *De Vita Libri Tres* (1482–89).[16] All men of letters are melancholy, says Ficino, but this is not altogether unfortunate, for Aristotle, Plato and Democritus all attribute great excellence to melancholy minds. Adust melancholy causes mania; natural melancholy – that is, the cold, dry humour normally present in the body – provided it is properly mixed with warmer humours, is kindled, without burning (which would cause the ashy, noxious humour of adust melancholy) and shines brilliantly.[17]

There are, therefore, two distinct and contradictory Classical conceptions of Melancholy simultaneously held by the Renaissance. Ironically, since behind one was the authority of Galen and behind the other the authority of Aristotle, scholars tended to deny the truth of neither, and accept both, although sometimes the two concepts appear to be very much in conflict. The Galenic – and predominant – idea of the Melancholy Man is a blockheaded and utterly disagreeable individual (presumably suffering a condition to which no one would readily confess); Aristotle's problem, however, popularized first in Italy and then in England, lent the condition of melancholia a distinct philosophic and artistic glamour, and a state to which many men were willing to declare themselves affected. This vogue left a permanent record in Elizabethan and early Stuart literature, and it was Aristotle's much more glamorous 'problem' that was the remote cause of Melancholy Men in the English drama, satire and character sketches of the late Renaissance period. It is this duality that is evident in the Renaissance Malcontent, who is

16   See Erwin Panofsky and Fritz Saxl (*Durers Kupferstich 'Melancolia I'* (eds Panofsky & Saxl, Leipzig-Berlin, 1923), who argue that Ficino was largely responsible for the popularity of the idea that melancholy and genius were allied. Although there was little interest in the Aristotelian conception of melancholy before Ficino, the Aristotelian problem was known and discussed during the Middle Ages (Panofsky & Saxl, op. cit. p.20).

17   Ficino gives the exact proportions: eight parts blood, two of yellow bile, two of black bile. He evidently regards this a high proportion of melancholy.

frequently portrayed as possessing simultaneously the Galenic features of moral and physical disease, and the wit and power that accompany great intelligence.

Burton's *Anatomy of Melancholy* adumbrates this double view. One fallen prey to melancholy is described as suffering from:

> Fear and Sorrow, which as they are frequent causes, so, if they per-
> sever long… they are most assured signs, inseparable companions
> of Melancholy… Suspicion and jealousy are general symptoms;
> they are commonly distrustful, timorous, apt to mistake and am-
> plify, testy, pettish, peevish, and ready to snarl on upon every small
> occasion… Inconstant they are in all their actions, vertiginous,
> restless, unapt to resolve of any business… Now prodigal, and then
> covetous, they do and by-and-by repent them of that which they
> have done, so that both ways they are troubled, whether they do or
> not, want or have, hit or miss,… erected and dejected in an instant;
> animated to undertake, and upon a word spoken again discour-
> aged. Extreme passionate,… and what they desire they do most
> furiously seek:… prone to revenge, soon troubled, and most vio-
> lent in all their imaginations, not affable in speech, or apt to vulgar
> [common] compliment, but surly, dull, sad, austere… neglect hab-
> it [clothing, etc]… and yet of a deep reach [intellectual capacity],
> excellent apprehension, judicious, wise, and witty…

It is in this last delineation – in the 'and yet' – that we can see the writer's acceptance of the Aristotelian concept as co-existent with the Galenic one, which suggests that Burton, like others, was reasonably comfortable with the discrepancy, an acceptance that can be attributed to the Renaissance scholars' respect for Classical authority, however divergent and apparently contra-dictory. But Burton's work was not current until after 1621, and he was to an extent writing in hindsight. Doubtless from a mod-ern scientific point of view, this contradiction might strike us through our post-Freudian lens as naive, unsatisfactory. From a strictly artistic point of view, however, such ambiguities and contradictions are far easier for us to accept. Dramatize Burton's delineation, and you have Hamlet, more or less.

If Burton's analysis might have been written for Hamlet, Sir Thomas Overbury's account accords rather better with the gentler Jaques. The Melancholy Man, according to Overbury, is:

> a strayer from the drove... His imagination is never idle, it keeps his mind in a continuall motion, as the poise of a clock: he winds up his thoughts often, and as often unwinds them... He'le seldome be found without the shade of some grove, in whose bottome a river dwells... He thinkes businesse, but never does any: he is all contemplation, no action. He hewes and fashions his thoughts, as if he meant them to some purpose; but they prove unprofitable, as a piece of wrought timber to no use.

The melancholy of Jaques is simply his 'humour', a quirk of nature: dramatically it is one more attitude to life among the many of which the play is composed. He is mocked by Orlando and Rosalind, and censured, not very seriously, by the Duke, but there is no suggestion that his melancholy is a serious pathological condition or that he represents any particular threat to a society which, on occasion, he likes 'to woo his company'. He has none of the sense of personal injury which characterises other, more obviously threatening, Malcontents. As Agnes Latham stresses in her introduction to the play,

> We never see him in a mood approaching depression and he is entirely free of the malcontent's sense of personal injury. He never suggests that the world has treated him more unfairly than anyone else. He proposes to 'cleanse' it, but not to pay scores.[18]

Of course, this position presents a different ambiguity: the puzzling paradox by which a character may be 'melancholic', yet at the same time be to all intents and purposes a happy man, existing comfortably in the eccentric balance of his humour, and in Jaques we see an important difference between the merely

---

18   William Shakespeare, *As You Like It*, Agnes Latham, ed. The Arden Shakespeare (London 1975), Introduction, pp. xlvi–li.

Melancholic and the Malcontent, for while many of the attributes outlined by Overbury would also predicate a malcontented condition, by no means does a Melancholic have to embrace the extremes of bitterness and malevolence associated with most Malcontents. Jaques is a Malcontent, but a mild one, and as such his evident benignity is somewhat unusual. He does of course exist in the kind of light-hearted romantic comedy in which a 'heavier', more obviously threatening Malcontent would set an entirely different tone, but this does not at all explain why *Much Ado's* much more malignant Malcontent, Don John, does not destroy that play's lightsome tone by his presence. Of course, Shakespeare's use of dramatic irony in *Much Ado* defuses much of Don John's potency - but one might be left wondering what is the point of Jaques in *As You Like It* if he is not to be merely a figure of fun – mocked more than mocking. Perhaps there is also another reading of Jaques in context. The society around him exists securely - and this is a comedy, and the 'ordered' world is ultimately secure – yet he does mock and rail, and his railings hit home. Jaques mocks and is mocked for his mocking, but his role has made its particular point: no ordered society is above mockery, and no human condition above satire.

CHAPTER TWO

MALCONTENTS BORN,
MADE AND PLAYED

i

The distinction between a 'born' Malcontent and a 'made' Malcontent is probably of as much significance as 'natural' and 'professional' Fools. To witness a Malcontent in the making is, potentially, 'good theatre' and the distinction is primarily a dramatic one: in the case of the born Malcontent, the malcontent personality is fully established from the outset, with no elaborate accounting for his state of mind or humour. He is recognizable because he is flagged-up, as it were, with the Malcontent's paraphernalia. He might be dressed in black, as Hamlet is, but not necessarily; it is primarily his language – his attitude – which will define and distinguish him. He might announce himself blatantly, like Richard or Edmund or Flamineo, or we might be allowed a more subtle perception of his purpose, but he is essentially *there,* a malcontented presence alienated and different from the other characters with whom he shares the stage. He need not necessarily be at a remove from the audience, however; Vice-like, he will probably insinuate a relationship with the crowd from the start. They, too, it is implied, are outsiders, looking on.

The made Malcontent is a different matter. His story, the tale of his alienation, is part of the dramatic narrative. We see his degeneration from an ordinary man with his moral matter, ambitions, inhibitions, and hopes in a decline towards alienation. The cause of this decline and its effects will be acted out before us, part of the plot. Inevitably, we witness something of ourselves in such a process: the average guy, as it were, lugged into extraordinary circumstances and emotional exigencies is forced to exceed certain bounds of moral convention and decency and is, potentially, any one of us, 'everyman', turned into a railing and disruptive cynic. Thus, of course, the distinction between the dramatic purpose and the moral one becomes essentially blurred. Anything that smacks of the Fall of Man can acquire a symbolic, even tragic, element. Sometimes the dramatist comforts us a little; some Malcontents whom we see made on the stage – Macilente, for instance, from Ben Jonson's *Every Man Out of His Humour*, and Malvolio from Shakespeare's *Twelfth Night*, even the hapless Timon – were always, we can construe, Malcontents *in potentia*: as it were, 'malcontent-material' awaiting the precise set of circumstances to tip the balance. Yet this potential need not lessen the dramatic impact: there is a cliff-hanger effect of watching the half-inevitable, a horror-factor in witnessing what amounts to a perversion of the human soul. Some of the most interesting examples of this at work in the drama can be found in those plays where a distinction between the two kinds of Malcontent – that is, where those characters who are established as malcontented from the beginning, and those who are brought to such a state in the course of the drama – can be seen in the same play.

Such a play is Shakespeare's *Twelfth Night*. Like Jacques, into the category of born Malcontents also falls Feste, at least superficially, but Feste is complex and problematic. He is primarily a Fool and, like all Fools, he has the licence to mock his betters from the safety of professional privilege. No apology is required for the way he is: he is 'my lady's corruptor of words' simply because it is his job. Moreover, Feste is very good at his job and that uncomfortable paradox, the un-foolish Fool. In no sense does his intelligence escape us. If he appears deliberately obfuscatory, then it is his power of language, his dexterity with certain semantic manoeuvres that is at work; his wits are not in doubt – it is ours that have failed to keep up. Feste the Licensed Fool is also a Malcontent with a Malcontent's bitter intelligence turned to malevolent ends. In *As You Like It* (and *The Malcontent*, to which the Fool-role – Passarello – was subsequently added) there is both a Fool and a Malcontent; in *Twelfth Night* the Fool's role serves a dual purpose. Like Jaques, Feste displays many of the characteristics associated with melancholy and, also like Jaques, he seems to be an essential part of, and to depend upon, the society in which he exists as a kind of essential outsider.

No Fool is portrayed as wholly benign, but Feste is a very far cry from the almost lovable Touchstone or Passarello. Feste denies us a sentimental view of him from the moment he reveals the active will to harm. He is also wholly unlike Lear's loyal and somewhat similarly wise Fool, in that he quite obviously 'belongs' to no one, except nominally to Olivia: he is 'nobody's fool', as it were. Perhaps partly as a result of this duality – where the Malcontent and the jester are one and the same – *Twelfth Night* is a very different kind of comedy from *As You Like It*. Feste is soon established as more than a bit sinister; a Fool who exerts an actively malevolent influence, all of a piece with the somewhat threatening atmosphere of the play. Like the Vice (and indeed like Jaques) Feste is invested with a certain 'stage-magic', apparently capable of being everywhere at once, a ubiquity which exacerbates his air of malevolence. Although some explanation for his particular bitterness is offered in the play (Malvolio has cast aspersions on his success in his profession and tried to have him dismissed from Olivia's household) it is never quite adequate to justify the degree and escalation of Feste's malevolence. His tormenting of Malvolio as the spurious Sir Topaz is peculiarly shocking to charitable Christian sensibilities, since he impersonates a priest supposedly visiting a prisoner in torment, with motives that are highly ambiguous: either he is rationally engaged in a redress of wrongs so severe that they warrant such measures (in which case we might sympathize with the motive if not with the method) or such unwonted malevolence was latent from the beginning – part of a 'back-story' we are not permitted to know. Given Feste's obvious intelligence, a merely uncontrolled excess of the 'pranking' he indulges – a thing that would have accorded well enough with the traditional Vice – is not a satisfactory explanation. There is a disturbing sense of lurking mischief, almost of chaos, threatening to push matters out of control and beyond reason. The punishment Feste inflicts upon Malvolio is not merely revenge for the ills that Feste has suffered at Malvolio's hands, but a punishment of the world – a dramatic declaration, evinced in its excess, of Feste's malevolent power and of society's impotence.[19]

On the one hand, of course, it is easy to see that Malvolio, a stock butt of the anti-Puritan joke, has deserved much of what he gets. Humiliations such as being persuaded into yellow cross-garters and wearing a permanent smile, belying his sobriety, is a fitting punishment for his sanctimonious hypocrisy. His vanity caused him to walk into Feste's trickery, and we can cheer. However, our sympathies are swayed falteringly to his side once Malvolio is presented as a hapless victim. He is trapped, literally, and caused to suffer a moral and spiritual penalty we feel he cannot entirely deserve. Our sympathies have been played on and played with: whatever sympathy we might have felt for Feste as the abused outsider getting his own back is surely exceeded; our sense of fair play - and the play does assume us 'fair' - forces us to revise our opinions . Feste's malicious revenge lets down whatever moral or sentimental expectations we might have had of him, and has repaid suffering in a way that is alien to any sense of Christian charity (which the pseudo-role of Sir Topaz directly mocks) let alone any sense of Stoical withdrawal from engagement with his fate. But there is something else at work, too. Not only is our sense of fairness being used against us, but so is our appetite for sentiment. Feste's last song, forlorn and lonely, attempts to claw back the sense of pathos, and we must

---

19 See A. C. Bradley: 'Feste the Jester' in *A Book of Homage to Shakespeare*, ed. I. Gollancz (Oxford, 1916), pp. 164–169.

owe it to the playwright's enormous and subtle sense of irony that the attempt succeeds.

Whatever the moral arguments of what has been called Shakespeare's bitterest comedy – a play perhaps best considered as a comedy of ideas, rather than regarded as having any single moral thrust – one can see in it a distinct trajectory of Malcontent. Prompted by his ill-treatment, which Olivia certainly acknowledges (but it will depend entirely on her tone of voice, and thus on the tone of the production, as to whether she is seriously concerned that 'He hath been most notoriously abused.'(V, i, 377)), Malvolio proceeds to become a Malcontent *in potentia,* and a would-be revenger; thus the dual nature of the Malcontent role undergoes another shift. Malvolio's habitual sneering and pomposity are not in themselves malcontented, however, and his less than attractive personality can be seen to be mitigable, however absurdly, once he becomes obsessed by the preposterous notion that Olivia returns his devotion. In the brief (and hugely comic) moment when we see an entirely different Malvolio preparing, literally, to embed himself at the top of that society to which he feels he belongs, we are forced to accept that, in Malvolio's case, circumstances apparently alter nature. It is only at the end of the play: 'I'll be reveng'd upon the whole pack of you!' (V, i, 376) that we perceive a capacity for true Malcontent in Malvolio, and to an extent can justify and sympathize with its cause. Malvolio, at the end of the play, is made Malcontent, preparing to continue his thwarted, vengeful malevolence into a future we can only guess at: what price the peace of the 'happy ending' of Olivia and Sebastian, Orsino and Viola, after such a threat?

The roles of Timon and Apemantus in Shakespeare's *Timon of Athens* also exemplify the born and the made, presenting two pictures of melancholia: the one apparently natural, in the character Apemantus (Ape-man?), and the other acquired by Timon after a series of slights and disappointments. *Timon of Athens* dramatizes the story of a real-life character who gained legendary status as the embodiment of misanthropy. Timon was not always this way. In Shakespeare's play, he lives happily and splendidly amid a crowd of supposed friends, persons attracted by his wealth and lavish generosity, but suddenly finds himself penniless and therefore friendless. Learning the bitter lesson that no one wants to know you when you're down and out renders Timon acidly melancholic. Disillusioned, he develops a deep antipathy for his former friends, his fellow citizens of Athens, and for mankind in general. He leaves Athens in order to live in solitude and to nurse his grievances. All men, he now believes, are deceitful flatterers:

> ... all is oblique;
> There's nothing level in our cursed natures
> But direct villainy. Therefore, be abhorr'd
> All feasts, societies, and throngs of men!
> His semblable, yea, himself, Timon disdains:
> Destruction fang mankind! (*TofA*, IV, iii, 18–23)

In his bitter retirement from the world, Timon plays unwilling host to a series of visitors at whom he rails corrosively. They comment, most of them sympathetically, on his mental condition and its causes. Prompted to suicide, he writes a surly epitaph for himself and apparently kills himself. The play (which Coleridge described as 'a *Lear* of the satiric drama') presents an ambivalent portrayal of its hero, and not surprisingly, critics have remarked that a serious problem is its uncertain vacillation between tragedy and satire. Timon can be seen as either a great man of flawed virtue who, like Lear is 'more sinned against than sinning', or as himself the object of satire, a mean and twisted prodigal, blaming others for his folly. We might incline to the second view, for Timon is a figure of little moral stature and consciousness, at the end of the play expressing no more awareness of his true situation than at the beginning. However, since his psychic disintegration is due to a mistaken faith in human nature – in other words, the fate of the disappointed idealist – his quarrel with the world is valid, if hopelessly naive. 'Human nature' cannot possibly deserve such 'faith', and the play makes this necessarily cynical point, regardless of the moral stature of its hero. Sympathy is rather a different matter, but since it is in the nature of the drama that there should be a powerful identification process at work between any hero-figure and the audience, Timon's abject despair is compellingly uncomfortable, whether or not we approve of its causes.

Timon's eventual hatred of mankind is so all-inclusive that even self-love disappears. Just as with Hamlet, this malcontented philosophy has a logical soundness which neither the prospect of vengeance nor the tentative offer of human affection can penetrate. This is, possibly, its truly tragic dimension: that at the same time the play should satirize the causes of such despair does not mean that despair itself is presented as some sort of sick joke. Rather, the fact that Timon has brought it on himself, as it were, emphasizes his inner loneliness, and his absence of enlightenment at the end is therefore all the more appalling. This play is, in effect, *about* despair, and the trajectory, from misguided but generous idealism to utterly loveless malcontentedness, is perhaps all the more powerful for its utter denial of redemption. Apemantus, who is characterized in the *dramatis personae* as 'a churlish Philosopher', is sharply contrasted with Timon. Apparently a Malcontent by nature and not as a result of a series of misfortunes, he deeply hates and distrusts all mankind, and he snarls and rails accordingly. While Timon is still in his prosperity, he receives Apemantus into his house and finds amusement in provoking his growling misanthropy. Then, when Timon himself becomes a railing melancholic, Apemantus scolds him for usurping his personality: 'Do not assume my likeness' (*TofA*, IV, iii, 219). Timon's new character, Apemantus says, is 'A poor unmanly melancholy sprung | From change of fortune' (IV, iii, 204–5), as if such 'change of fortune' invalidates the condition (which, from the born Malcontent's point of view, it well might.) The two Malcontents spiritedly express their disgust with each other. Apemantus, despite his eccentricities, is an intelligent, candid and honest man. In Timon's heyday, it is Apemantus alone who tells him the truth about the sycophants who surround him and about the foolish course he is taking (I, ii, 39 ff.).[20]

ii

This essentially truthful element of the Malcontent nature – whether born or made – is of vital importance. Without it, the Malcontent, however variable his guise, would be inevitably a negligible figure, of no significant thrust, either dramatically or morally. Invested with *truth* – as opposed to rectitude, good will, civil and religious moral values, however, he is highly potent, not only as a role in the context of the plot, but to the impact of the play as a whole.

The Malcontent *in potentia* – one whose balance can be seen to be precarious and who only needs a switch of circumstance to turn him from being a law-abiding citizen into an alienated malevolent force is one thing. The impact of external forces upon the personality and individual will of a seemingly incorruptible and just character is another, and makes for a powerful, harrowing dramatic study. Nowhere, perhaps, is this impact more horrifically apparent than in Thomas Kyd's *The Spanish Tragedy*, (entered onto the Stationer's Register 1592, but almost certainly performed earlier) where we see Hieronimo, a decent and just man, a loving husband and father, finally left with nothing but his single-minded and ingenious obsession to avenge the murderer of his son. For much of the play, the moral tension concerning Hieronimo lies in his reluctance to change his moral

---

20 Timon seems not to have been characterized as a melancholic in the classical sources (Plutarch, Strabo, Lucian) or in William Painter's *Palace of Pleasure* (1566). It would appear that Timon had melancholy 'thrust upon him', as it were, by Renaissance commentators. It should also be borne in mind that the first 'Dramatis Personae' for *Timon of Athens* was produced for the Folio of 1623, probably to even out compositorial problems, and there is no evidence that Shakespeare himself designated the character of Apemantus 'a churlish philosopher'.

nature, his refraining from leaping to conclusions despite his terrible grief, and his cautious desire for proof of the culprits' guilt so that he can bring them to the proper court of justice. He has sworn revenge, but he intends it lawfully; he will bring Lorenzo and Balthazar to justice before the King in the proper approved manner without taking the law into his own hands. At all points, we are made to sympathize with Hieronimo; and his essential decency, established from the start, is vital to that response. We are outraged on his behalf, and his extreme grief for his murdered son and his initial belief in the machinery of justice (as befits his honourable commitment to his office of Knight Marshal) presents a complex (and entirely credible) picture of human and civil decency maintained in spite of his own suffering, and despite the revelations that the machine of justice is hopelessly corrupt. The escalation of suffering as the play proceeds, with his wife Isabella's grief-crazed suicide, and with the apparent conspiracy of circumstances which prevent Bel-Imperia's testifying (she has been taken prisoner by her brother), followed by the murderers' plausible story to account for the lovers' disappearance, ultimately weaken Hieronimo's resolve, a weakening which is plausible and highly sympathetic. This is partly because, despite his elevated office, Hieronimo is that rarity on the Elizabethan stage, the essentially *ordinary* hero: a decent man with a decent job who becomes a victim, both of the evil will of others, and of a state justice machine which cannot protect or defend him. Our sense of the impotence of his position is compounded by the King's disinclination to believe Hieronimo's witness-less testimony because of his increasingly deranged behaviour at court. His sanity is put in doubt, but not to us, because we have been allowed to see why it has altered. We are the witnesses. We share the agony of truth uncredited.

The culmination is shocking on two levels, apart, of course, from the contrived theatrical horror of having Hieronimo bite out his tongue on the stage. The first 'shock' arises from the fact that we know Hieronimo is essentially not 'malcontent material'; that is, that there is nothing, apart from the accumulation of events, which indicates the declivity into which he finally falls. Given this dreadful concatenation of circumstances, we can identify with his sense of helplessness and with his obsession. His exultation in his revenge is final and fatal, but the biting out of his tongue, far from being merely a gratuitous piece of horror (although it is profoundly horrific in its effect) is symbolic of the virtuous man biting out his own terrible words, the more powerful because it occurs shortly after a very long speech, in which he has told his story at last, but which has come far too late to remedy matters, even if it were believed. The second 'shock' lies in the knowledge of the impotence even of kings – the Renaissance world's last resort and veto of the justice-machine, and next to God only in earthly judgement – and therefore of the impotence of simple truth on a human level. In this play, supernatural forces supervene (the Ghost of Andrea, and the Allegory of Revenge) but this divine interference does not detract from our perception of Hieronimo as essentially human, and a very unwilling Malcontent. Rather, his dislocation from himself is the inevitable state conferred on the human protagonists by the supernatural ones, and is thus inescapable. His malcontentedness is 'made' beyond his control, in the manner of the Senecan drama – Classical aspects of the play which I shall be discussing in Part II – but it is Hieronimo's essential humanity which makes the play innovative: his almost obscene capitulation affirms his humanity rather than denies it.

Seemingly at the opposite end of the spectrum, we have the mere evil-doing of Iago. In *Othello* we are made to feel the full and inexorable force of the Malcontent element. Apparently simply evil in nature, Iago is constantly seeking to destroy, exulting in his own cleverness. No entirely satisfactory explanation is ever given for his malevolence, nor do we witness any moral 'struggle', except for his own 'trying-on' of several explanations for himself. A long-running scholarly pursuit was triggered by S. T. Coleridge's famous reference to Iago's 'motiveless malignity', but Iago's elusive motives remain just that: no rational human explanation quite accounts for him. There is his resentment of Othello's choice of Cassio rather than himself as lieutenant, a slight he regards as especially wounding because Cassio is a mere 'theoretician' without experience in the battlefield. Later, Iago states that he hates the Moor for having cuckolded him – a thing which is left entirely ambiguous and unproven (I, iii, 392–93 and II, i, 305–6); and then there is Iago's hint that he himself has a lust for Desdemona (II, i, 300). Finally, he complains bitterly that Cassio's virtues cast a moral shadow over his own depraved life: 'He hath a daily beauty in his life | That makes me ugly' (V, i, 19–20). Perhaps it is here and here only that we perceive a hint of Iago's personal tragedy, a tiny glimpse of the distorted humanity in what is otherwise a comprehensively – and incomprehensibly – vile character.

It has been suggested that Iago requires no rational motives because his Elizabethan audience would have recognized him as a dramatic descendant of the Vice.[21] However, while the medieval 'pedigree' of this supreme Malcontent, as with the others, is undoubtedly important, the assumption of such a direct ancestry here is surely too simple, and for two reasons. While Iago's relationship to the Devil is acknowledged by Othello at the end of the play when he stares at Iago's feet, expecting to find them cloven, the assumption of a direct and obvious relationship to the Vice as such seems far less certain, since the Vice is pre-eminently witty and amusing, and Iago is neither. I suggest that the Elizabethan audience was far more likely to have recognized Iago as something rather different. A Malcontent in a modern Renaissance sense, Iago is (whatever else) unrecognized and unrewarded for his talents, which include a mordant apprehension of the moral weaknesses of others. This play requires no supernatural agent of chaos, for chaos is embodied in Iago himself. And however unexplained the causes, ultimately Iago's

---

21 Bernard Spivack, *Shakespeare and the Allegory of Evil* (New York 1958), pp. 52–3.

malevolence is logical and human if explained by relentless and pitiless envy. Iago's destructive impetus is that of the ambitious politician – albeit crazed and taken to extremes, and *Othello* is essentially a modern tragedy of thwarted ambition. On Iago's apparently purposeless malignity rests the tragic tension of the play, so that structurally, Iago's role as agent of chaos is central, 'inhuman' because human. Is Iago a 'tragic' figure? Possibly: rotten humanity cannot help being this. But whatever explanations he offers for himself, or are offered in his behalf, these are insignificant compared with his effect on Othello and on Desdemona, and it is to them that the tragedy properly belongs.

The Revenger's Tragedy probably remains the iconic Jacobean drama: Italianate, wordy, violent, full of revenge and counter-revenge, poison, assassination, virtue wronged and compromised, several vile villains, and – of course – everyone heaped dead on the stage by the end of Act Five. Its hero, Vindice, is a Malcontent – but the Malcontent-role is in fact (once again) shared: between Vindice, avenging his murdered lover, his dead father and wronged sister, and Spurio the evil duke's bastard son, who claims 'malcontenthood' from the outset. The comparison is interesting, for in Vindice can be seen one set of possible causes at work – his disillusion with any justice meted out by the Duke's corrupt court, and his grief; in Spurio, we have quite another: the fact of his bastardy. Both characters rail against the moral world that mankind has created, and against the universe generally, but the interesting difference at the start is that Vindice states a positive intention to right wrongs, his purpose as a revenging hero – a reformer, in effect – whereas Spurio's only purpose seems to be to make life as uncomfortable as possible for everyone around him. Matters have gone way beyond the retrieval of 'justice': his very birth means that his is an unjust existence. He parades his viciousness, and 'has the courage and attractiveness of a character with convictions, believes in his own evil.'[22] Spurio

---

22   *The Revenger's Tragedy*, R. A. Foakes, ed., The Revels Plays,(Manchester, 1966), Introduction, p. xxviii.

is, to all intents and purposes, a born Malcontent, but he is given a different and importantly social, as opposed to a merely ill-humoured context: he is a Bastard, marginalized from the ducal family and the possibility of inheritance, and his malignant nature is therefore supplied with an a priori cause and motive.

Bastards (and Jews as another traditionally vilified stratum of society) therefore form a rather separate strand of 'born' Malcontents, since they are presented as literally having been born into that condition which society describes as outcast. This has nothing to do with their 'humour', necessarily, although their social condition is frequently seen to condition their states of mind, and to be both the cause of, and excuse for, their hatred of the world. Thus, Barabas from Christopher Marlowe's *The Jew of Malta* (c. 1589/90) and Shylock from *The Merchant of Venice* (1596/8) rail against the society which has ostracized them for their race, but react in accordance with the bitterness and ultimate malevolence which, ironically, society expects of them: 'The villainy you teach me, I will execute...' (*M of V* III, i, 76). Likewise, with Spurio in *The Revenger's Tragedy*, and Edmund in *King Lear*, the fact of their bastardy conditions everything they do and, even more importantly, everything they are. Edmund views his own bastardy as an almost pathological condition: after denouncing the tendency for people to blame the stars for personal disasters in ironic tones as 'excellent foppery' and 'admirable evasion', he follows up with:

> My father compounded with my mother under the dragon's tail, and my nativity was under Ursa major; so that it follows I am rough and lecherous. Fut! I should have been that I am had the maidenliest star in the firmament twinkled on my bastardizing.'
>
> (I, ii, 135–140)

thus rejecting the 'stars' and claiming his bastard nature for his own. While the primary thrust of Edmund's speech is a 'modern', humanistic seizing of control of personal fortune and a rejection of the medieval superstitions evinced by his father, nevertheless in justifying the seizing of his own destiny in this way - the stated intention to evil deception - he has, in effect, replaced one moral superstition with another. 'Bastardy' has taken the place of astrology in predetermining his nature and therefore, we can infer, he is as helpless in its power as if he were prepared to abrogate responsibility to an adversely-aspected star. Spurio makes a similar claim while planning adultery with his stepmother:

> ... hate all I;
> Duke, on thy brow I'll draw my bastardy.
> For indeed a bastard by nature should make cuckolds
> Because he is the son of a cuckold-maker.   (I, ii, 201–205)

'Hate all I...' The adultery is not undertaken in passion, nor even truly in lust, but in a spirit of fulminating hatred: 'Step-mother, I consent to thy desires, | I love thy mischief well, but I hate thee...'(I, ii, 192–94). Lechery, being the cause of bastardy is, *ipso facto*, taken for granted as a condition of bastards; but this is no mere excess of libido; this is a lechery made aggressive and vile by a hatred of the world. Similarly, the Jews Barabas and Shylock can be relied on to behave 'Jewishly': that is, born with the Jews' supposed love of money – but their miserliness and ambition is conditioned and exaggerated by their hatred of the Christian society which shuns them.

This makes for a powerfully ambiguous moral judgement from the stage. *The Jew of Malta*, as Robert Jones puts it, 'repeatedly knocks our conventionally self-flattering expectations off balance through the responses to Barabas it demands from us.'[23] Although Marlowe uses the Morality Play's tactics of alienating us from the malicious knave who entertains us, he puts his own special twist on them. Barabas at once elicits our hostility by crowing on behalf of all Jews: 'We have scrambled up | More wealth by far than those who brag of faith' (I, i, 120–21) but then proceeds to expose our hypocrisy:

---

23 See Robert Jones, *Engagement with Knavery: Points of View in Richard III, The Jew of Malta, Volpone, and the Revenger's Tragedy* (Durham, Duke, 1986), pp. 63–98.

Who hateth me but for my happiness?
Or who is honour'd now but for his wealth?
Rather had I, a Jew be hated thus
Than pitied in a Christian poverty;
For I can see no fruits in all their faith,
But malice, falsehood, and excessive pride,
Which methinks fits not their profession.   (I, i, 110–16)

Barabas, Jones suggests, has invited our hisses and then pointed to their hidden motive: in this case, the envy that underlies
the audience's Christian contempt for Jews, and its ostensible
sanction of Jew-baiting. If we (a typical Elizabethan Christian
audience) take consolation (or excessive pride) in the fact that
Christians govern the world in which Jews prosper, so be it; Barabas will grant us that and be content in the 'peaceful rule' that
wealth (as opposed to princely rulership, government, 'degree'
and so on) allows him. If we align ourselves against the Jew, as
the play invites us to do, we are adopting a position that the play
will make entirely unflattering.

iii

Physical ugliness produces a similar double perception, since
our revulsion and our sympathies are played on simultaneously.
In the real world, Fools, who were frequently physical oddities:
deformed, midget or somehow ugly and unable to compete in
a society which demanded, then as now, aesthetic regularity of
form as a pre-requisite, nevertheless had the protection of patronage. Physical deformity was for the Elizabethans notoriously indicative (and therefore emblematic) of spiritual deformity;
and where there was no such patronage to be had, many crip-
ples and misfits must have experienced the full force of such entrenched belief and lived in misery. This is one of the reasons
why the conquering Tudors so emphasized (and, it is said, greatly exaggerated) Richard III's crook back, and Shakespeare's play
is, on the one hand, endorsing the popular myth: pandering to
the prejudice that all external ugliness points to a disfigurement

of the soul within. On the other hand, by manipulation of the sympathies of the audience for the disadvantage of deformity, the play exposes such an attitude as flawed. Richard's declaration at the beginning of the play that he is 'not shaped for sportive tricks' (I, i, 14) is his initial justification for, and announcement of, his villainy. His shape precludes him from proving 'a lover', so he is determined instead to 'prove a villain'. Not only has his outward shape predetermined his inner, spiritual shape, but his deformities must explain and justify his deformed outlook, given the aesthetic pre-occupations of the age – and the theatre, which cannot countenance him in a virtuously heroic role. Because he is not shaped like other men, therefore he claims the right to not be judged by other men's standards, and the audience has been invited to perceive that in this he has no choice.

The constant allusions to Richard's deformities in the play not only emphasise this moral paradox, but achieve a kind of poetic fetishism when he does, after a fashion, become a 'lover'. Anne ruefully admits that her 'woman's heart | Grossly grew captive to his honey words...' (IV, 79–80) even as she loathes him. We are never in doubt that, briefly, Anne has been *seduced* by Richard, as opposed to terrorised and effectively raped by him.

The role of De Flores, in Middleton and Rowley's *The Change-ling* (first registered in 1622) – 'this ominous ill-fac'd fellow' – is a similar case in point. De Flores justifies his relentless pursuit of Beatrice–Joanna partly on account of his ugliness – he cannot woo her in the ordinary way because she will find him revolting, but, being obsessed with her, he will nevertheless prey on her to the point of wearing down her resistance. His eventual triumph is partly that of his personal disadvantage, and in this play too, the ugliness itself becomes the focus of a strange obsessive fascination: De Flores' own, in continually testing Beatrice–Joanna's resistance, and hers, both before and after she has submitted to him. But her repugnance becomes ever more ambiguous as the play proceeds, and a twisted erotic tension mounts as, whatever her stated motives (and certainly she reiterates her revulsion again and again) it is also obvious that her protestations are at least ambivalent, part of a monstrous flirtation with a man she finds more and more fascinating. It is highly significant that her only real experience of sex is with the vile but charismatically compelling De Flores, while courtly Alsemero remains a fantasy, actually to be enjoyed by the sexually uninhibited Diaphanta. Beatrice–Joanna's submission, ostensibly the 'payment' extracted for Alonzo's murder, is the beginning of a potently perverse enjoyment, of a piece with all of the other 'inversions' which preoccupy *The Changeling*.[24]

It is vital to this psychologically sophisticated play that we are allowed to see complex psychologies from all sides. De Flores, undoubtedly ugly – *and* a thoroughly unpleasant character, predatory and pitiless – must be charismatic enough for us to perceive the sexual fascination he is able to exert upon Beatrice–Joanna. Likewise, Beatrice–Joanna is a complex enough stage-presence to allow us to see through her unconscious fascination with De Flores: she believes she is using him, but we can see, ironically, that despite her belief in her control of him as her cat's paw, it she herself who is the victim of manipulation. (Beatrice–Joanna would almost qualify for a female Malcontent, were it not for her self-ignorance: but a Malcontent is never self-ignorant.) As an ambitious upper-servant, De Flores' hatred of the world, especially of the *beau-monde* of pampered aristocrats, is fairly typical, but because of his ugliness, he has been born alienated rather than merely socially disadvantaged: an accident of nature has effectively excluded him from attaining that position in the social sphere (and therefore – powerfully, in his case – the sexual and emotional sphere also) to which he feels he should and could belong. One implication of this is that mere social disadvantage is surmountable. In the real, changing world of late Renaissance England, too, this was beginning to be true: education, brains and ambition were the qualifications

---

24   See Nicholas Brooke, *Horrid Laughter in Jacobean Tragedy* (London, 1979).

with which most of Elizabeth's most trusted advisers gained their posts.

In *The Revenger's Tragedy*, (first performed c. 1606) Vindice, a minor courtier of brains and parts on the margins of grand society, embodies no less than three distinct types of malcontent. He plays, for the purposes of insinuating himself into the Duke's court, a villainous pandar: 'some strange-digested fellow... of ill-contented nature... such a blood, | A man that were for evil only good' (I, i): a born Malcontent in the crudest sense. Later, when this disguise has been all but penetrated, he takes the role of a hired assassin, prescribed by Lussurioso as 'a fellow of discontent and want | ... the best clay to mould a villain of' (IV, i): a 'made' Malcontent, in other words, responding to the sufferings of poverty and unemployment (although the syntax of Lussurioso's prescription leaves it unclear whether the discontent predetermined the want or the other way round.) But these disguises are both predicated upon an underlying state of melancholy in Vindice's 'real' nature, a state prompted or at least exacerbated by the murder of his betrothed. Her skull – his 'study's ornament' – serves as a continual reminder of death in general, a *memento mori* , and of her particular death, by which he is obsessed, and determined to avenge. The chief difference between this Vindice and the crude travesty he adopts as a disguise is his role as hero-revenger – a desire which quickly extends beyond revenge for his lover's death to plotting the destruction of the whole corrupt court.

When we consider the fact that his very name means 'revenger', and that this play is, more than most, a late experiment in the allegorical drama, it is pointless to consider mere causes, or to imagine a world in which Vindice were a happy man (as we are almost invited to in the case of Hamlet) with a live and beautiful bride. Vindice has a mission which goes beyond any individual consideration or causal psychology. Once the 'mission' is complete, Vindice is effectively redundant, and in recognition of his unfitness for the new court he has been responsible for 'cleansing', he goes down stoically with the ship he has destroyed. He has only partly been accounted for 'psychologically' in a play which is not so much about the fortunes of Vindice, as a *reductio ad absurdum*: what happens when certain attitudes and motivations are taken to their logical extremes.

On the other hand, complex psychological conditions are revealed, and a considerable dramatic tension produced , by Vindice's role-play. It is not simply a matter of 'putting on an act'; Vindice partly is Piato, and his final rage at the end of the first scene involving his mother and sister applies equally fitly to both the moral-seeking son and to the procurer-tempter:

> Were't not for gold and women, there would be no
> Damnation; Hell would look like a lord's great kitchen
> Without fire in't...   (II, i, 257–9)

The inversion of the imagery: of a cold – and because 'hearthless', therefore 'heartless' – Hell, without 'gold and women', is highly suggestive of the integration of the two roles, as is the 'great lord' who surely doubles for the Devil. Sin is necessary for fire and warmth, even for centrality, hence the hearth – and the paradox produced by the imagery makes a dramatic paradox of Vindice/Piato. In another scene (IV, iv), Castiza (whose name means 'chastity') must play the whore so convincingly that her mother is truly shocked. This implies that, in order for the scene to 'work' properly, it is necessary, as Nicholas Brooke put it, for Castiza to 'discover the whore within herself... her performance demands thought about role-playing, not simply about 'being' chaste.'[25]

A similar dramatic paradox exists between the several facets of Hamlet, and equally it is a vital part of the dramatic tension of the play that it is impossible to make clear distinctions between what might be the 'real' Hamlet and the 'antic disposition'. As Philip Edwards points out, everything he says to Polonius,

---

25   Nicholas Brooke, ibid., pp. 17–19.

Rosencrantz and Guildenstern during the long scene II,ii, 'has its irony, and if his hearers do not know when he is being sane and serious, nor do we.'[26] So much of *Hamlet* considers 'acting' in two senses: as in performing a deed, and as in playing a role, both in the legitimate sense of the acting profession, and with intent to deceive – and we are forced to consider the implications of acting and action throughout. Any attempt to identify the 'seam' between Hamlet's madness and sanity is a pointless exercise, since it does not exist as a clear division; and thus any answer to the question 'How mad is Hamlet?' would need to address itself to the highly ambiguous nature of the problem (of a role embraced with so much conviction as to become 'real') as presented in the play.

In Marston's *The Malcontent*, however – another play very much concerned with the playing of parts and psychological disguise – ostensibly we know the answers: Altofront is the 'real' personality; Malevole is the 'role', and the distinction is apparently clear and unambiguous. The clarity is quickly exposed as illusory, however. We are given the first direct indication that Malevole is a disguise in I, iv, during the dialogue between the disguised Duke and his trusted henchman, Celso. Celso's urging of his master to 'mutiny and die' (in itself a remarkable combination of the Herculean and the Stoical) is rejected, not so much because of the futility of such an action as for the simple truth that Duke is having a great deal more fun being a malcontent. 'Being' is the operative word here. Although he says:

O, no, climb not a falling tower, Celso;
'Tis well held desperation, no zeal;
Hopeless to strive with fate; peace, temporize...   (I, iv, 26–8)

---

26   William Shakespeare, *Hamlet, Prince of Denmark*, Philip Edwards, ed., The New Cambridge Shakespeare, (Cambridge, 1985). See Introduction pp. 46–7.

in a manner which suggests a less impulsive acceptance of 'fate' and the tactical need to play for time, this quickly gives way to: 'Hope... bidst me live, and lurk in this disguise!' and 'What? Play I well the free-breath'd discontent?'

This is smugly rhetorical; he does play the role far too well for mere dissembling, and his claim that 'Discord to malcontents is very manna' rings greedily with enjoyment. We are now in no doubt of his gleeful anticipation of his chosen part, and of his delight in banishing, however temporarily, his other self: 'When the ranks are burst, then scuffle Altofront.' The 'burst ranks' signify not only the dissolution of order at Court that permits Malevole to exist, but to the breaking out of Malevole from the constraints of the conservatively aristocratic Altofront, and the word 'scuffle' is powerfully dismissive. When Celso, evidently far more fearful of this course than the death-or-glory option he himself proposes, asks: 'Yes, but durst?', Malevole's reply: ''Tis gone; 'tis swallow'd like a mineral' announces the *fait-accompli* which is now very far removed from any sense of noble martyrdom, or of an unpleasant duty undertaken in a virtuous cause. Moreover, a 'mineral' is ambiguously a medicine or a poison, but evidently not, given Malevole's quick despatching of it, a metaphorically unstomachable draught. 'Some way, 'twill work...' Poison it possibly is, but only in the empowering sense that Malevole intends to be poisonous. His confidence of control over what he will become is beyond question.

That Malevole is far more than a mere disguise is reinforced in the play's structure: Altofront is a tiny role compared with that of Malevole, and indeed the whole play seems dedicated to a process of inversion, whereby 'good' characters – Altofront himself, his duchess Maria, and Celso – are largely absent from a stage which is monopolized for the most part by the far more amusing exploits of the 'bad' ones. The remarkable exception to this is Pietro. He also adopts a disguise under the direction of Malevole, who has revealed to Pietro his true identity, and with whom Pietro, penitent, but also pragmatic, has now joined forces. While at first it seems as if Pietro's 'Hermit' is entirely spurious, a mere ruse invented by Malevole to outwit Mendoza, the penitence is nevertheless real, as is his reported grief at the infidelity of Aurelia, even though, of course, the Hermit's highly-coloured report of Pietro's suicide on that account is an elaborate fiction. By the end of the play, however, the priestly Hermit, far from being a mere mockery of the Stoical sage (although of course it is this as well) is as much of a release and literal alter-ego for the materialistic usurping Duke Pietro as Malevole the Malcontent is for the high-minded Altofront:

> I here renounce forever regency.
> O Altofront, I wrong thee to supplant thy right...
> O, I am changed... (IV, v, 122–7)

Eventually, Altofront apparently tires of playing Malevole, and re-assumes his 'real' self. This elaborate device – the rejection of a role within a role – is used by Shakespeare when he has Edgar sicken of playing Poor Tom at the sight of Lear's distress and later in witnessing the despair of Gloucester. However, the device is put to a different purpose in *Lear*, where it is Edgar's remorse for his duplicity which threatens to get the better of him, and an apparent emotional exhaustion of the assumed role is seen to impinge on his feeble moral nature. This is not the same thing at all as Malevole's indignation when the Malevole role forbids him to assert his proper ducal authority, and it is only when Malevole is acting pandar for Mendoza to his own unsuspecting wife that we see his repugnance for the Malcontent role which he has 'become' so thoroughly as to have abrogated his ducal prerogatives. Malevole reasserts himself as Duke Altofront for reasons of power.

In neither *Lear* nor in *The Malcontent* is the role-within-a-role at all simple or straightforward, and we are forced to see in both not only the psychological, practical and emotional problems inherently faced by one personality deliberately maintaining another, but the theatrical truth that such a device involves: The 'Poor Tom' act forces a social perception, not only upon Lear and his father, but upon the audience. To all intents and purposes, Edgar really is Tom o' Bedlam *pro tem*. We are made to feel with his hunted misery, both from his own lips and Lear's. Tom is convincing as the 'bare, forked animal' because that is what he presents on the stage.

Similarly, Malevole forces an in-role perception of malcontenthood that is confusingly realistic, not at all lessened because we know he is in disguise. While much of the comic thrust of *The Malcontent* derives from the clear divisibility of the two roles (this is Comedy, and if the play is to achieve comic resolution, as it does, Altofront must supersede Malevole and regain his dukedom – Order must win) quite another imaginative thrust is at work. This strange play is not merely a lightsome comedy with a happy ending. Marston works in sinisterly uncomic elements which involve many of the tropes of serious tragedy.

A witty satire of theatrical convention *The Malcontent* undoubtedly is, and it is naturally tempting to suppose that the very title of the play is a tease, since the Malcontent in question is spurious: not a real Malcontent at all, but a clever device. Malevole's nastiness has been established as a sham in Act One. Yet, Malevole has to be sufficiently convincing for the illusion to work on stage, and from it, it is we who are being teased, played upon, invited to enjoin with him in his bitterness. He has the edge on us: like so many other more serious Malcontents, he is the Vice-like presenter of a horrid-funny comedy of the human power-play, its chief intelligence. None of his observations lose truth in the telling, for all that the play partially invites us to comfort ourselves with the knowledge that he is only playing. To assume otherwise would be at assume that this play is for (rather than played by) children, an assumption that John Webster's Induction for the public theatre is at pains to dispel.[27]

---

27 *The Malcontent* was written and performed in 1603, and printed in three editions in 1604. A third edition contains the Induction by John Webster in

Morally complex, emotionally ambiguous, this parody of theatrical convention appears to mock the ultimate triumph of the
Stoical virtue of Temperance until the end, when it endorses it
in spades – universal forgiveness instead of the almost standard heap of murdered corpses – but by this point we cannot be
entirely certain which 'side' it is on. We will cheer the 'goodies',
but 'temperance' is largely an off-stage abstract. For much of the
play, a sheer enjoyment of wickedness has invited our laughter
and thus our complicity. Virtue and order make for poor entertainment, in the theatre and out of it. The Genoese Court was
a dull place when presided over by a Duchess who 'had almost
brought bed-pressing out of fashion' (V, ii, 89–90), and, by implication, the 'suburbs' will be much enlivened when Maquerelle
the Bawd is eventually banished there. Moreover, it is plain that
Altofront is primarily the victim of his own stolid clinging to
conservatism, a quality which failed to allow him to perceive
political machination when it was under his nose:

> I wanted those old instruments of state,
> Dissemblance and Suspect...
> My throne stood like a point in midst of a circle,
> To all of equal nearness, bore with none,
> Reigned all alike, so slept in fearless virtue,
> Suspectless, too suspectless; till the crowd,
> (Still lickerous of untried novelties),
> Impatient with severer government,
> Made strong with Florence, banished Altofront.   (I, iv, 9–17)

Altofront the feudal ruler has been forced to become the precarious politician, acknowledging the demands of the 'lickerous'
crowd for bread and circuses, starkly acknowledging the met-

---

which Richard Burbage, Henry Condell, John Lowin and William Sly, all
members of the King's Men, converse with the audience about Marston's
play, about a rival company of boy actors at the Blackfriars theatre, and about
the Globe theatre itself, where *The Malcontent* is about to be performed with
Burbage in the title role.

aphor of a fixed hub of rule in an unchanging concentricity of command as unworkable, something breaking apart – a rueful admission of a realpolitik which now demands a Machiavellian approach to government, not to be found within the compass of 'fearless virtue' or the old established order. How much Altofront intends to change his governmental practises once he regains power (he will – this is a comedy) is left unclear, and we have to consider the possibility that he will make the same political errors in the future. This applies equally well to events that were taking place off the stage.

iv

The Malcontent figure is frequently the instrument through which the play-world is exposed as morally and politically flawed. So, too, in the manner of any meaningful satire, is the world outside the play. Thus we, the audience, are forced to ponder in our discomfort the values not only of the play-world, but of our own. The Malcontent is perforce often a highly uncomfortable element in a play, possessing at once qualities which are both alienating and incontrovertibly truthful, and this is as true of Malevole as of any other. Frequently, Malcontents are presented as the most intelligent characters in their plays and because of this, they possess a verbal succinctness which serves as a scourge to lash others for their sins and follies, regardless of the Malcontents' own behaviour. One of the more profoundly disturbing aspect of the Malcontent figure is that he perceives such uncomfortable truths. This far from precludes his being a liar. Like his Vice ancestor, he often engages in double-dealing and deception. Yet, his duplicity and lies are possible (and effective) only because of his accurate perception of the true weaknesses of others. Thus can Malevole win back a dukedom, Iago bring down a great general, Richard of Gloucester seize a crown.

The power of such figures derives partly from a powerful stage tradition, transmogrified to appeal to an audience which was becoming attuned to such inversions of a perceived natural or-

MALCONTENTS BORN, MADE AND PLAYED

der. Partly, however, that power was reinforced by a gritty social realism, and the appeal lay in a compound of the fear and exhilaration experienced when people begin to question established order for themselves. The theatre itself increasingly became a focus for radical ideas. The stage Malcontent figure was no mere fictional invention upon which to hinge such radicalism, but was already manifest on the fringes of a changing, exciting and troubled society.

CHAPTER THREE

THE ROLES AND
THE MODELS: THE
MALCONTENT AS SOCIAL
PHENOMENON

i

I have already indicated that Diccon in *Gammer Gurton's Needle* provides an early example of the dramatic fictional representation of a social phenomenon. A highly entertaining stage figure, part Fool, part Vice, he is also something else as well: the savant-idiot, enjoying the harsh Elizabethan version of care in the community. A substantial part of his entertainment-value derives from his being recognizably 'real'. We might meet his like in the street, be pestered by such a person, jeer at him perhaps, give him alms because we feel pressured, or, more insidiously, because we wish to feel, for a moment, 'good', buy a little private pardon. To cross his palm with a copper or two is to bless ourselves. Diccon's creator had closely observed real people.

Why those archetypal elements, Vice, Fool and the Melancholic, should have coalesced so significantly to form the late Elizabethan-cum-Jacobean stage Malcontent is largely explained by the emergence of a phenomenon in real life: in the shape of a significant tranche of young men who came to be known as 'malcontents' in late Elizabethan society and who seem to have grabbed what in those days passed for headlines, and thus the dramatists' attention as, amongst other things, excellent entertainment fodder. These so-called Malcontents were regarded variously as subversive, contemptible, awesome, glamorous, a little crazy, and without doubt dangerous; representing for many a sort of social malaise. It was not so much their literal numbers or power (or not nearly so much as their reputation suggested) but more the result of a popular fear of radicalism: insecurities prompted by changes to the old order in late Elizabethan and early Stuart society were making themselves felt. These so-called Malcontents became mythologised in their own time, and, since many of them were more than adept at self-advertisement, they seem to have deliberately fed the fear and the fascination they held. There is more than a touch of the caricature about the stage figure, but popular myth was already generalizing and caricaturing the real-life model.[28]

This process by which a relatively minor social phenomenon acquires, in the popular imagination, an ambiguously glamorous and vicious reputation, having the effect of inflating its power in one way, and in another inviting hissing and protest (a fashion icon for some, an object of fear and loathing for the rest) can of course be pointed to in other times and other places. Certain youth cults of the mid-twentieth century are good examples. The 'Punk' movement, for instance, seems to have had precisely this effect. Ravishingly appealing to some, perceived by others as heralding the virtual collapse of civilization, it had its nucleus of serious intellectuals, its outer rings of fashionable hangers-on who learned the dress-code and the argot but who would have been hard pressed for a meaningful utterance, and, of course, its alarmed detractors. These were anyone from elderly ladies frightened by the safety-pins and army boots, to members of the Establishment convinced of the rise of anarchy. Dangerous as it would be to place too much importance on this, or upon such other anachronistic phenomena as, say, the 'rebel without a cause' of the nineteen-fifties, it is highly interesting that dramatic fiction (in the case of the 1950s, largely the cinema) followed very quickly upon real life, and just as quickly

---

28 See Mark H. Curtis's essay, 'The Alienated Intellectuals of Early Stuart England', *Past & Present* 23, pp. 25–43.

exacerbated its cult status among the young. It is without doubt significant that the sixteenth-century phenomenon of the Malcontent was primarily, although not exclusively, also a cult of the young, embodying disaffected decadent youth, perceived by the majority as undesirable misfits.

Melancholy was already established as a precondition for 'malcontentedness' in various prose portrayals of melancholy and the melancholic type. The Galenic tradition had it that melancholy was an intractable medical condition, one which (not unreasonably) had the power, like many medical conditions, to infect: a disease, caught like the pox. In contrast, the 'malcontent disease' had also acquired both authority and a certain fashionable *cachet*, for melancholy was also the 'malady' of poets and the divinely inspired. This 'infection' was most likely to be contracted abroad, and especially in Italy, where the much more glamorous Aristotelian idea of melancholy had been generally current among scholars and artists in England since the later years of the fifteenth century. Thus the acquisition of melancholy had its irreproachably Classical roots, and the 'disease' was especially noted by English observers as having not only a direct causal link with the study of Humanism, but with foreign travel. Foreign cities, foreign courts or the fringes of them, had a wide appeal among young men of a certain education. Europe was the ultimate finishing school for the young aristocrat and others rich and ambitious enough to undertake such an adventure. In Europe, educated or semi-educated young gentlemen would acquire the melancholic attitude and bring it home with them, where it was to become an indispensable attribute, almost a fashion-statement. Robert Greene relates that, just after his continental travels in his youth, he affected malcontented melancholy. He confesses proudly that he travelled in 'Italy, and Spaine, in which places I sawe and practizde such villainie as is abominable to declare… At my return into England, I ruffeled out my silkes, in the habit of Malcontent…'[29] He returned from

---

29   Robert Greene, *The Repentance of Robert Greene*, in Works, ed. Grosart

his continental tour probably in 1580 to live a bohemian life in London, by which time the disgruntled, essentially exotic, traveller type of Malcontent had been well established in the public imagination.

ii

The Tudor age had produced an urge to travel generally, not just to imitate the great explorers of distant lands and capture colonies. Indeed, travel to the nearest countries of continental Europe – principally France and Italy – had become a favourite ambition among well-to-do young Englishmen by the middle of the sixteenth century.[30] (It is important to note that we are not thinking, yet, in terms of what came to be known as the Grand Tour, which came quite a lot later and which had far more to do with a broader sense of discovery of places as well as people, and of diverse peoples and cultures more than courts, of strange and wonderful geography that might inspire sublime Romantic poetry. The Grand Tour was perforce undertaken on foot, in a carriage, astride a horse; the travelling being as much about the journey itself as the getting there, and the 'there' might be a mountain range or a pyramid...) This earlier student would have been travelling in search of an education of a rather different kind, less to do with the stirring of the poetic fancy by means of natural wonders than a sort of communications exercise, through which he might absorb the lessons that sophisticated modern Europe could teach him. These young Tudors who visited their continental neighbours would have travelled by sea across the Channel to Calais, or by the fastest route to their destination, for the destination was the prize.

(London and Aylesbury, 1881–6), 12, p. 172.

30   See Z. S. Fink, 'Jaques and the Malcontent Traveller,' *Philological Quarterly*, 14 (1935), pp. 237–52. According to Fink, Frenchmen as well as Italians affected melancholy and encouraged the imitative English traveller to assume the pose. The French, however, copied the attitude from the Italians.

Francis Bacon, in his Essay 'Of Travel' lists for his young readership the ideal itinerary: 'the things to be seen and observed are: the courts of princes, specially when they give audience to ambassadors; the courts of justice... the churches and monasteries, with the monuments which are therein extant; walls and fortifications... havens and harbours; antiquities and ruins; libraries; colleges, disputations and lectures; shipping and navies; houses and gardens of state; exercises in horsemanship, fencing, training of soldiers; treasuries of jewels and robes; cabinets and rarities; and whatever is memorable...' While Bacon advises that triumphs, feasts, weddings, funerals and public executions might be low on a young traveller's list, he also says that these too are not to be neglected, and as for the theatre, he allows as edifying 'comedies, such whereunto the better sort of person doth resort'.

By the time Sir Francis Bacon wrote 'Of Travel' (published in 1597, but almost certainly written earlier for a narrower circulation during the previous ten years) the notion of traveller-student, travelling for the sake of his broader education and ambition, is well-established. Nowadays we would call it a gap-year: not such a silly anachronism as one might suppose for, according to Bacon, students should expect to be away for several months, improving themselves, learning as much about their new environment as they could, in however short a time, and preferably with the help of a guide-book ('some card or book describing the country where he travelleth') a human guide ('some tutor or grave servant') who speaks the language and knows the country and, as Bacon strongly advocates, 'some entrance into the local language' on the part of the student himself. He urges that the diary or travel journal should be brought into use, that the young student-traveller might note his observations, not for his own edification merely, but for the purpose of true reportage home.

There is plenty of evidence that during the 1500s, travel to the near continent became positively modish. That great English Renaissance man, Philip Sidney, had done it extensively, travelling to Italy, France, Spain, Poland, Hungary and the Low Countries. The young, rich and well-connected fetched up at foreign courts as the escorts of royalty, and there was much competition for places. It was in this respect that foreign courts became a sort of finishing school for young English aristocrats. Some were effectively amateur ambassadors. Indeed, some of them became official ambassadors, reporting back on a regular basis to the heads of government in the courts of Henry, of Mary, of Elizabeth, of James. Illustrious careers began in foreign courts; but some ended ignominiously, young men ruined financially after living the high life abroad. Patronage was all, yet the lack of a suitable patron doesn't seem to have deterred the less well-connected student. This less than salubrious existence (it has to be imagined: for all but the grandest, this was a sort of early hitch-hiking and living on one's wits in a foreign country without Consuls and without Tourist Information – indeed potentially without friends at all) was the reality of travel abroad for many young university graduates, and often involved a very precarious existence. But they did it, and it was highly popular; it was also regarded as a necessity by some, for the times had produced, amongst other things, a glut of unemployed and more or less dispossessed university graduates, whose future was uncertain. Francis Bacon warned James I in 1611 that an excess of grammar schools had produced more educated men than the state could hope to usefully employ.

The humbler traveller wound up, inevitably, in less than grand circumstances, seeking his fortune as he might; and of course there were those who were merely hangers-on: spies, some said; and they were not necessarily wrong. In the sprawling networks of the lower strata of great foreign houses, an observer of the comings and goings and covert conversations might be an innocent abroad, or he might not... Yet others, hopeful young adventurers, many of them graduates, some of them drop-outs, from Oxford or Cambridge who had come down without any clear direction of a future career, sought their fortunes if not in London then in the even darker terrains close to the walls of foreign cities, living on their wits and, when they could, often engaging in, amongst other things, journalism. Many of these young adventurers wrote pamphlets describing their experiences which were sent home and read, avidly. Pamphlets, one of the precursors of the modern news commentary (and only slightly less reliable) often had the advantage of being essentially freelance, but they were also often highly biased, subject to censorship and, inevitably in those days, out of date as far as went reportage of 'news'. Nevertheless, pamphlets as opposed to more official reportage were a powerful means of communication on matters abroad and the dissemination of ideas, some of them highly dangerous ones.

iii

The perceived threat of European travel was associated in particular with Italy. It was here – in the cradle of Humanism, the home of the notorious Machiavelli, as well as the infamous Borgias, and the powerful Medici family who more or less invented modern banking – that a young man dislocated from Tudor England and Englishness might acquire any number of vices, from Catholicism to homosexuality, and where he might begin to question England's relatively newly re-ordered Protestant values. The notion of 'Italian wickedness' was axiomatic by the later sixteenth century; Italy with its reputation for lawlessness and danger, spies lurking behind high walls, friends bearing cups of poison, hired assassins... There was also its reputation for the spirited exchange of ideas, and this double-vision of Italy seems to have been established a good generation before Shakespeare was born. Italy, and all things Italian, had begun to fascinate an increasingly wide educated English public from the early 1500s. Throughout the century, works in Italian or from the Italian language came to be in increasing demand, many published in the original before they became available in translation. Towards the middle of the century, there was a veritable flood of publication in translation, especially of prose-fiction: old tales and newer ones, as well as plays and poetry.

Not unnaturally, Italy began to attract a great many young travellers seeking to broaden their educations and further their careers, and no less than two Italian phrase books were published before the turn of the century, and probably the first English/Italian dictionary. Italian universities, Padua in particular, became a magnet for foreign students from all over Europe but especially from England. As late Renaissance Italy gained a reputation as the graduate school of Humanism and the *vita civile,* the place where might be found, as the critic Kenneth Bartlett has put it, the 'patina of culture, manners and social finesse which had made the image of the *cortegiano* a model of aristocratic behaviour throughout Europe, but especially in England...'[31] so also grew its reputation for something more sinister, a place where assassins could be had for hire, where the legend rather than the truth of Machiavelli's writings lent to Italy a glamour of an altogether more amoral, anarchic nature. As well as the poetry and fiction, the myth – including hearsay, myth of the urban kind – there was Italy's reputation for a certain political freedom, as well as for savagery between its rival dukedoms and principalities. And Italy, of course, was home to the Pope – the Antichrist for an England that had so recently and bloodily broken away from Rome.

For the English dramatists, Italy and things Italian provided a rich source of inspiration. Italianate plays became highly fashionable, some directly adapted from Italian works of literature, others which merely borrowed an Italian setting. Many of Shakespeare's plays follow the fashion. It is established beyond reasonable doubt that Shakespeare had never visited Italy himself, unlike some of his dramatist confreres, but in any case verisimilitude of location is relatively beside the point. Italianate

---

31   Kenneth Bartlett, *The English in Italy, 1525–1558: A Study in Culture and Politics,* (Geneva: Slatkine, 1991).

settings, from the utopias of grand palazzi, where it is possible, despite the lack of perspective scene-painting, to imagine through the power of the language the *città ideale* of the great Renaissance paintings, to the far grittier urban city settings, which do indeed capture a realism of a kind, but which could also double, metaphorically speaking, for London. Where the plays portray something more like an actual location – the Venice of the *Merchant*, for instance – the city ambience is more recognizable as late Elizabethan or Jacobean London than anywhere else. It is important to remember that these play-makers were, in most important respects, *London* dramatists, so that it is perhaps inevitable when Vindice in *The Revenger's Tragedy* describes the delights of urban luxuries to his mother and sister, it is the seductive pleasures of London that Middleton's audience is asked to remember rather than some unspecified Renaissance Italian city; and in the nominally Italianate world of a tragedy like Middleton's *Women Beware Women* (c. 1625), the Florentine court is a cipher for the decadence of Jacobean Whitehall. As for the semi-magical forests outside Milan, say, or Florence, or Mantua – as with the Forest of Arden of *As You Like It*, or the 'Athens' of *A Midsummer Night's Dream* or *Twelfth Night's* Illyria – these could be almost anywhere, sort of mythologized never-never lands, as 'real' as the original fairy tales that begat them. A certain fuzziness of location is perhaps essential to romance and fairy-tale; and the dramatic characters who journey between Italian cities on the stage do so with a freedom that is just dangerous enough to be exciting to the audience, just familiar enough to be amusing. Mythologized, demonized, the stage 'Italy' is an ambiguous, duplicitous place: an alluring foreign paradise with a seamy underside of fervid crowds, theft and double-dealing, and chicanery and bitter rivalry between powerful families behind high walls and grand locked doors.

To consider this ambivalence in its proper context, we have to go back a little. Crucially, the early Tudor age saw translations of two very important texts. These were Baldassare Castiglione's

Il libro del cortegiano, 'The Book of the Courtier', and Niccolò Macchiavelli's *Il principe*, 'The Prince'. These had both been published in England by 1530, in Italian, but they had been widely read and had had a considerable impact. *Il cortegiano* appeared in an English translation in 1561; the translation of *Il principe* took quite a lot longer, but it was read avidly. Perhaps it is not too far fetched to say that these two books were the twin poles on which the ambivalent English perception of modern Renaissance Italy really rested.

The Book of the Courtier was, amongst other things, a 'courtesy manual', one that superseded all others in the arc of a fashion for such things. *The Courtier* was essentially different from other home-grown courtesy books: an etiquette book meets philosphy meets a sort of dining-table soap-opera: a dialogue-drama on the page, one which constituted powerful stuff for the lumpen English aristocracy of the time who had been brought up on far stuffier matter. Baldassare Castiglione was inspired to write the *Book of the Courtier* by his experiences in the court of the Duchess Elisabetta Gonzaga of Urbino, and it takes the form of a dialogue in four books on the subject of what constitutes the ideal manners and behaviour of a perfect courtier, and in book three, a perfect lady. It took him almost twenty years to write, and it was, and remains still, the definitive account of Renaissance court life. Beginning with Elisabetta Gonzaga asking for a topic of conversation for the evening, the work is narrated by Ludovico da Canossa, Federigo Fregoso, and Giuliano de' Medici among others. The ensuing dialogues are witty and amusing; but it is the subject-matter: what, precisely, constitutes the perfect Courtier – that fascinated. Crucially, the Courtier is described as having a cool mind, a good voice (with beautiful, elegant and brave words), and proper bearing and gestures. At the same time, though, the Courtier is expected to have a warrior spirit, to be athletic and an expert horseman, as well as possess a wide knowledge of the humanities, classics, let alone know how to draw and paint. However, with all these skills he does everything with certain nonchalance or *sprezzatura* – a sort of self-deprecating modesty that wears its learning lightly. It was from this work that the idea of 'Renaissance Man' gained ground in Tudor England, uniting a modern, European cosmopolitan ideal with those already established, including that of Chaucer's 'parfait gentile knight...' And it was from this book that Sir Philip Sidney developed the Tudor ideal in his *Defence of Poesy*, having devoured *Il cortegiano* with the avidity of a disciple.

On the other hand, *Il principe*, written by Niccolò Machiavelli and addressed to his boss when he occupied the office of *consigliere* to Lorenzo (the Magnificent) de' Medici was a rather different matter. Machiavelli wrote *The Prince* to prove his proficiency in the art of statesmanship, addressing Lorenzo directly in the matter of gaining and maintaining power; yet it offered guidance for any budding politician, and its rapid notoriety ensured its equally rapid success. The views expounded by Machiavelli in *The Prince* may seem extreme even for the period in which they were written – and indubitably it provided an insight into power-politics that had never been exposed before. The theories expressed in *The Prince* describe methods by which an aspiring prince can acquire the throne, or an existing prince can maintain his reign. According to Machiavelli, the greatest moral good is a virtuous and stable state, and actions to protect the princedom justified even if they are cruel. Machiavelli strongly suggests, however, that the prince must not be hated. He states,

> ... a wise prince should establish himself on that which is his own control and not in that of others; he must endeavour to avoid hatred...' also pointing out. 'it is best to be both feared and loved; however, if one cannot be both it is better to be feared...

Thus, Machiavelli appeared to advocate rule by force rather than by law, and accordingly, *The Prince* seems to justify a number of actions done solely to perpetuate power. Concerning the behaviour of a prince toward his subjects, Machiavelli writes:

... a man who strives after goodness in all his acts is sure to come to ruin, since there are so many men who are not good.

In other words, since there are many possible qualities that a Prince can be said to possess, he must not be overly concerned about having all the good ones; and although a Prince may desirably be perceived to be merciful, faithful, humane, frank, and religious, he might only *seem* to have these qualities, for crucially, a Prince must be prepared to dissemble, against those times when it will be necessary to act against them. Although a bad reputation should be avoided, this is not crucial in maintaining power. The only ethic that matters is one that is beneficial to the Prince in dealing with the concerns of his state.

In short, *Il principe* is a classic study of political power – its acquisition, expansion, and effective use. Never intended to be a scholarly treatise on political theory, this is in fact what it became. It is Machiavelli's pragmatism that shocks. Machiavelli observes that most men are content as long as they are not deprived of their property and women. A Prince should command respect, because a Prince who is highly respected by his people is unlikely to face internal struggles. A Prince who does not raise the contempt of the nobles and keeps the people satisfied, Machiavelli assures his boss, should have no fear of conspirators. There is much of 'bread and circuses' here, and Machiavelli alludes to ancient Rome very often. He deplores Republicanism vehemently (apparently) but by now, we cannot be at all sure what Machiavelli really believes. Apparently, he is no ordinary snob, no mere adherent to those of the Blood for their own sake. A Prince earns honour by accomplishment. King Ferdinand of Spain is cited by Machiavelli as an example of a lowly monarch who gained esteem by showing his ability through great feats and who, in the name of religion, conquered many territories and kept his subjects occupied so that they had no chance to rebel.

Not surprisingly, in the aftermath of the publication of *Il principe* in England, both the Catholic and the newly formed Protestant Church condemned the book and it was banned in Elizabethan England. The papacy placed it on its *Index Librorum Prohibitorum* in 1559, but it was nevertheless read widely by the Elizabethan political class during this period. Although an English translation was not made until 1640 – unsurprisingly, given the ban – there were Latin, Italian, French and Spanish versions of the book in print and circulation more or less from 1532. Machiavelli's somewhat tamer lesser works, *The Art of War* and *A Florentine History* were translated into English c1560 and 1595 respectively. *Il principe* became a virtual handbook for such as Thomas Cromwell, Gabriel Harvey, Francis Bacon and Lord Burghley among others, and must have stated obvious truths, however cynically expressed, to those who observed the machinations of Henry VIII's court and into the next reigns.

It is not hard to imagine the impact of this book, not least to appreciate its application to the drama, yet it was not from *Il principe*, as such, that Elizabethans derived their fear and awe of Machiavelli, but from a vehement attack on it in a book called *Contre-Machiavel* published in France in 1576 by a French Huguenot, Innocent Gentillet. This deeply hostile and distorted work, translated into English in 1602, but well-known in the French long before, helped to spread among Englishmen the impression of Machiavelli's *Il principe* as a monstrous, atheistic and totally immoral handbook written for the 'devil's disciples'. Indeed, it is fair to conclude that Tudor England was aware of 'machiavellianism' before it was aware of Machiavelli.

In the drama, Thomas Kyd's arch-villain Lorenzo in *The Spanish Tragedy* (c. 1585) is often cited as the first 'Machiavellian' villain on the English stage, but that is to confuse Machiavellians with Machiavels – in other words, to confuse those characters who follow the precepts of the historical Machiavelli, author of the work on the science of statecraft, such as (arguably) Prince Hal/Henry V (*Henry IV* pt 2) – with villains like Kyd's Lorenzo who seems to be based on the 'mythical' version of Machiavelli exemplified in the work of Gentillet among others. It is these stage Machiavels who, although probably not conceived in ignorance of Machiavelli's actual writings, bought into the myth with a cruder, crueller, more amoral version of Machiavelli's statesman; one who delights in 'sleights, scrues, engins... rare tricks': in a word, 'policy', of which there had long been a pejorative connotation (of lying, chicanery and duplicity) in England. While Kyd did not invent the taste for the tragic intriguer, his contribution was in developing dramaturgical techniques for staging the kind of action which allows the audience to 'eavesdrop' on the plotting. Similarly, Othello's henchman, batman and trusted colleague, Iago, has his own agenda, exploiting the impulsive, trusting and emotionally gullible nature of Othello as he steers him towards destruction, and hiring other villains – cat's paws and assassins – to do his dirty work. It makes for powerful theatre; we watch Macbeth commit murder, but we watch Iago play a pitiless, savage game.

Othello is an 'Italianate' play, essentially. Others, such as Marlowe's *Edward II*, (1592) are essentially 'English', but the villain, Lightborn, is nevertheless a specialist Italian assassin, even though his nationality (and we assume him to be English) is never entirely clear. The main evidence linking him with Italy is his catalogue of the lethal skills he has learned in Naples, that most murderous of Italian cities. It is tempting to suppose he is simply an Italianate English traveller of the sort the scholar Ascham so mistrusted. Whatever, Edward is presented as a king corrupting England's national integrity by introducing foreign influences.

iv

Inglese italianato è un diabolo incarnato: the Italianate Englishman is a devil incarnate... This well-known proverb was quoted by the inveterately nationalistic English scholar Roger Ascham, whose seminal work, *The Scholemaster*, was published in 1570,

THE STOIC, THE WEAL & THE MALCONTENT

shortly after its author's death. This was a popular user-friendly manual aimed at private tutors of upper class English schoolboys. Ascham's most famous student, of course, was a girl: the young Princess Elizabeth. Ascham was famously a little xenophobic, an orthodox, classically-educated Englishman; but he was modern, too, in his own way, and argued sensibly for an unadorned English style, supporting good writing in the 'vulgar tongue' – that is, the plain language everyone used, deploring over-elaboration and foreign importations. Not surprisingly, he was a fan of Chaucer (less obviously, perhaps, he rather detested the Arthurian romances of Malory.) On the other hand he was a true scholar, an alumnus of St John's College, Cambridge, and a Classicist to his boots: although he was suspicious of what he termed 'rhyme', deriding it as an invention of 'Goths and Huns', he recommended that poetry, if written at all, be written in imitation of Classical models.[32]

The Classical model was of course a desirable one, perhaps the only proper aspiration for the modern literary arts, and many a classically educated Elizabethan Englishman would have agreed with this sentiment. Sir Philip Sidney is a shining example of such Classical imitation in modern English poesy; Sidney's most obvious model was Francesco Petrarca (Petrarch), himself a modern Classicist: that is, he made a vernacular, modern Italian language fit the Classical model, something that Sidney would go on to do with modern English. It is in his reverence for the Classical period that Ascham appears to have been most offended by 'modern Italy', and for ethical and moral reasons rather than artistic ones. He was clearly alarmed by what he took to be Italy's moral lapses, asserting that great cities such as Rome

32   Roger Ascham began writing *The Scholemaster* (1570) after a debate on school punishment occasioned by some frightened pupils running away from Eton College in 1563. He was particularly committed to the idea that the young might be brought to enjoy their lessons by patience and love rather than by punishment. Such enlightenment was rare, however, and the majority of schoolmasters continued to whip their students just as preachers continued to threaten their congregations with eternal damnation.

'once the best breeders and bringers up of the worthiest of men, not only for wise speaking but also for well-doing in all civil affairs that ever was in the world' are now so enslaved to vice that the English who travel there exemplify the Italian proverb: 'you remain men in shape and fashion, but become devils in life and condition'. From Roger Ascham's suspicion of the Italianate Englishman we can safely infer that Italy and things Italian had begun to have a profound impact in England by 1563, when Ascham was penning *The Scholemaster* (and this was quite a long time before what came to be regarded as the Golden Age of the English theatre) and can begin to see in the indignation of this 'schoolmaster' the ambivalence with which Italy was coming to be regarded. By contrast, an older contemporary, William Thomas, in his *History of Italy* (1549) and his *Italian Grammar* (1550) had presented a generally favourable, positive image of the modern sixteenth century Italy.

More than other near neighbours such as France, Italy had gained a reputation for a kind of political freedom unknown in England. The freedom of Italian cities takes on a decidedly sinister cast from Ascham's perspective: 'And being brought up in Italy, in some free city, as all cities be there, where a man may freely discourse against what he will, against whom he lust – against any prince, against any government, yea, against God himself and his whole religion – where he must be either Guelf or Ghibelline, either French or Spanish, and always compelled to be of some party, of some faction, he shall never be compelled to be of any religion, and if he meddle not overmuch with Christ's true religion, he shall have free liberty to embrace all religions and become, if he lust, at once without any let or punishment, Jewish, Turkish, papish and devillish...' Ascham sees freedom degenerating into mere political factionalism and religious apostasy, and he was far from alone in his opinion. But this was the freedom that others would find intensely alluring, and the lure of Italy, doubtless glamorized in reputation and thus in fiction, was irresistible. William Thomas and Roger Ascham were both writing for an audience of young scholars, scholars who, more-over, were travellers, or at least potentially so.

That Renaissance Italy should have been of concern to the wider scholarly fraternity is more or less obvious: the well-educated Englishman (we are talking of men rather than women, but not exclusively) would have read the most prestigious of the Classical writers: Virgil, Homer and Ovid; and indeed Plato, (whose influence was omnipresent via the Latin, French and Italian, but which was not translated into English until well into the seventeenth century.) These constituted a major part of the school curriculum – indeed in grammar schools such as Shakespeare's, as did Roman dramatists such as Plautus and the tragedian Seneca (as well as the later plays of Euripides, on which Seneca based many of his own tragedies.) Seneca's Stoicism was a school and university staple. By way of these Classical works and ideals, moral and artistic, Renaissance Italy captured the imagination of the English scholars, just as they had those of the Italian Humanist scholars themselves. Quite evidently, there was a lively market for untranslated Italian texts of all kinds. Between 1584 and 1589, the London printer John Wolfe was publishing editions of Machiavelli's works, including the erotic drama, *La mandragola*, (which may have contributed much to *Antony & Cleopatra)* and of Pietro Aretino's *Quattro commedie* and the sexy *Ragionamenti,* not to mention Aretino's scurrilous parody of *Il cortegiano* – 'La cortegiana', followed by Giovanni Battista Guarini's play *Pastor Fido* and Torquado Tasso's pastoral *Aminta* in 1591, the popularity of which doubtless demonstrates the keenness with which literary London of Elizabeth's time followed any new development of Italian letters, even to the point of reading plays in text. Tasso especially was a model for Elizabethan courtly poets. This flood of publication was part of a commercial venture designed, according to the scholar G. K. Hunter, 'to exploit English fascination with Italian wickedness and the desire to read, even in a half-understood language, works never likely to be available in English.'[33]

Travel to Italy may have been derided by wiser counsels as having only wickedness, moral turpitude and heresy to teach, and at least some of this sinister reputation had foundation. There are well-documented accounts of hired assassins, notably the *bravi*, in Italy. Venice, in particular, passed numerous edicts against *bravi* in the late sixteenth century, and the very existence of legal controls only indicates the extent of the problem. Yet despite – or perhaps perversely because of – these dire warnings, fictional and otherwise, travel and especially to Italy became ever more fashionable. Thomas Nashe's *The Unfortunate Traveller* (1594) includes Italy in the forbidden ports of call in terms far harsher than Ascham's: 'Italy', he says, 'the paradise of earth and the Epicures' heaven - how doth it form our young masters? ... From thence he brings forth the arts of atheisme, the art of epicurising, the art of whoring, the art of poysoning, the art of Sodomitirie.' And in his *Pierce Penniless* (1592), Nashe attacks Italy as being the 'Academie of Manslaughter, the sporting-place of murther, the Apothecary-shop of poyson for all Nations...' And while we have to acknowledge Nashe's irony in his giving this speech to his hero, a dispossessed English earl, there is no doubt that these sentiments echo not only the prejudices, but the perverse fashion of the times. And the fact that this found its way into fiction demonstrates just how recognizably normal, at least for a certain stratum of English society, Italian travel actually was.[34]

---

33 G. K. Hunter, 'English Folly and Italian Vice: the Moral Landscape of John Marston' in *Jacobean Theatre*, eds J. R. Brown & B. Harris, Stratford-up-on-Avon Studies (London: Arnold, 1960).

34 Thomas Nashe, *Pierce Penniless his Supplication to the Divell*. See *Works*, ed. Ronald B. McKerrow (London 1910), which contains a definitive biography and a full account of Nashe's role in the Martin Marprelate and Harvey controversies. See also Stanley Wells, *Thomas Nashe, Selected Writings* (1965).

V

I have already remarked that the aristocratic or at least gentrified condition of Melancholy caused it to be an essentially 'fashionable maladie', the more attractive for its association with great minds, and thus the 'sufferer' projected a certain intellectual mystique. The condition of the world-weary and often well-travelled melancholic had acquired nothing short of snob-value and, at its outer fringes, it was the conceit of the *poseur* rather than anything more politically significant. Nevertheless, this misfit youth began to constitute a social type in dress, attitude, language and affectations, even though, unlike Robert Greene, many had never actually been abroad. The melancholy *poseur*, lampooned in fiction, was at pains to remind his inferiors of their place. In Lyly's *Midas* (printed 1592 but written probably two years earlier) a page rebukes a barber for complaining of melancholy: 'is melancholy a word for a barbar's mouth? Thou shouldst say heavie, dull and doltish: melancholy is the crest of Courtiers' armes, and now everie base companion… says he is melancholy.' Armado, in Shakespeare's *Love's Labour's Lost* (c. 1593–94), regards the melancholy he affects as a token of his superiority to the 'rude multitude' (V, i, 97), and in Ben Jonson's *Every Man Out of his Humour* (c. 1599), Carlo Buffone instructs the loutish Sogliardo in how to be a gentleman: 'You must endeavour to feed cleanly at your Ordinary [local tavern], sit melancholy, and pick your teeth when you cannot speak.' (III, i, 445). A passage in Nashe's *Pierce Pennilesse* furnishes a summary of the pseudo-melancholic/malcontent's pretensions:

> All malcontent sits the greasie son of a Cloathier, & complains (like a decaied Earle) of the ruin of ancient houses… Sometimes… hee will bee an Inamorato Poeta… All Italionato is his talke… Hee will despise the barabarism of his own Countrey, & tel a whole Legend of lyes of his traviales unto Constantinople… [He] hath been but over to Deepe…

The snobbery, even the sheer silliness, cannot be disputed; and obviously, Nashe's 'greasie son of a Cloathier' is a social and intellectual impostor and one upon whom Nashe, a genuine traveller-scholar, whose tutor in Italy was no less than Pietro Aretino, might well have poured his customary violent scorn. Yet this melancholy posing, far from being dismissed as nonsense, was taken seriously and with some cause. Melancholics were, or affected to be, disappointed and disgruntled by their fellow countrymen's failure to recognize and reward the talents and accomplishments they believed themselves to possess, and were given to railing at their unappreciative contemporaries. This melancholy class included many persons who appeared to be actively seditious, dissatisfied with the status quo and ambitious to overthrow it. Behind the posing of the young men of fashion, there existed a genuinely disgruntled faction, who felt secure in the knowledge of its superiority, if secure in little else:

> Some thinke to be counted rare Politicians and Statesmen, by being solitary: as who would say, I am a wise man, a brave man, Secreta mea mihi: Frustra sapit, qui sibi non sapit: (and there is no man worthy of my companie or friendship...)

Often desperately poor, and frequently unemployed, these Malcontents railed at an unappreciative world. Marston's Bruto, the cynical fictional commentator of the *Satires* who recounts his scurrilous escapades in great detail, is highly conscious of what he regards as self-improvement abroad and rails at the 'corrupted age' which has slight regard for 'men of sound carriage', at the 'ungrateful sots', the 'oily snails' who are 'respectless... of my good parts.'[35] John Earle provides socio-psychological apologies for the malcontented state: 'a hard father, a peevish wench...' as well as the inevitable 'ambition thwarted' which he sees as producing a dangerous state of mind in which the 'discontent-

---

35   John Marston, *The Metamorphosis of Pymalion's Image... and Certain Satires* (1598), verse satires published under the pseudonym W. Kinsayder.

ed man' is 'much displeased to see men merry, and wonders what they can find to laugh at,' and who, 'at the last falls into that deadly melancholy to be a bitter hater of men and in the most apt companion to any mischief.' Advancement in the state has gone to undeserving dullards, and the Malcontent's sense of injured merit makes him 'the sparke that kindles the Commonwealth, and bellows himself to blow it.'[36]

In this dissatisfied rebelliousness lies the Malcontent's actual menace perhaps; his education, both abroad and in the English Universities, has equipped him with an anarchically-inclined learning which fits him only dubiously for responsible office. Thomas Lodge reviews the intellectual vices which the real-life Malcontent has picked up on his travels:

> well spoken he is, and hath some languages, and hath read over the conjuration of Machiavel: In beliefe he is an Atheist, or a counterfait Catholicke... He hath been a long traveller, and seen manie countries but... from al those Provinces he hath visited, bringeth home nothing but corruptions to disturbe the peace of his countrie, and destroy his own body and soule.

Lodge's prose pamphlet, *Wit's Miserie* (1596) presents an actively misanthropic figure: 'This fellow spares neither nobility, clergy nor laitie but... desireth that the whole people and commonalitie had but one head that he might cut it off at one stroke.'[37] Melancholy malcontentedness was a frequent accusation against those who held unorthodox or heterodox religious opinions, Catholic or Puritan. John Davies, a notorious anti-Catholic, was anti-Puritan, too. He describes malcontents as proud and envious men, 'Exclaiming on the tymes,' complaining that 'Men of

---

36   John Earle (with others?) *Microcosmographie* (1601) is a collection of character sketches. Ed. by Edward Arber, (Westminster, 1895) No. 8 'A Discontented Man', p. 28.

37   Thomas Lodge, *Wits Miserie and Worlds Madnesse* (1596). Satirical character sketches. See *The Works*, ed. by Edmund Gosse, 4 Vols, (New York, London 1883) iv, 'Wit's Miserie' pp. 1–117.

woorth' are neglected.[38] 'These unwise wittie Malcontents', says Lodge, are instigators of rebellion against royal authority. Robert Anton attacked Roman Catholics absconding from the English universities: 'Discontented graduates' who leave their country and renounce its religion to seek preferment abroad and write 'scandalous volumes against the King and State.' These are 'recusants both in faith and loyaltie... deep malcontent[s].'[39]

Many of these satirists would of course fit the Malcontent mould themselves, and it is impossible to discount a considerable amount of self-portraiture in their work. They were almost all University men: Greene was a graduate of St John's College, Cambridge, as was his protegé, Nashe; Lodge attended Trinity College, Oxford, after which he entered, briefly, Lincoln's Inn to study law; Marston was a Brasenose man who also briefly studied law in his father's footsteps until he abandoned law for literature. All had come from relatively comfortable circumstances. Some, like Davies, a graduate of Queen's College, Oxford, who found favour with King James, were in fact committed conservatives, men of public affairs; but all could bend the idea of malcontentedness to anything that came within their compass of disparagement. Nashe, especially, was ferociously anti-puritan, and for him the 'puritan' was the Malcontent, but a 'malcontent' could be almost anyone: rogue, clever, anarchic, in the business of upsetting the ever-precarious balance of a state in flux. The hysterical tone grew, inevitably, and thus did the reputation of the anarchically-inclined rebel nurtured on scholarship and travel.

vi

The traveller and the scholar both suggest sophistication, self-cultivation and, often, literary ability. But while there might

---

38   John Davies, Microcosmos, (Works, vol. 1). Cf. Nicholas Breton's *Against Murmurers, and Murmuring* (*Works*, vol.II) (London: Robert Raworth, 1607).

39   Robert Anton, *The Philosopher's Satyrs*, (London, 1616) pp.9–10

be some distinction between traveller and scholar-malcontents, there is a metaphorical, as well as an obvious sociological and intellectual, overlap between the man who travels literally in order to acquire a wider learning of the world and the book-learned scholar who travels in his mind. A university education, and learning in general, where it is not directed to good and sober purpose and constitutes a training in civic duty, was regardedby many as sinister. In fiction, the melancholy scholar becomes virtually indistinguishable from the traveller. In Lyly's *Sapho and Phao* (c. 1582) Pandio is called a Malcontent. He is clearly not merely a disgruntled traveller, but accords more closely with the view of melancholic genius presented by Ficino and the other Florentine Humanists. It is significant that both Hamlet and Flamineo, of Webster's *The White Devil* (1612), have both at some time returned from university; that *King Lear's* Edmund has been, as his father proudly boasts, 'out nine years, away he shall be again…' (I, i, 27–8), and Macilente of Jonson's *Every Man Out of his Humour*, is 'A man well parted, a sufficient Scholar, and travel'd, who wanting place in the world's account which he thinks his merit capable of, falls into… an envious apoplexy.' (III, i, 423). His scholarship is considerably emphasised in the play. At the same time he has many of the traits which distinguish the Galenic melancholy malcontent type. A 'lean moungrel', he possesses 'a lank raw-bon'd anatomie', one who 'looks as if he were chap-fall'n, with barking at other men's good fortunes.' He dresses in black, is wretchedly poverty stricken, a 'poor seam-rent fellow' who rails continually at the fools who have fared better in life than he. He is also a satiric author, who 'carried oil and fire in his pen.'

The scholarship and learning of such individuals is often viewed as superfluous and worthless. Marston presents Lampatho, in *What You Will* (1601), as a scholar who has been rendered melancholy not so much by material misfortune as by intellectual confusion and frustration. After what he considers a wasted youth spent studying the conflicting opinions regarding the nature of the human soul and stuffing his notebook with quotations from the philosophers, Lampatho has 'crept abroad', and 'Finding my numbness in this nimble age, | I fell a-railing.'(II, ii, 190–2). In Webster's *The Duchess of Malfi*, Antonio's friend Delio remembers Bosola's student days with contempt:

> I knew him in Padua, a fantastical scholar, like such as study to know how many knots was in Hercules' club... he hath studied himself half blear-ey'd, to know the true symmetry of Caesar's nose by a shoeing-horn: and this he did to gain the name of a speculative man. (III, iii, 40–6).

Thus Delio dismisses Bosola as a repository of useless information, acquired solely for the purpose of self-aggrandisement.

The anonymous Parnassus trilogy (c. late 1590s) is probably the most elaborate satirical treatment of the scholar's melancholy.[40] The unknown author, who was evidently a scholar writing for an academic audience, is bitterly critical of the neglect of learning, the pitfalls of patronage, and the uncertain plight of scholars after graduation. These allegorical plays contain many allusions to contemporary writers, such as Dekker, Greene, Jonson, Lyly, Marlowe, Nashe, Peele and Shakespeare. The first of the trilogy, *The Pilgrimage to Parnassus*, is an allegory describing the 'pilgrimage' of two idealistic scholars, Philomosus and Studioso, to Mount Parnassus to drink from the holy spring of learning. Their metaphorical climb takes through them the trivium of Logic, Rhetoric and Philosophy. In Logic, they encounter a bewildering maze created by the conflicting schools of Aristotle and the anti-Scholastic Peter Ramus;[41] in Rhetoric

---

40   This anonymous trilogy of satiric plays was written c. 1598–1602, and performed in St John's College, Cambridge before 1603. The first part was printed in 1606, the other two parts not printed until 1773.

41   Petrus Ramus: the Latinized form of Pierre de la Ramée (1515–72), French philosopher and grammarian. His *Dialectique* of 1555 systematically refuted Aristotelian and Scholastic logic. It was introduced into England in the late sixteenth century by Andrew Melville and William Temple and ob-

– or poetry – they encounter equal disillusion, this time with the subtle ('sourlie sweete') eroticism of Ovid; in Philosophy, the steepest ascent of all, they encounter the philosopher Ingenioso, who curses learning because it has impoverished him, and he clearly means spiritually as well as materially. Study 'is wonte to eat mens marrowes, drye there bloude,/And make them seem leane shadowless pale ghostes.' The pair remain undeterred, and at the end of four years, they reach Parnassus: that is, the B.A. degree.

The theme of the two later parts of the Parnassus trilogy is one of sad disillusion, as our heroes experience the reality of the poverty and misery of scholars. The second play finds the two graduates in search of a living. In London, they again meet with Ingenioso, the philosopher, who is now scratching for work among ignorant printers and miserly patrons, and Luxurioso, a profligate would-be poet. Ingenioso talks of putting his wit 'out to interest' – become a hack in other words – to 'make it return two pamphlets a week,' but he is dismissed by his affected patron, and the hard-headed publisher, Danter, who is only attracted by the offer of libellous satires. At the end of the second play, all four are reduced to mean labour, abject poverty and total despair. The third play, subtitled *The Scourge of Simony*, shows the scholars in even more desperate straits. The pilgrims, failing miserably as quack doctors, turn to the 'basest trade': the theatre. Dismissing their talents as writers as uncommercial, because too scholarly (their plays 'smell too much of that writer Ovid… and talk too much of Proserpina and Jupiter') Richard Burbage and Will Kemp, (in real life Shakespeare's colleagues, chief actors in the Lord Chamberlain's Men) try to teach them acting, suggesting they might do well in Kyd's *Spanish Tragedy* or Shakespeare's *Richard III*, but in the end both scholars abandon all hope of profit and retire, bathetically, to Kent to become shepherds.

---

tained wide academic currency, especially at Cambridge. His followers were known as Ramists and his anti-Scholastic system of logic as Ramism.

The *Parnassus* plays present a vivid account of the woes and disaffections of college-trained intellectuals of the Elizabethan period, as well as tilting not a little at the smugness of theatre-writers associated with the public stage. Few scholars, it seems, were fortunate enough to find patronage or even gainful employment after graduation. Most of these young men, over-educated for their likely position in life, drifted into the Church, languished at the doors of nobles, or, if they were insufficiently well-connected to clamber on to the lowest rungs of the administrative ladder, worked at hack journalism, which notoriously paid extremely badly. There was no system of royalties, and printers made outright payments for manuscripts (typically around £2) often to their current possessor rather than to their authors, a misappropriation facilitated by the habit of manuscript circulation. Success was therefore unlikely to benefit the author directly. On the face of it, writing for the theatre looked more financially promising, but here, too, it was less profitable to receive outright payment for a particular play (Henslowe paid a flat £6) than to be a company shareholder, regularly receiving a fixed proportion of the takings, as Shakespeare did. In practice the university men were often less versatile than the full-time professionals such as Heywood, Dekker or Shakespeare. As the Globe actors remark in the third *Parnassus* play, 'Few of the university men pen plays well… Why, here's our fellow Shakespeare puts them all down.'

Learning is tinged with mystique – even oddness, inevitably. Dowsecer, in George Chapman's *An Humorous Day's Mirth* (c. 1597) is melancholy to such a degree that other characters consider him half mad. We are not allowed to know the cause of Dowsecer's melancholy, but the King of France is deeply impressed by his scholarship and eloquence: 'Nay, he is more human than all we are'; Dowsecer's 'humour' is a *'holy fury, not a frenzy'*. The distinction is made. This tendency toward mysticism in the scholar-malcontent, harking back to the Aristotelian delineation, is highly significant, both of the veneration and of the

[89]

THE STOIC, THE WEAL & THE MALCONTENT

fear they tended to generate. The two things began to be synonymous on the stage. As Lawrence Babb pointed out, 'So strong is the association between melancholy and learning that not only do the scholars of the drama tend to be melancholy, but the melancholics tend to be scholarly. Bussy D'Ambois, Bosola... are supposed to be scholars. Hamlet is a scholar. Melancholy men so often come upon the stage reading a book that reading almost seems to be a dramatic convention of melancholy.'[42] Scholarship in itself was suspect, and it was this the dramatists (many of them serious scholars themselves) satirized. Bosola's learning may be pointless to one such as Delio, but the sense of his having seen and learned too much for anybody's good, including his own, is stressed in the play.

Learning has a double disadvantage, therefore: the scholar knows and can criticise those things a hidebound and corrupt world will not permit him to express. He is henceforth alienated from his fellows, and doomed to persistent frustration. For the early Humanists, those ancient Classical scholars, Cicero and Seneca, became established as moral authorities partly because of the Humanists' identification of their own predicaments. These English 'alienated intellectuals', as Mark H. Curtis termed them, were not so much economically oppressed and exploited as frustrated.[43] Alienated intellectuals had to accept posts or roles which, no matter how remunerative, could not entirely satisfy them, and the opportunities to use their training and talents to the full were not available to them. As Francis Bacon warned King James I, an excess of grammar-schools had resulted in 'ther being more scholars bred than the State can prefer or employ, and the active part of that life not bearing a proportion to the preparation, it must needs fall out that many persons will be bred unfit for other vocations, and unprofitable for that in which

42 L. Babb, op. cit.

43 Mark H. Curtis, 'The Alienated Intellectuals of Early Stuart England', ibid, p. 28.

they were bred up, which fill the realm full of indigent, idle and wanton people, who are but materia rerum novarum.'[44]

Given this atmosphere, it is not surprising that the legend of Dr Faustus should have captured the artistic imagination. At its most poetic, the vision of the alienated intellectual is one of unattainable desire, of the inevitable destruction of contentment as the result of a vaulting ambition to *know*. Nowhere is the destruction of contentment more apparent than in Christopher Marlowe's *Doctor Faustus* (c. 1588). This play, the troubling and sinister story of a scholar who over-reaches himself in a contract with the Devil, possibly based on an historical figure (a magician named Georg Faust, possibly born in 1480) derives from a German-language legend, many variations on which appeared in Germany after 1587. Editorially problematic, Marlowe's play survives in two quite different (but almost equally corrupt) editions, the authenticity and authorship of which have long been argued.[45] It opens with a long soliloquy in Faustus' rooms as he broods over the 'four faculties' of humanistic study: philosophy, medicine, law and divinity. He has gained an easy mastery over them all, and concludes that all learning is banal and simplistic except magic. He then conjures up a devil, Mephistophilis, Satan's minion, and offers to sell his soul in return for twenty-four years of luxurious living and complete obedience from Mephistophilis. In spite of the admonitions of his Good Angel to 'lay that damned book' aside, and console himself with works of Holy Scripture, Faustus heeds his Evil Angel and determines to command the elements like a god. In parody of these weighty matters, Faustus' silly but sly assistant, Wagner, tries to persuade a village oaf to bind him for seven years and actually succeeds

---

44   Francis Bacon, *Essays*, cited by L. C. Knights, 'Seventeenth Century Melancholy', in *The Criterion*, 13 (1933–4) pp. 105–34

45   The A and B texts have been edited in the same volume by W. W. Greg for the Clarendon Press (1950)and in *The Complete Plays*, ed. Irving Ribner (1963), but see especially the Manchester University Press Revels Plays series ed. Eric Rasmussen & David Bevington (1993).

in conjuring up two minor devils. Wagner more than echoes the medieval Vice, but he is chiefly a comic foil (and comic scenes with him are interspersed throughout the play, some scenes of buffoonery involving Faustus as well as Wagner). However, the sinister focus is upon the intellectual man who, in echoes of Adam, seeks to know more than is 'good' for him, but who does not see a 'good' reason why he should not, since the acquisition of knowledge contains the ancient theological conundrum: the desire for knowledge, intelligence, is also the gift of God. He is too much the intellectual to believe in God's forgiveness (Marlowe's detractors thus condemned him as an atheist) and the play concludes with Faustus eventually being condemned to Hell with the words: 'Cut is the branch that might have grown full straight, | And burned is Apollo's laurel bough | That sometime grew within this learned man.' (Epilogue, 1–3).

Dr Faustus is a powerful re-working of the traditional Morality play conflict between good and evil in man's soul. It is also innovative in its perception of the power, appeal, and the danger of learning. In it, the power of intellect is clearly linked to a rejection of God, yet we do not necessarily sympathize with the Good Angel and his exhortations, for all we see that Faustus's rejection of his advice can only lead to disaster. An abrogation of God seems to be the Scholar's only course, and God is relegated to superstition. Yet the play's conclusion is highly ambivalent: learning is God-given, or at least god-given, dignified by 'Apollo's laurel', but learning (as opposed to scholarly indoctrination) must imply challenge. Marlowe makes Faustus overweeningly ambitious but, taken to its logical extreme, learning inevitably makes man ambitious. In many ways the ultimate Malcontent, Faustus challenges the Devil and defies God, becoming the ultimate representation of all that human will can achieve. At a mid-point between having Mephistophilis in his power and before God catches up with him, Faustus is powerful indeed.

At a more mundane and practical level, the attitude to education and learning was inevitably ambivalent. The conviction that if only learned clergy preached, and the literate laity read their Bibles, society would come to agree in a comfortably united Protestant faith turned out to be very seriously mistaken. Similarly mistaken was the notion on the part of the English humanists such as Ascham (who were more directly responsible for laying the foundations for the kind of education provided in Elizabethan schools than the Protestant reformers) that Christian moral uplift and civil responsibility would be the outcomes of reading good Classical authors. Education, as opposed to indoctrination, is potentially an unruly instrument and always was: good students tend to be inspired with questions, and to acquire ideas of their own. It is therefore hardly surprising that, later, Thomas Hobbes (1588–1679) was to assert (albeit somewhat idealistically) that the universities were 'the core of rebellion', and attribute at least some of the causes of the Civil War to courses of study at Oxford (his own alma mater) and Cambridge, not just because they disseminated radical Presbyterianism, but also for the potential danger in reading the Classics:

> There were an exceeding great number of men of the better sort, that had been so educated as that in their youth having read the books written by famous men of the ancient Grecian and Roman commonwealths concerning their polity and great actions, in which books the popular government was extolled by the glorious name of liberty and monarchy disgraced by the name of tyranny, they became thereby in love with their forms of government. And out of these men were chosen the greatest part of the House of Commons...[46]

While it is unlikely that the seventeenth-century House of Commons was invigorated by anything like the passionate republicanism that Hobbes attributed to it, these educated misfits were observed to possess three potentially dangerous attributes: pov-

---

46 Thomas Hobbes, *Behemoth* (before 1668, but published posthumously in his *Tracts*, 1682) in *The English Works of Thomas Hobbes of Malmesbury*, ed. by Sir William Molesworth, 11 vols,(London, 1840), vi, p. 236.

erty, morbid envy and erudition, together with a reputation for having acquired notorious vices and seditious opinions abroad. On the Jacobean stage, many of the malcontented characters, not surprisingly, are portrayed as impoverished intellectual would-be gentlemen with chips on their shoulders.

vii

De Flores, in Middleton and Rowley's *The Changeling* complains that 'Though my hard fate has thrust me into servitude,/ I tumbled into th'world a gentleman.'(II, i, 48-9), and so justifies his relentless pursuit of the aristocratic Beatrice–Joanna. Vindice and his brother, in *The Revenger's Tragedy*, are 'placed', socially, as hard-up gentry, and upon this social context rests much of the satire of the sub-plot involving the rest of his family: Vindice's father died of 'discouragement' (I, i, 119–30); Vindice himself has no employment; his mother and sister suffer from a poverty to which they were not born. The disguised Vindice's attempt to procure his sister Castiza for Lussurioso almost succeeds, largely because of their mother's complicity. Her motivation and moral abasement is rooted in poverty, together with chronic disappointment, envy and greed, which is seen to threaten all the decent moral traditions of the humbler gentry. In *The White Devil*, Flamineo justifies the prostitution of his sister on his lack of means, and directly cites his university education as the cause of both his dissatisfaction and of his moral degeneracy. When challenged by his mother: 'What? Because we are poor/Shall we be vicious?' He responds with:

> Pray what means have you
> To keep me from the galleys, or the gallows?
> My father proved himself a gentleman,
> Sold all's land, and like a fortunate fellow,
> Died ere the money was spent. You brought me up
> At Padua, I confess, where I protest
> For want of means - the university judge me -
> I have been fain to heel my tutor's stockings

At least seven years. Conspiring with a beard
Made me a graduate; then to this Duke's service;
I visited the court, whence I returned,
More courteous, more lecherous by far,
But not a suit the richer...   (I, ii, 306–20)

Like Bosola in *The Duchess of Malfi*, Flamineo is an alumnus of
Galileo's university at Padua; Hamlet is a former student of Martin Luther's university at Wittenburg (to where, not unreasonably in the circumstances, Claudius does not wish him to return.)
Their association with such universities is yet another instance
of dramatic fiction hinging itself upon fact.

In 1610, Galileo Galilei, using a telescope, finally offered scientific proof of Copernicus' deduction (c. 1543) that the earth circled the sun, and not the other way round. For a society taught
to accept geocentricity for countless generations, this is 'revolution' in revolution, and in every sense. Likewise, the potent religious reformist, Martin Luther, had already developed, by 1517, a
highly 'revolutionary' thesis of religious practice which radically
challenged the 'free-will and works' theodicy taught and accepted by the Catholic church as a whole, and indeed by such notable humanist-reformers like Erasmus. Both Luther and Galileo
were, in their very different ways, regarded as dangerous intellectual challenges to orthodoxy, and it is highly significant that
the fictional scholars, Hamlet and Bosola, should have graduated
in real-life seats of radical learning. Both are presented as possessing the afflictions associated with the Renaissance or 'Galile-
an man', rejecting the 'old certainties'. Fredson Bowers remarked
that Webster had humanized his villains by substituting, for the
religious tradition of 'the devil incarnate' some 'real persons
with more than their share of vice yet treated so poetically as to
argue the sympathetic as opposed to the antagonistic interest of
the audience.' [47] And although, as René Weis observes, 'between

---

47 Fredson Bowers, *Elizabethan Revenge Tragedy* 1587–1642 (London,
1940), pp. 181–2

them, Flamineo and Bosola epitomize… the villain cast in the roles of disillusioned intelligencer, pimp, speaker of malicious asides, misogynist, and murderer' (which of course they do, as well) their placing in a real-world setting of academic, as well as social, challenge, invests them with a worrying credibility.[48]

Many stage-Malcontents possess an informed cleverness when it comes to exploiting the superstitious weaknesses of others. *King Lear's* Edmund constantly reminds us of his superior intelligence, and thus his wider knowledge of the world. He triumphs over 'A credulous father' and manipulates Edgar's gullible nature which 'is so far from doing harms | That he suspects none; on whose foolish honesty | My practises ride easy!' (I, iii, 186–9). He throws out references to the 'stars' to convince Gloucester of the inevitability of Edgar's perfidy, and then proceeds cleverly to cover his back by providing a ready-made explanation for the accusation redounding upon himself should Gloucester ever challenge Edgar for the truth. The entirely mendacious report of a conversation with his brother, in which Edgar is supposed to have scorned the idea of Edmund's being believed – 'Thou unpossessing bastard! dost thou think, | If I should stand against thee, would the reposal | Of any trust, virtue, or worth in thee | Make thy words faith'd?' (II, i, 67–9) – intend the dual effect of ensuring the discredit of anything Edgar might plead in his own defence, and of bringing the whole question of Edmund's own position to his father's attention but in a wholly positive light, a manipulation which elicits the promise that 'of my land, | Loyal and natural boy, I'll work the means | To make thee capable.' (83–4). This double-bluff (a thing which the audience has come to expect with relish) shows us not only Edmund's superior wits but also a seemingly instinctual sense of the weak spots in others. Similarly, Iago works on the possessive insecurity of

---

48   René Weis, *John Webster, 'The Duchess of Malfi' and Other Plays* (Oxford World's Classics, 1996).

Othello; De Flores on the neurotic, unconscious libido of Bea-trice–Joanna.[49]

While neither Iago nor De Flores is a university graduate, both are highly articulate in a way which suggests learning, and in any case both are invested with a sheer superiority of mind which is capable of intellectual detachment, a quality their victims in their emotional superstition do not possess. Whatever the stated antecedents of these characters in the matter of actual learning, it is this facility for detachment from the normal, fearful, superstitious and morally-awed sphere of human existence that gives them their potency.

It is logical that the intellectually superior Malcontent perceives malcontentedness, envy and greed in others, and that the humbler man with a grudge against the world might be induced to play what E. E. Stoll termed the 'tool-villain': a cat's-paw for villains of higher social rank.[50] One of the Earl of Essex's secretaries, Henry Cuffe, is said to have been '… in many ways Essex's evil genius. Outwardly he was one of those Malcontents whom dramatists were so fond of portraying, a man who affected learning, and would utter his mind with such candid frankness that he passed for honest. Inwardly, he was overweeningly ambitious, and hoped by following his master to insinuate himself into great place.' We can see many examples of such recruitment of tool-villains in the drama, many cynically and blatantly exploited for their poverty, ambition and discontent. Richard III instantly recognizes such a potential in Tyrrell, (and, interestingly, his Page does also):

RICHARD: Knowst thou not any whom corrupting gold
Will tempt unto a close exploit of death?

PAGE: I know a discontented gentleman
Whose humble means match not his haughty spirit:

---

49 See Nicholas Brooke, *Horrid Laughter in Jacobean Tragedy,* op. cit.
50 E. E. Stoll, ibid.

Gold were as good as twenty orators,
And will, no doubt, tempt him to any thing.

(R III, IV, ii, 32–38)

Richard is not disappointed in his Page's choice. With the Page as go-between (and we must infer that the Page knows his master's wishes intimately) Tyrrel is the Malcontent recognized by another of the same kidney, and exploited accordingly. Thus does Macbeth work upon the resentful feelings of the Murderers, and Iago similarly recognizes and exploits the disappointment and moral weakness of Roderigo with deadly intelligence. Roderigo is doomed, of course: he cannot be expected to survive such a dubious faith as Iago has placed in him, even had he succeeded.

Ironically, the melancholic–malcontented humour predisposes itself to such use. In *The Duchess of Malfi*, Bosola's melancholy is a positive asset to the brothers' horrid schemes. Ferdinand, as he engages Bosola for criminal services, instructs him to continue his customary melancholic manner:

> Be yourself:
> Keep your old garb of melancholy: 'twill express
> You envy those who stand above your reach,
> Yet strive not to come near 'em. This will gain
> Access to private lodgings, where yourself
> May (like a politic dormouse... (I, ii, 198–204)

It is as if the melancholy intriguer has a ready-made disguise and needs no other; Ferdinand merely desires Bosola to use his natural properties to advantage. There is a wonderful incongruity in the oxymoronic image of the 'politic dormouse' – in other words, a sleeper constantly on the watch – a dual propensity apparently entrenched in the melancholy psyche. Since a melancholic may be supposed to be somewhere near the borderline of sanity, others are therefore inclined to regard him as a relatively harmless eccentric: interesting, but not to be taken too seriously, and thus he may act as a spy and an informer without arousing suspicion. His abstraction is taken for granted, and thus he can hide in plain sight: a quality that is tantamount to invisibility, essential to the spy. While the Duchess is giving birth in great secrecy, no one thinks to lock up Bosola for the night along with the other officers. Indeed, no attention is paid to the oddity of his presence; it is simply in his nature to skulk.

Thus, Altofront/Malevole in *The Malcontent* capitalizes on being both ignored and confided in by others. Mendoza is taken in by Altofront's disguise, fooled into recognizing what he believes is excellent murderer-material (although it is an essential part of the comic plot that it backfires.) Similarly, Vindice enters the services of Lussurioso in *The Revenger's Tragedy*. Lussurioso orders a pander, preferably:

> ... some strange-digested fellow...
> Of ill-contented nature, either disgraced
> In former times, or by new grooms displaced.   (I, i, 76–79)

Vindice duly presents himself disguised as 'Piato', and Lussurioso examines him, discovers that he is as shrewd, blunt, and satiric as any Malcontent could be expected to be, and hires him. Vindice-Piato uses his position to carry out designs of his own and then disappears, just one of a number of 'tool-villains' who are not necessarily what they seem, and sometimes get the better of their hirers. George Chapman's *Bussy D'Ambois* offers a further variation on this theme, this time with the unwitting co-operation of the audience. The eponymous Bussy is a soldier to whom Fortune has been unkind; he is obviously poor and wears threadbare clothes. He appears to have such potential as a tool that Monsieur deliberately seeks him out and takes him into his service. Bussy proves to be a very unmanageable instrument, but for much of Act I, the audience is probably as deceived as Monsieur.

The mere 'tool-villain' – that is, one who is solely devised as an instrument in a larger scheme of villainy – has little dramatic weight, not surprisingly. He serves his purpose and then exits, a minor role, as much the 'tool' of the drama as anything else. It is only perhaps when the dramatist's concern is with such a worm turning that any significance can be attached to him. And there are subtleties. In *Richard III*, the role of Tyrrel is minor, undeveloped and, in a sense, perfunctory; but it is by no means straightforward. A tool who hires tools, Tyrrel has his moment of strange poetic glory when he comes on to the stage alone at the beginning of IV, iii, and describes for the audience the murder of the Princes as 'a tyrannous and bloody act'... and an 'arch deed of piteous massacre', and goes on to describe the actions and feelings of the two men who actually committed the deed: 'this piece of ruthless butchery' at his own behest. He describes how, 'albeit they were fleshed villains, bloody dogs', when confronted by the sight of the little corpses, they were as 'melting with tenderness and mild compassion', men who 'wept like two children in their death's sad story'. Tyrrel relates the success of the murders to the 'bloody king' as a mission accomplished, but not before he has left the audience with the impression of 'the gentle babes... girdling one another | within their alabaster innocent arms: their lips... four red roses on a stalk, | which in their summer beauty kissed each other. | A book of prayers on their pillow lay...' (IV, iii, 10–15).

Thus Tyrrel's speech hints at a complex moral and aesthetic ambivalence: we have a poetically beautiful understanding of human pity and compassion, ironically made more beautiful by its tableau of innocent death, juxtaposed with a necessarily ruthless imperviousness to either compassion or beauty. The irony is compounded by the use of the past tense: the murder has already been committed, and compassion, however sincere and heartfelt, did not win out past its royal order – indeed, how could it have? Tyrrel's role, being largely perfunctory, does not so much invite us into a perception of the ambivalent state of Tyrrel the individual as into this poetic truth; and his personal remorse and that of the two murderers (if that is what it is) is of less consequence than the suggestion of the general human moral dilemma between the ruthless inhumanity of a bloody action and the soul-scared, sentimental pity of committing it. The act of assassination, moreover, is inextricably linked to the command that orders it: Tyrrel is in the double bind of one who is human enough to be revolted by bloody orders which he dare not defy, and one who has been chosen precisely because of the (correct) assumption that he possesses the necessary inhumanity to ensure that he will do it, and efficiently. Elsewhere, Shakespeare exploits the plight of the officer under foul orders to a seemingly opposite purpose: Camillo's defiance of Leontes' orders to kill Polixines in *The Winter's Tale* and his subsequent moral prominence in the play. Antigonus, too, softens under the orders to abandon the baby Perdita: '... Weep I cannot, | But my heart bleeds: and most accursed am I, | To be by oath enjoined to this.' (*WT*, III, iii, 51–3). Significantly, however, Camillo and Antigonus are both far from malcontented, and it is important to the plays in which they appear that they have been chosen, not for their villainous potential, but for their loyalty, in Camillo's case, and as punishment for attempted defiance in Antigonus's. Where the thrust of the play is the overwhelming evil of its tyrant, however, and the tool is a villain, there is only the tantalizing possibility of being swayed by sentiment, which inevitably the tool resists. The ultimate fate of Tyrrel as a soul is unimportant in *Richard III* except for this one speech, in which he is functioning partly as a 'chorus', voicing in effect the condemnation of a compassionate society upon the evil of Richard's will and actions. Richard, of course, is the extreme villain as well as the Malcontent of this drama. The play itself must rely for some of its moral subtlety on the choric revelations of its subordinates.

Much more prominence to the personal plight of the morally-beset tool-villain is given to Bosola in *The Duchess of Malfi*. Bosola is a highly-developed figure upon whom much of the tension of the play rests. Partly prompted to remorse through Ferdinand's reluctance to pay up for the Duchess's assassination, his sudden change of heart has nevertheless far more resonance than a mere switch of allegiance for reasons of venality. Here, too, operates the structural device of the villain-plus-tool-plus-tool's-conscience and, in this case, Bosola's conscience is given a present-tense immediacy which increasingly appears to be about to affect the outcome, to harrowing dramatic effect. In realising he has served a false master, Bosola further undergoes what appears to be a total moral conversion: ' What would I do, were this to do again? | I would not change my peace of conscience | For all the wealth of Europe...' (IV, ii, 333–5). His vain attempts to resuscitate the Duchess are desperate, a harrowing moment in the play made all the more so because we have been forced to see the possibility of Bosola's own spiritual salvation if he can only save her. His speech after she finally dies is full of tragic resignation, to his malcontented nature which 'cannot be suffer'd | To do good when we have a mind to it!'; to his present remorse and to the hell awaiting his own soul; to the now irredeemable condition of his 'dejection', which he can only divert to serve his resolve to save Antonio and kill the Cardinal, a 'damage-limitation' exercise which, of course, goes tragically wrong. In *King Lear*, Edmund's death-bed 'conversion' produces a similar frisson. At this point in the play, we care less for Edmund himself than with what such a change of heart might achieve in the saving of Lear and Cordelia. Yet, arguably, this is the only moment in the play when we are forced to turn our attention to Edmund as a morally rounded character, and his 'Some good I mean to do, | Despite of mine own nature' (V, iii, 217–8) is resonant, however ironically: Edmund the Malcontent-bastard apparently has seen a path other than the destruction of others. A pro-active villain and no 'tool', Edmund's death-bed retraction is that of one who has perceived his error for himself, in spiritual terms, at a moment when ambition for anything other than his immortal soul can amount to nothing.

The penitent Malcontent is perforce a powerful figure. Webster's furnishing of Bosola with what might be considered a tragic dimension – that is, with a conscience and an awareness of damnation – forces the audience into a sort of double-perception, whereby ruthless cruelty (at which we have hissed) is radically overturned by a sudden access of remorse, at which point we can identify with his human despair. Bosola begins by being virtually a 'stock' Malcontent figure, recruited by Ferdinand and the Cardinal for the usual telltale signs of corruptible malcontented melancholy. He is a witty and acid railer, 'The only Court-Gall.' (I, i, 23) His 'foul melancholy,' says Antonio, 'Will poison all his goodness... want of action | Breeds all black malcontents...' (I, i, 80). As we learn that he has been rendered bitter by the Cardinal's failure to reward him for past services, we might afford his plight some fleeting sympathy, but his unspeakable deeds destroy any good will. The Cardinal and his brother Ferdinand, the two arch-villains of this play, see in Bosola the ideal instrument for their cruel practices upon their sister. Bosola accepts the offer of this ignoble employment with no illusions regarding the foulness of it, and is co-opted as the brothers' agent throughout most of the play. Yet once we witness Bosola's helplessness, his entrapment not only as the brothers' pawn, but the far more serious moral enslavement by his own nature: the 'foul melancholy' that poisons from within, and whose only satisfactory purpose will be in out-fouling the brothers' villainy, we are forced onto the moral margins of the play along with its Malcontent. We must, and do, to some degree, share his alienation, and applaud his bravery.

Any 'goodness and bravery' in this play are, as elsewhere, abstract concepts; that is, they transcend the character of Bosola. There exists a far more profoundly consistent evidence of goodness and bravery in the play in the Duchess herself, and to a lesser degree in Antonio. Equally, the evil of the Cardinal and Ferdinand is also consistent to an extent that Bosola's is not. Bosola's struggling ambivalence embodies a paradox which ironically makes him more 'human' than the more consistent characters in the play. This life-like quality is not the apparent function of

Malcontents. Mostly, they appear to possess the reverse of any reasonable moral expectation, and the dramatic development of Bosola in this respect is somewhat unusual.

In Bosola, all the ingredients of the Malcontent at his most complex would appear to coalesce. His traditional theatre ancestry of Vice and Fool are present, if subsumed, but he shares the Vice property of direct addresses to the audience (largely in asides) and in the Fool-like qualities of ubiquity and obscure intelligence. He is also, essentially, the melancholy-natured university man, down on his luck and turned villainous adventurer; and he is the mistreated individual with a grudge for doing his 'time' in the galleys. His most remarkable dimension (and thus the feature that makes *The Duchess of Malfi* a strikingly dual-focused play) is the playwright's concern with Bosola's moral conscience. Bosola's moral fate holds sway over an audience increasingly involved with him, alongside the fates of the other, much more ostensibly sympathetic characters of the Duchess, Antonio, Cariola and the children. The fact that the crazily-evil Ferdinand and the Machiavellian Cardinal are ultimately vanquished largely as a result of Bosola's change of heart constitutes an inevitable and vitally significant concentration of sympathy with Bosola as the (albeit unexpected) source of the power of right-doing. This is compounded by Bosola's personal sacrifice of his life in such a finally worthy cause.

But does the play actually reinforce a sense of the ultimate power of goodness and conscience? It is not so much a question of doomed individuals; harrowing tragedy is not necessarily an obstacle to an overtly optimistic message as many examples of tragedies of this period show. Neither is it merely a question of the death-ridden ending, although it is surely a little problematic, to say the least, that a play which, unusually for its time, stresses what we now would call 'family values', faith, loyalty, the transcendence of caste and the power of love, should allow its chief proponents of these to die alongside the evil-doers, and if anything more horribly. Conventional tragedy, that is to say, tragedy which, despite such horrid fates meted out to right-eous individuals, does endorse the message of justice and hope, achieves this frequently through a sense that some sort of Divine Will is at work. A necessary sacrifice is made, but through it, the quality of spiritual life is enriched and altered for the better. There is probably no better example of this than *Romeo & Juliet*, where the lovers' deaths effectively and uncomplicatedly ends the feud between the Montagues and Capulets and forces a sense of spiritual humility upon proud, frail humanity. *The Duchess of Malfi*, by contrast, would seem to more than hint at an underlying despair: goodness, justice, where they are seen to exist, reside in mortals; God holds very little influence over the ultimate fate of man's soul, as Bosola's acknowledgement of his immortal damnation testifies. And while it is undoubtedly true that there is an unassailable note of optimism in Delio's (of all people's) testimonial to 'this young, hopeful gentleman' and his urging of those decent courtiers remaining to establish Antonio's son 'In's mother's right' (V, v, 110–1) at the end, there is the ultimately hollow ring that that 'right' was not proof against injustice. It is not that we doubt the 'right', or the righteousness – surely the Duchess has shown us this; yet there is also surely a sense, too, that all human endeavour is eventually impotent, whether it is good and true from the start, like that of the Duchess, or eventually undergoes an epiphany, like Bosola's.

Bosola embodies a spirit of doom which is rooted not merely in his character as Malcontent, but one which permeates the play. His malcontented nature is essential to this view, however, and there is a striking contrast between the solipsistic ambition of the villains and Bosola's own troubled perceptions of existence, where mere ambition, and winning, counts for very little. This existential pessimism is implied in many plays and is present, either in a Malcontent figure, or as an insinuated part of the plays' wider message. It may not, as with *Twelfth Night*, be obvious or central, but may take a subtler form, be a marginal, black insinuation that pollutes a comedy with its threat however much the play has invited our laughter.

The Malcontent figure may be as central and developed as Bosola, as eccentric and marginal as Feste or, in some cases not actually present in the form of a *dramatis persona* at all. Such plays are all 'malcontented' dramas, however; that is, they convey a sense of the edge, an end of comfort, the idea that the 'man who sees' possesses a formidably intelligent maturity far removed from either the worldly serenity implied by the Stoics, or any Christian ideal of after-life reward. In such drama lurks the potential for destruction of contentment with the human, as well as the civil, condition.

PART TWO

THE MALCONTENTED
STAGE

CHAPTER FOUR

CONTROVERSY CONCERNING THE THEATRE

i

Long before the ferocious Puritan attacks on the drama in the mid-sixteenth century, the English medieval stage had already provided a more than troublesome influence. The nature of the 'trouble' would appear to lie in the nature of theatre itself, or indeed of any art which includes entertainment as one of its functions. Once sin is portrayed as recognizably human, and temptation as attractive, even if only temporarily so, the moral message cannot be wholly straightforward; a thing which Chaucer exploits over and over.

This inherent contradiction – between the apparent purpose of a work and its actual effect – can be seen in pre-Elizabethan works of non-dramatic prose, some not necessarily at all intentionally comic. Occasionally, even where the intentional message is stated from the outset, the effect on the readership may be considerably at variance with the author's stated intention. Thus it is that in some non-dramatic writings, such as Robert Mannyng's *Handlyng Synne* (c. 1300), an ostensibly homiletic work[51] there is an ambiguous intention to amuse as well as to edify. Mannyng's moral message is plain enough: a priest's daughter, compelled to dance incessantly for a year for disobeying her father's order to stop revelling with her friends in the church-

---

51 Based on translations of William of Waddington's *Manuel des Péchés* written in Anglo-Norman, c. 1220.

yard, promptly drops dead when the time is up, but the tone is satirical and the reader's sympathy is at least partly engaged on the side of the sinner. Rolle's *The Pricke of Conscience* (c. 1340), far from seeking to amuse, sets out the terrors of Hell in horrible detail, and would appear to be far less ambiguous: a piece of homiletic writing with the straightforward intention of ensuring that its readers never put their immortal souls in danger of being sent to such a place. Yet it fascinates while it disgusts, and in this fascination lies its imaginative, as opposed to its moral, power.

Obviously formidable are the prescribed Anglican sermons of the Elizabethan Church, such as the famous 'Homily on Obedience', called in full 'An Exhortation Concerning Good Order and Obedience to Rulers and Magistrates', which makes unashamedly selective use of the more lurid passages from the scriptures to enforce an ideal of public order, but it is probably the dramatic power of oration, of the spoken word from the pulpit, that makes for such a persuasive rhetoric. Dramatization, in some form or another, therefore seems to have been perceived as central to the power of the message in prose, and dramatic devices were borrowed freely.[52]

Secular 'conduct books', which became increasingly popular from the middle sixteenth century onwards, exploited dialogue and other dramatic devices. These were produced in bewildering numbers, and seem to have been more or less unambiguously homiletic, essentially didactic, and addressing all manner of matters from the proper conduct of state rulers to the homelier 'family values' desirable in the English middle-class home, including such weighty matters as education and religious observance. They tended to be prescriptive of ideal behaviour,

---

52 The reigns of Edward VI and Elizabeth I saw the need for local congregations to be taught Christian theology and practice. Before the Reformation the liturgy was conducted entirely in Latin, to which the common people listened passively. Since parsons, vicars and curates often lacked the education and experience needed to write sermons and were often unfamiliar with Reformed doctrine, scholars and bishops wrote out a collection of sermons for them, which were appointed to be read each Sunday and holy day.

clothes and manners, and were taken very seriously by an age much concerned with appearances. The famous ones, aimed at the ideal Renaissance aristocrat, had been obviously influenced by Castiglione's *Il cortegiano*, and were Humanist in tone and purpose.[53]   The most popular seem to have been those which adopted dramatic devices for effect. While some, such as Nicholas Breton's *The Mother's Blessing* (1602) are merely sententious (and very much sent up in the speeches of *Hamlet's* Polonius), the ones with most impact adopted the Socratic conversational rhetorical device, thus providing the illusion, at least, of dramatic debate.

To read vivid prose is one thing; to witness vivid spectacle another. The involvement is much more immediate, and more intense. Vivid verse-drama combines the double function of reading and performance, a point which Shakespeare makes forcibly in *Hamlet* when the First Player apparently recites from Virgil's *Aeneid* in II, ii. Verse-drama enables vivid word-scapes and spectacle. It was the growing fashion for staged spectacle – especially gruesome ones as opposed to vivid verbal reportage, together with a fascination with horrors in the Elizabethan theatre, which provoked negative criticism of 'Senecan' drama in the sixteenth century. This extended to the drama of Seneca himself, although such criticism was complicated and partly mitigated by a tradition of reverence for the classic dramatist. Drama is in its nature ambiguous. It might moralise on the one hand, but display and invite enjoyment of the opposite of that morality on the other. This ambiguity was evident in virtually all the sources of the drama of the Elizabethans, but the schoolboys who grew

---

53   Baldassare Castiglione's *Il cortegiano* was translated into English as *The Book of the Courtier* by Sir Thomas Hoby in 1561; an Italian work of lesser influence was by Stephen Guazzo, translated as *Civil Conversation* by George Pettie in 1581. Other 'landmark' works include *A Book Named the Governour* (1531) by Thomas Elyot, (who was much influenced by Plutarch, Isocrates and Aristotle and translated Plutarch's *The Education of Children* in c. 1535), and Roger Ascham's *The Scholemaster* (1570) which prompted a flood of pedagogical conduct books.

up to be writers for the public stage would have noted a further, special ambiguity in regard to the Roman tragedian Seneca, who provided the great Classical model for so much of their work. For Seneca also formed an essential part of their educational curriculum as a great Stoic moralist.[54]

In his prose writings, Seneca praises the patriarchal king who bases his rule upon reason rather than passion, who exercises clemency in judgement, who receives the obedience of his subjects through love, not fear. As a writer of dramatic tragedies, however, it was Seneca's business to present the reverse side of this picture, and he portrays in several of his plays kings who are carried away from proper governance by their passions. In other words, the playwright seems to dramatize the very evils which, apparently, it is the play's ultimate purpose to abhor. Thus Atreus is vengeful, Lycus is ambitious, Nero is wrathful, and Eteocles, in the *Phoenissae*, is a usurper who seizes a kingdom by force. W. A. Armstrong points out that Eteocles has much in common with the 'worst tyrants in Elizabethan drama', citing the Senecan convention frequently imitated by Elizabethan dramatists: namely, the device of introducing a discussion of rule and obedience between a tyrant and a subordinate character, in which a 'case' for tyranny is argued and won. Thus Atreus praises compulsion, in contrast to obedience willingly given, as the highest attribute of royal power, contending that a king is not subject to the moral code of common men but may act as he pleases. The Attendant argues that compulsion changes subjects into enemies and that considerations of honour, virtue, and faith should guide the exercise of royal power, but he argues in vain. The form of this debate-scene between tyrant and subordinate was consciously

---

54 There is nowadays persuasive suggestion that Seneca *ethicus* and Seneca *tragicus* were not, in fact, one and the same. The Renaissance accepted that they were, however, and for the purposes of this argument, I must do likewise.

imitated by several Elizabethan dramatists, and, in some cases directly 'lifted' from the Senecan debates.[55]

In the drama, the Elizabethan perception and the Senecan differed, and significantly. Whereas Seneca depicted his royal protagonists rather as, in Armstrong's words, 'super-human villains consumed by passion' and their offences as 'an affront to the gods and as a negation of morality', the Elizabethans' view of such tyrants held them much more immediately accountable to their fellow men (as opposed to God) – defective guardians of the commonweal, in short, who paid the penalty of evil rule with social disruption. At the end of Marlowe's *Edward II* (c1592) it is not divine right but revenge that is stressed in the powerful climax when Edward's young son takes over as a strong ruler and sends the usurping Protector and alienated Queen to their doom. In the Elizabethan drama, moral retribution was far more likely to be represented as human than Divine; and depiction of rulership on the Elizabethan stage had come not only to represent something quite different from the Senecan model, but to have evolved a quite different purpose.

ii

Drama is problematic. There is the underlying property of drama which more or less dictates a 'double vision' whereby evil characters and, increasingly, evil deeds, are animated with as much fidelity as good ones, and this was true of the revered Classical Roman drama as of any other. The essentially experimental drama on the English stage from the early 1580s onwards was the result of other dramatic and literary 'strainers' through which the ancient Classical drama had arrived on the Elizabethan stage. Thus we have a sort of cultural soup, in which the Miracle

---

55 See W. A. Armstrong, 'The Influence of Seneca and Machiavelli on the Elizabethan Tyrant', *RES* 24 (1948) pp. 19–35. He points out that in *The Misfortunes of Arthur* the imitation is 'so slavish that the discussion between Conan and Mordred in Act II,ii, is little more than a conglomeration of translations from similar debates in Seneca's *Octavia and Troades.*'

Cycles, the Moralities and Interludes, English vernacular drama like *Gammer Gurton's Needle*, Terence, Ovid, *The Mirrour for Magistrates* among diverse literary and dramatic ingredients contributed to a form of drama that was uniquely English, and very specifically 'of its time'.

The seeds of 'malcontented drama', or at least pugnacious, challenging, subversive drama, had been sown already, and had, of course, been from the beginning part of the nature of theatre itself, quintessential to Classical and medieval theatrical traditions. Theatrical innovations – literally, experiments with dramatic conventions and sources – accounted for a great deal in the 'revolution' that occurred on the English stage during the latter part of the sixteenth century. The merely dramaturgical could never have existed in a vacuum, however, and its motivating force almost certainly had as much to do with the relationship which was developing between the playwrights and their public as with innovation in the dramaturgic art. This 'public' was of course massively diverse; dramatists were rather less so, inasmuch as they were all educated, lettered men, whether they had been up at Oxford or Cambridge or (like Shakespeare) not. Those who wrote for the public stage – and this was to account for most of them eventually – might have been driven as much by the intellectual excitement generated by a public mood of fear, unrest, reformation and counter-reformation and above all, debate, as by an artistic desire to rework the dramatic medium. Both of these motivating forces probably occurred simultaneously more or less, the one influencing the other. When one of the chief intellectual influences on moral debate – Seneca – also happens to be its most eminent classical dramatist, in both emanations highly contradictory, this can have scarcely failed to be the case, at least at one end of the spectrum.

But we must go back via the folk-theatre route, where the traditional Vice and the Fool trace their descent to the point when the drama began to tease its audience with images of its own capacity for the enjoyment of disruption. From the moment when early English medieval dramas, originally no more than the act-ing-out of the more overtly dramatic portions of the celebrato-ry Masses – such as the dialogue between the Angels and the Three Maries at Christ's tomb inserted into the Mass for Easter Sunday – became more concerned with the secularly humorous, and therefore human, elements of biblical stories, an ambigui-ty concerning the theatre is immediately apparent. Clearly the main practical purpose of the Miracle Cycles was to 'animate' Bible stories for a largely illiterate audience, but the 'theatre', or the theatrical side of the business, was beginning to represent a threat for those in charge of public morals, and therefore of public order, as can be seen from the fact that the Church be-gan to frown on the increasing involvement of the citizenry in these plays, and eventually to disallow the involvement of cler-gy in any play which took place outside the church building. Anything which did not convey a straightforwardly virtuous message was potentially threatening; but in the drama, actors provide the living embodiments of Evil as well as Good, from Satan himself to the venial moral temptations and lapses of mere mortals. In their representative battle on the stage, Good will triumph over Evil, and thus provide the moral message, yet the play must entertain, and it is here that we perceive the nub of the problem, for if the moral message were not also entertaining, the audience might just as well be edified from the pulpit.

In the sixteenth-century Morality Play *The World & the Child*, the figures of Folly and Vice are, by their opening expositions, enough to place the play 'on the side of the angels' as it were, since neither 'wins', and the representatives of Good triumph. Vice enters on a note of vulgarity common to all medieval stage Vices: his is essentially a comic role, even though the overall moral purpose of the play is a serious one. Farce apparently serves to demonstrate the irreverence of the satanic crew. In the Miracle Cycles (for instance in the lewdness of the Detractors in *The Trial of Joseph & Mary*) and in the Morality Plays, the far-cical representations of sin simply serve – so it is said – to provide a vehicle by which the audience can express its contempt. This vulgarity is not, so the argument goes, something which the audience is required to share; if anything, it should serve to distance the Devil's representatives from the sympathies of the watching crowd. These commentators had presumably not reckoned with the gift of laughter. Those that did were more than aware of its potency. Perhaps such 'minions of the devil' represent the unregenerate instincts of playwright and audience? The 'grave theme' of these plays – the perpetual fall of Man – was undoubtedly accepted and respected in the manner of ones hearing a well-worn lesson, but the human condition is one of little falls, constant adversities, and laughter is often the only antidote. The Morality players presumably considered the average audience and its attention-span. Without the ironic promptings and rumbustious doings of Devils and Vices, the audience might well have fallen asleep.

Many of the early Moralities were actively subversive in a highly theatrical way. In *Mankynd* (c. 1465), the figure of Mercy extols temperance: 'beware of excess' – to an audience of tavern patrons carousing as it watches. Moreover, the roles of the priest Mercy and the devil Titivillus are probably doubled since they are not present on the stage at the same time (leaving the cast requirement of six actors) and this was a theatre 'trick' the audience would have been allowed to know and share. Thus Devils may serve Angels in the wider context of the play's message, but angels *are* devils once released by the token alteration of a stage costume. Moreover, Mercy and Mischief are, significantly, brothers: offspring of the same parent source, and the 'message' as presented by this play would seem to be a great deal more complex than one of simple polarities. The moral dichotomies of wheat and chaff on the Last Day of Judgement as intoned by Mercy are rudely contradicted by Mischief who, suddenly bounding onto the stage, reminds the audience that horses eat straw and men burn straw, in a parody of his brother Mercy's sermonly rhetoric. Since straw is demonstrably not useless, it is misapplied as a symbol of uselessness: the workaday metaphor extracted from the familiar scriptural commonplace makes the point very plainly. Mischief, by exposing Mercy's homily as flawed, exposes Mercy as, at the very least, trite.[56]

Mankynd himself is not a hero but an artisan with a spade, a figure with whom many members of the audience might have identified. Mercy, on the other hand, is a recognizable caricature of the pompous landowning priest, the butt of Wycliffite satire with his over-Latinate, alienating language, but it is this language which Mankynd is forced to adopt in conversations with Mercy and which Mischief parodies and mocks. At a crucial mid-point in the play the audience is 'invited' to pay to see the devil Titivillus, 'Ellys ther xall no man hym se' – that is, the Devil will not appear on the stage without their paying for the privilege, and of course they won't see him in the next world, it is implied, since all are destined for heaven. General laughter, and the busker-actors bargain for their fee. The Devil, not Mercy, is the star turn (but both roles are presumably played by the same senior actor) and the play assumes correctly that the Devil is the main attraction for the audience. Even before the end of the fifteenth century, the moral message of such 'Moralities' had become nominal. The prominence of the devil-role, and the amusing fun-poking of Mischief, are dramatic commonplaces established long before *Mankynd*. Even more ambiguous, perhaps, is the portrayal of Mankynd himself, who is any humbler one of us, as being pushed into a kind of personal heresy when confronted by figures of authority like Mercy, of whom he is not unreasonably afraid.

iii

The stuff of theatre is frequently threatening and frightening, since conflict, violence, plotting, crime and so on provide much more obviously dramatic material than do peace, goodwill,

---

56   See A. P. Rossiter, *English Drama from Early Times to the Elizabethans* (London, 1950).

harmony and Stoical detachment. They are also far more *fun*. Drama, to be *dramatic*, must be concerned in some way with conflict. Another inherently distinguishing feature of the drama is the 'conflict' of personation. The drama will represent vice and villainy through exactly the same medium – actors' mouths, bodies and actions – as it does virtue. Opposing moral abstracts will therefore enjoy the same 'virtual reality' whatever the outcome, whichever is the victor. Explored by Shakespeare in *Hamlet,* and a frequent discourse in many other plays, 'personation', that is 'acting', presents, at an extreme level, the problem of 'truth'. This is just one reason why the drama itself and the theatre – the venues themselves, and the licence inside them – was so frequently in conflict with both Church and State. Despite attempts at control, the theatre came to be seen as a law unto itself, and Authority's ability to keep this increasingly popular medium in check was severely challenged. While its apologists and supporters sometimes propounded the unlikely notion that horrors, lewdness, criminal behaviour and moral turpitude were necessary tools of moral instruction, even claiming that this was the theatre's main purpose, 'moral instruction' as such was fairly low on the agenda of even the Moralities. Ambiguity and questioning was what took place in the theatre, however much the stated purpose was otherwise. Almost none of the earlier Tudor plays were confined to mere indoctrination.

Plays, players and playmakers were suspected, and with some cause, of producing entertainment that was at least potentially subversive. Arguments against the theatre escalated, and ran more or less continuously from John Rainold's lectures at Oxford in Henry VIII's reign to the interminable diatribes of William Prynne in the 1630s. Many of the Puritanical rants are absurd: extreme and hysterical, and defined by a chop-logic that became a gift to the satirists, often it is impossible to discern to what, precisely, the objectors were objecting. Critics who cited the theatre itself as a venue of vice and corruption frequently gave way to attacks on the subject-matter of the plays, and vice-versa.

To all but the most extreme, however, there seems to have been an assumption that, in theory at any rate, plays are permissible if they consist of edifying matter or, among the more moderate voices, plays were more or less defensible provided they be shorn of their various 'abuses'.

This acceptance tended to include Classical drama for its unassailable antiquity, partly because such works tended to be regarded as 'literature' – that is, to be read, lesson-wise, rather than as 'drama' to be performed. While the works of Seneca and his sixteenth-century imitators certainly were performed in schools and at the universities, the purpose was educational and the audience was intellectual, as opposed to entertaining and plebeian. These Classical works were of course 'pagan', but their general acceptance partly rests on a moral framework and 'messages' that accorded fairly comfortably with the Christian ethic. Thus, Classical, or classically-derived, drama had its stout defenders among the educationalists. The early English Humanists, Thomas More, Thomas Elyot, and later, Roger Ascham, generally supported the theatre, especially in terms of its Classical antecedents and because of their regard for the classical playwrights. Moreover, the Humanist emphasis was on the accommodation of both Classical and Christian virtues within a single moral view.

Erasmus, like the Italian Lorenzo Valla whose works he treasured, philosophically espoused a kind of Christian hedonism, justifying earthly pleasure from a religious perspective, and there is much emphasis on the delight to be derived from a study of the comedies in the commentaries of many of these early dramatic critics. In an epistle to an unnamed friend, Erasmus recommended the educational use of both great Roman comedy writers, Terence and Plautus, exhorting his reader to beware 'lest the chatterings of those little men… who say it is wicked for Christians to read the stories of Terence… influence you', and condemning the 'religious types' who are capable of seeing only naughtiness or wickedness, and who 'fail to see how much morality, how much silent exhortation there is… in this kind of writing which was … adapted, indeed invented, for condemning human vices….' He condemns as 'oafish' any who have not learnt to value Terence's purpose as moral instructor, a theme taken up by many, including Thomas Elyot in *The Governour* (1531), who argues that if Comedy, by showing Vice, should be the cause of corruption, then the same should also, logically, apply to Interludes and even to sermons 'wherein some vice is declared'. He assumes a basic moral rectitude on the part of the reader | audience, likening the contact with vice to the fleeting and forgettable sting of a nettle when walking in a garden.[57]

The comic dramatists themselves later spoke up for their own art. Richard Edwards, in the prologue to his only extant play *Damon & Pithias* (1561, and styled 'tragicall-comedie') points to the necessity for dramatic realism: '… in Comedies, the greatest Skyll is … to touche all thinges to the quicke….'. Thus a roister must sound like a roister, a whore like a whore: it would be unnatural for such characters to preach or to use language otherwise out of character, and he points to the principle for this set by Horace. Lewis Wager, in his prologue to *The Life & Repentance of Marie Magdalene* (1566), criticises the 'Hypocrites that would not have their fautes reveled' who set themselves against the theatre, and points to the 'godly myrth' enjoyed there. Nicholas Udall, in the prologue to *Roister-Doister* (probably performed c.1552, and printed 1566-7) regards comedy as necessary for health, and a positive antidote to pensiveness, or melancholy.

There is a striking difference between the seemingly 'radical' sympathies expressed by the early Humanists and the severely censorious and prescriptive opinions advanced later by an increasingly hostile army of divines and Establishment figures. One possible reason for this difference is that the Humanists were almost all of them writers, whereas, in the artistic sense, the divines and polemicists mostly were not. Erasmus (again,

---

57   *Collected Works of Erasmus* (U. of Toronto Press, 1974–2011) and *The Correspondence of Erasmus* (U. of Toronto Press, 1975–2011).

like Valla and the entire rhetorical 'arm' of Italian Humanism, which included such figures as Petrarch, Machiavelli, Castiglione and Tasso) gave philology prominence over philosophy, and described himself as a poet and orator rather than an enquirer after truth. His influence was very considerable both in France (especially on Rabelais) and in England, significantly on the work of Sir Thomas More, to whom he had dedicated his *Moriae encomium* better known as *The Praise of Folly* (1511), a poetical satire directed against theologians and Church dignitaries.

In the middle of the century, Martin Bucer, Regius Professor of Divinity at Cambridge, expressed a typical Establishment suspicion engendered by dramatic art. He asserts (in *De Honestis Ludis*, a section of *De Regno Christi*, presented to Edward VI in 1551) the value of training the young in the performing of comedies and tragedies, but insists that plays, if they are to have any value must be sermons in performance, as it were, and stresses the need for 'pious men, trained in the ways of God... who would compose [them]' ...ensure that 'nothing trivial or *theatrical* is allowed in performance...' [My italics.] Very obviously, 'theatrical' is synonymous with 'frivolous'. He goes on to enjoin: 'Let there be shown not only the subject itself and the actions of men, their emotions and anxieties but also their attitudes and characters, and let them be shown in such a way that they incite keen imitation in the spectators; however, for those ways of life and deeds in them that are otherwise, let them most diligently encourage detestation and avoidance,' while on the subject of Classical plays, he opines: 'There survive today some not displeasing comedies and tragedies... in Latin and Greek...'praising the charm and grace of speech in the comedies of Aristophanes, Terence and Plautus, the skill and elegance of Sophocles, Euripides and Seneca, but clearly prefers modern works with a more overt Christian message, adamant that theatrical merit is of far lesser importance than the pious lesson conveyed: 'it is preferable to perform...tragedies and comedies, in which even if there is no poetic art, the knowledge of eternal life is clearly depicted, than those in which a certain style of wit and language delights while mind and manners are polluted by impious and scurrilous exchanges.'

In 1559, the scholar William Bavand, translating *A Woork of Ioannes Ferarrius Montanus touchynge the good orderynge of a Commonweale* - a work he dedicated to Queen Elizabeth, seems in no doubt about the power of the theatre to influence, and the emphasis is more firmly pragmatic: piety as a means of maintaining public order. While he supports the theatre, he assumes it to have a specific role as moral instructor: 'There shall be no Tragedy, no Comedy, nor any other kind of play, but it may increase the discipline of good manners...if thou either hearest, or seest anything committed that is evil, cruel, villainous, and unseemly for a good man, thou learnest thereby to beware and understand that it is not only a shame to commit any such thing but also it shall be revenged with everlasting death. Contrariwise, if thou doest espy any thing done or said well, manfully, temperately, soberly, justly, godlily, & virtuously, thou... may labour to do that thyself, which thou likest in another... With which discretion, who so beholdeth Tragedies, Comedies... plays of histories, holy or profane, or any pageant...shall not mispende his time...' He obviously imagines, naively, an audience made up of 'good men' with the discretion to make moral distinctions. Like Bucer, he of course makes no allowance for ambiguity in the play, or for the moral confusion that could arise from such ambiguity, but whereas Bucer is actively prescriptive of both the play and its effect on the audience, Bavand describes a moral condition in the theatre he assumes already in place. It makes for a hearty support of the theatre that is essentially unrealistic.

Roger Ascham, in *The Scholemaster*, is more equivocal. On the bringing up of youth and the teaching of Latin, he recommends Terence and Plautus as well as the Classical tragedians, but warns that skilful censorship must be exercised by the master when instructing a pupil in Plautus, particularly in the need to censor 'olde and unproper wordes'. He then goes on to contradict his own recommendation of both dramatists, criticizing their treatment of the baser side of life and likening them to 'meane painters...as if one were skilfull in painting the bodie of a naked person, from the navell downward, but nothing else.' Ascham's equivocation on the point of the relative educational merits of 'scholastic plays' was frequently voiced by others, and is typical of Ascham's own particular prejudices. A good Humanist and a notable pedagogue, Ascham was acutely aware of the need for correct (ie, Ciceronian) Latin, which was long perceived to have lapsed, to be taught and taught properly via those classical media deemed sufficiently authoritative. The linguistic purism associated with Cicero was frequently associated with his moral authority, and this might partly explain Ascham's insistence on the Greeks' supremacy (by this time the subject of intense study in Florence, where Greek scholars and manuscripts had long been eagerly sought after by rich intellectual patrons such as Cosimo de' Medici, and translated into 'proper' Latin). In his suspicion of the Latin comic dramatists, Ascham seems less concerned with their subject-matter than their handling of the Latin.

At the opposite end of the spectrum we have the 'angry divines', whose chief quarrel seems to be with public theatricals, as opposed to the valid and proper study of drama in schools. Where these views overlap with the educationalists it is in the assumption that the drama and especially the *theatre* has an instructional function by default if nothing else, one which, in the opinion of these divines, is notoriously abused, especially given the moral susceptibility of the average theatre-goer. John Northbrooke, a Gloucester minister, was evidently in no doubt of this, any more than he doubted the power of the theatre as an instrument of instruction. *A Treatise wherein Dicing, Dauncing, Vaine playes, or Enterluds, and other idle pastimes &c., commonly used on the Sabboth day are reproved* (1577) is a tract, ironically in the circumstances, 'made dialoguewise' between Youth and Age. He denounces the theatre, asserting that 'Satan hath not

a more speedie way, and fitter school to work and teach his desire, to bring men and women into his snare of concupiscence
and filthie lusts of wicked whoredome, than those places, and
playes, and theatres are,' recommending that 'those places and
players shoulde be forbidden, and dissolued, and put down by
authoritie, as the brothell houses and stewes are', accusing the
theatre of having so blinded the people that they are unashamed
to 'affirme openly that plays are as good as sermons... that they
learne as much or more at a playe than they do at God's word
preached'. He recommends particularly that 'women (especially)
should absent themselves'. After giving such a diatribe to Age (it
is highly doubtful that Northbrooke ever attended a theatrical
performance in his life, although he must have seen the crowds
outside, and would certainly have known of the notorious reputation of the adjacent 'stews') it is significant that 'Age' con-
cedes 'scholastic plays' as permissible in certain circumstances:
'I thinke it is lawfull for a schoolmaster to practise his schollers
to playe comedies, observing these and the like cautions: first,
that those comedies, which they shall play be not mixt with any
ribaudrie and filthie termes and words...Secondly, that it be for
learning and utterance sake, in Latine, and very seldome in Eng-
lishe...'

Northbrooke's reference to the direct rivalry between Sabbath
observance and theatre performances had begun to be as commonplace as the (often grudging) concession to the scholastic
study of Classical plays. However, it is impossible to ignore an
overt relish, not to mention much chopping of moral logic, in
the cataloguing of evils to be encountered in and around the
theatre in much of this type of sanctimonious Puritanical crusa-
ding. Thomas White, (vicar of St Dunstan-in-the-West, and later founder of Sion College and of White's Professorship of Moral Philosophy at Oxford) in a sermon preached at Paul's Cross
in 1577 'in the time of the Plague', and printed the following year,
gleefully intones, in a tract full of puns, quibbles and other rhetorical devices, the following remarkable syllogism: 'sumptuous

Theatre houses, a continuall monument of London's prodigalitie and folly... are now forbidden because of the plague... I like the policy well if it holde still... the cause of plagues is sinne... and the cause of sinne is playes: therefore the cause of plagues are playes.' John Field, another zealous Puritan minister and activist against stage plays (and whose son, Nathan, became, ironically, an actor-dramatist and was a protégé of Ben Jonson) claimed in an epistle 'to the Lord Mayor, the Recorder and the Aldermen' (1583) that the collapse of a gallery at the Paris Garden which killed several people was the judgement of God upon those who broke the Sabbath, ending with the ominous warning that this was proof, if any more were needed, that the theatres must close, for 'God hath given them as I have heard, many faire warninges already.'

It was one thing for Church ministers to rail against the the-atre: the rivalry between theatre and pulpit for audience (or congregation) had long been noted. More problematic were the converts to extreme Puritanism among the writing fraternity. An important influence on the anti-theatrical debate from this faction was Stephen Gosson, (1554–1624), an ex-playwright who apparently underwent a religious conversion in 1579 and pro-ceeded vehemently to attack English literature, poetry as well as plays. Like certain other divine zealots, he evinces a distinct-ly voyeuristic delight in all he denounces, watching, apparently with great relish, the whores at the theatre ply their trade. He dedicated the first of his vitriolic attacks, the *School of Abuse* (1579), to Sir Philip Sidney and was, according to Edmund Spenser, 'for his labor scorned.' The pamphlet was, possibly, one of the prompts of Sidney's *The Defence of Poesie* which was writ-ten not long afterwards, although there is no evidence to show whether Sidney wrote the essay in reply to Gosson specifically or was (as is more likely) responding to a general trend. *School of Abuse* sparked a long-running argument with, among others, Thomas Lodge, who did respond to Gosson directly in *A De-fense of Poetry, Music & Stage Plays - A Reply to Stephen Gosson*

Touching Plays (c. 1579), and Gosson continued the argument in an appendix to his *The Ephemerides of Phialo* (1579) and in a pamphlet aimed at Lodge personally, *Plays Confuted in Five Actions* (1582). At first, it is the playhouses, as opposed to the plays themselves which seem to have caused him the greater offence. In later tracts, he reverses this position, and the players and their audiences come in for most of the blame. He regards women as particularly susceptible (*Epistle to the Gentlewomen Citizens of London*), and there is no little degree of snobbery on the matter of personation, for Gosson objects to the way that actors ape the gentry 'under gentlemen's noses in suits of silk… prating on the stage' and to the preponderance of 'hangbyes' – fans – who surround these impostors.[58] In response, Lodge acknowledges that there is an 'abuse of playing', by which he presumably means excessive lewdness and Sabbath-breaking, but remains tolerant of the 'abuses' for the sake of the Art in general. Lodge's *Defense*, as well as being far less hysterical in tone than Gosson's harangues, is also amusing for its satirical attacks upon Gosson, and the semi-playful accusation that Gosson's own play was plagiarised. Gosson's *Plays Confuted*, though aimed at Lodge, was dedicated to Elizabeth's Secretary of State, Sir Francis Walsingham. In a fawning plea to that eminent statesman, he claims that 'Plays are an Augean Stable to be cleansed', and hints that the 'Hercules in the Court' is Walsingham himself. *Plays Confuted* contains a wonderfully embarrassing confession-cum-refutation of two of his plays put on since the publication of *School of Abuse*, which, although he 'cannot deny, they were both mine' but 'epenned two yeeres at the least before I foresoke them…'[59]

---

58 Gosson's concern here alludes to the 'Sumptuary Laws'. After 1363, repeated efforts were made to legislate against forms of personal expenditure, particularly on clothing, or to limit it to certain social groups in status-conscious mediaeval and Tudor societies. Tudor statutes for financing military expenditure by taxation that was estimated on the contents of female wardrobes were particularly ludicrous, but busily enforced up to the 1560s. Thereafter enthusiasm faded and the laws were rarely enforced.

59 See 'Stephen Gosson, Plays Confuted in Five Acts (1582)' in W. C. Hazlitt,

Into this fray came *A Second and Third Blast of Retrait from Plaies and Theatres* (1580), attributed to Anthony Munday, another 'converted playwright'. The tract offers Gosson the writer's general support, calling the *School of Abuse* 'a title not unfitly ascribed unto plays', and listing the now familiar catalogue of evils of which the theatres stood accused: 'publicke enemies to vertue, and religion: allurements unto sinne; corrupters of good manners...meere brothel houses of Bauderie: and bring both the Gospel into slander; the Sabboth into contempt; mens soules into danger; and finalie the whole Common-weale into disorder.' To this he adds the corruption of the young, calls the Theatre the 'Chapel of Satan', plays 'a snare to chastity', and goes on to denounce actors as being in their private lives as corrupt as their roles on the stage.

In the prose of these Puritan writer-converts any moderate tone rapidly degenerates into the bitterest diatribe once the particular abuses come to be described. Nowhere is this more obvious than in Phillip Stubbes's *Anatomie of Abuses* (1583), where a measured beginning acknowledging that tragedies and interludes 'all Abuses cut away' can be 'very honest and very commendable exercises', containing matter '...of doctrine, erudition, good example and wholesome instruction...' gives way to a near-hysterical if rather wonderful catalogue of vices observable in the theatre audience: 'but marke the flocking and running to Theatres and curtens, daylie and hourlie, night and daye, tyme and tyde, to see Playes and Enterludes; where such wanton gestures, such bawdie speaches, such laughing and fleering, such kissing and bussing, such clipping and culling, such winkinge and glancinge of wanton eyes ... is wonderfull to behold... Then these goodly pageants being done...very friendly, and in their secret conclaves... they play the Sodomits or worse...' In a final fulmination, he urges all players and founders of plays to leave

---

The English Drama and Stage (1869). See also E. N. S. Thompson, *The Controversy Between the Puritans and the Stage* (1903).

their way of life, claiming that supporters of the theatre court eternal damnation.

The evident relish in this type of denunciation must have contributed a great deal to the reputation of Puritans in general as hypocrites.[60] Through a modern lens, there is more than a suggestion of the 'disgusted of Tunbridge Wells' mentality – the slightly pathetic and unconsciously humorous rantings of the harmlessly unhinged. There was a certain eloquence, however, and with the frequent appeals to the magistracy or higher influences to either control or effect a total ban on the theatre on the grounds of the threat of serious public disorder, these rants could not be merely dismissed. Gosson must have been perfectly aware of the likely effect on Walsingham to be told: 'In a common-weale, if privat men be suffered to forsake their calling because they desire to walke gentlemanlike in sattine and velvet, with a buckler at their heeles, proportion is broken, unitie dissolued, harmony founded, that the whole body must be dismembered and the prince or the heade cannot chuse but sicken.' In the 1580s, there still existed strict sumptuary laws concerning appropriate dress which the theatre perforce had to break. Gosson's allusion to the diseased 'body-politic' – a staple metaphor of the unchangeable social order of things as a 'body' with the 'prince' (in this case, Queen Elizabeth) as the God-appointed 'head' – contained a direct appeal to those in charge of maintaining the old balance. Such appeals had a certain validity. The increasing use of colloquial language for political affairs in the newer plays, the recognizably contemporary aspect of the politics themselves, together with the humanization of kings and public figures, the direct exposure of the human – and frequently corrupt – element of politics and policy-making, as well as upon the inherent dichotomy between the sacredness of royal

---

60   'Puritan' was a term of opprobrium: according to Thomas Fuller in his *Church History of Britain* (1655), the 'odious name of Puritan' came into use in 1564 when the Anglican bishops attempted to impose strict conformity of ritual and vestments in the Church.

office and the fallible human individual who held it was, potentially, seriously inflammatory.

The theatre, always potentially subversive, was becoming more so. From the inception of public commercial theatres in 1576, it became a supremely powerful medium in England, both as an increasingly popular pastime and as an experimental artform: in both respects highly influential, attracting people from far and wide in great numbers, testimony, of course, of the theatres' commercial success. Labourers from the counties travelled to Town and enjoyed a 'season' on their wages and took in a show or two between the bear-baiting, the taverns, and the nearby brothels. In London, peers and prostitutes, merchants and the respectable middle-class, ambassadors, apprentices and 'mere riff-raff' gathered together under the same roof in the name of dramatic entertainment. The theatre itself embodied a certain ambiguity. Since the theatres were both under cover and out of doors, the playing area and galleries being roofed, meant that all but the grandest members of the audience sat or stood in the open, depending on how much they could afford at the entrance. Women's roles were played by men; gentlemen's parts were played by actors who enjoyed only an equivocal position in society. The theatre in the later sixteenth century embodied, literally as well as metaphorically, a characteristically contradictory status, on the margins of public order and morals, literally on the margins of the city. These public playhouses operated outside the city boundaries in the so-called 'liberties' in order to evade the jurisdiction of local authorities which made (albeit unsuccessful) attempts to close the London theatres down at least once in each of the last three decades of Elizabeth's long reign, in addition to enforcing more reasonable closures when plague-casualty figures rose, as in 1593-4.[61]

Plague-risk aside, together with the more obvious fears for public safety from the criminal elements – pickpockets were rife in those close-packed crowds – and the general fear of public

---

61   See Julia Briggs, *This Stage-Play World*, (Oxford, 1983).

laxity engendered by a pastime that encouraged apprentices to skive, students to waste their time and all sorts of people to be tempted away from their proper attendances at church, the public theatre was seen to provide an ideal platform for inspiring seditious sentiment. It is no accident that an office for public censorship was created at around the same time as the public theatres. The fact that many plays actually endorsed those very precepts of morality which it was accused of undermining: issues concerning self-indulgence, greed, ambition, sexual licence, hypocrisy, irresponsibility, and extravagance tended to escape the notice of the notoriously mulish Revels Office which (fortunately for the theatre) was also often inclined to be unsubtle in its rulings and miss the obvious. The public theatre was enjoying its heyday by the time Henry Crosse in *Vertue's Commonwealth* (1603) demanded, 'For what more fitter occasion to summon all the discontented people together than plays?… At a stage play… the horrible rebellion of Kett and his accomplices, by a watch word given, broke out to the trouble of the whole kingdom.' By this time, 'discontented people' were almost a commonplace, mythologised on the stage as well as off it. But the 'public' is always potentially discontented, and licensing good public entertainment is often good pragmatic politics. The public theatre was potentially a rogue force, and drew together some notorious ingredients: people from all unlikely walks of life, and the artistic and entertaining presentation of unorthodox ideas in forms that the majority of such a diverse audience could and did respond to. It hardly needs to be stated that these dramas were written and presented by companies whose leading lights included Marlowe, Shakespeare, Jonson, Middleton and Webster.

CHAPTER FIVE

THE WEAL WITHIN THE WHEEL

i

It is axiomatic that the popular stage of the late Elizabethans and early Jacobeans was dominated by some quite exceptional dramatists and some quite exceptional plays. Although a veneration of Shakespeare from the eighteenth century onwards has led to our tendency to think, inevitably, of Shakespeare's contemporaries as the 'Others', if one thinks of the brilliance of those 'others', and the fact that their eclipse was none other than Shakespeare, then we have to reckon with a very short period (thirty-five years? less?) over which the stage was presided by genius. The reason why such a commonplace is worth reiterating is to emphasize two things. The first is that the drama became immensely popular in this extraordinary atmosphere; plays penetrated the consciousness of far more than a very literate few, and Shakespeare – and the 'Others' – were virtually legend in their own time. The second is that while their plays often incorporated amusement of a fairly uncomplicated kind – most of the tragedies have scenes of 'comic relief', clowns, and bawdy, topical humour – the greatest of these works were highly complex and sophisticated. More than a few were troubling, radical. Many did not end up on a neatly affirmative note: far from it; 'happy-ever-after' endings are notably lacking in even the comedies, and comedies often had a bitter edge. Yet the late Elizabethan and Jacobean audiences positively revelled in them. Market forces, then as now, would – *must* – have dictated the terms: if the product was unsatisfactory, it would have been roundly rejected. Audiences would have hissed, thrown rotten vegetables, and walked out. They did not, as we know. They clamoured for more and more. This evident popularity of plays as complex and wordy as, say, *Romeo & Juliet, Julius Caesar, Hamlet,* etc, has caused bewilderment in our own age, when schoolchildren struggle with antique texts and theatre audiences tend to be the educated middle-class. But an audience need not necessarily understand all the more obscurely 'lettered' ironic references in order to enjoy the show: as John Cleese has pointed out, half the *Monty Python* jokes were not 'got' by half the audience, which did not seem to detract from its immense popularity. Jacobean drama seems to have enjoyed a similar appeal in its own way.

One explanation is the dramatists' skill at telling a tale, at stage narrative, at making everybody laugh, cry, gasp in horror, or bite their fingers in suspense. There was something else, too, that seems to have attracted the attention of so many, and so much: a political and philosophical climate that was at once inspiring while it was acutely disturbing. When A. P. Rossiter spoke of a 'typically Jacobean play', in which 'ideas' were more important than 'characters', in works which were 'concerned with the questioning of values in the new and sceptical atmosphere', he was speaking of a world in which the perplexities of Renaissance individualism occupied the attention; where the 'dismissing of the old stable Mediaeval universals leaves thoughtful minds with the discovery that if every individual thinks freely for himself and follows his own will, then chaos results, in which all order is lost...' But this discovery – of a new re-ordering, and the emphasis on individual determination, of personal destiny – carries an almost irresistible allure. The theatre responded to – and doubtless helped to prompt – a radical, even explosive social change. And if 'thoughtful minds' seems to point most obviously to intellectuals, we must remember just how diverse the public theatre audience actually was. 'Letters', essays, treatises written and circulated among a literate, amateur few had been current for virtually ever; some undoubtedly containing material considered subversive (often on charges of atheism which, given the 'special relationship' between God and His 'anointed' monarch, was emphatically not a mere matter of personal belief) but the subversion, while doubtless worrying to an Establishment constantly in fear of plots and counter-plots, was contained. University plays, such as the *Parnassus* trilogy, and those of the Inns of Court, had voiced some highly radical ideas, but their audience was small, private. Now, on the public stage, there was a much more strident voice, speaking in a tone and a language and through the dramatic media of dialogue, spectacle and immediate action that addressed massed and diverse audiences. 'Thoughtful minds' – or at least 'thought' – was being provoked in public.[62]

Rossiter's comments occur at the beginning of a specific discussion of Shakespeare's *Troilus & Cressida* (1601–2), but they equally apply to a number of plays which force highly uncomfortable views of the political machine, expose the essential fallibility of the political framework. In the actual world, many things were changing. The supremacy of 'Englishness' was being challenged despite the conquering explorer heroes, the colonies and the Armada triumph; an old Queen whose hard-won stability of a frequently embattled nation was dying without an obvious successor, and plotting and counter-plotting in government was rife, extreme and violent; the passive Christian behaviour which could be relied upon to keep the oppressed and over-taxed in their place was being challenged, not only by the obvious disturbances created by extremist Catholic and Protestant factions, but by a growing mistrust of indoctrination. We are not speaking of mere abstracts to be debated by scholars – the Humanist concepts which had sought to widen, but in essence mostly endorsed, the age-old medieval Christian theodicy and values. These had been kept within the narrow spheres of intellectual debate rather than entering

---

62   A. P. Rossiter, *Angel With Horns and Other Shakespeare Lectures,* ed. Graham Storey (London, 1961).

practical politics. Nevertheless, the central Humanist precept: of Man's taking responsibility for, and therefore control of, himself, inevitably implied practical, even radical, politics if it was to have any meaning apart from an utopian abstract. With leadership, representatives of the Church, and monarchy itself more or less openly challenged from the popular stage, together with the value-systems – religious, philosophical, and mythical – which upheld them, it is no wonder that the stage was perceived as threatening.

The playwrights – most of whom had had a thorough grounding in the Classics and the emergent Humanist arguments – were not unreasonably accused of manipulation, of not only responding to, but actively inflaming, a mood of questioning and mockery. Mostly, their plays did not contain an obviously politically didactic agenda as such – the Censor would have seen to that. But iconoclasm, some of it experimentation in strictly dramatic terms, involving re-workings of Classical and other traditional dramatic models, inevitably spilled over into the challenging of authorities of other kinds. In this sense, inevitably, the theatre 'educated' its audience to the extent that it refined public awareness that questions were there to be pondered at all, and through that most powerful of media – dialogue. This made the theatre a far more potent danger than if it were a mere alternative to the pulpit, and was presumably the main reason why the 'angry divines' of all colours feared and loathed it so vehemently.

The few of the early public texts which survive suggest that they relied at least partly on old allegorical formulae. Such a one is Robert Wilson's *Three Ladies of London* (?1584) in which the comic rustic Simplicity shrewdly detects the four 'knaves of the pack': Fraud, Dissimulation, Usury and Simony, who operate in the mercenary city ruled by Lady Lucre. He can never get the better of them. Usury, whom he exposes as the swindler of the poor, continues to trade respectably at the Royal Exchange, while Simony, the corrupt churchman, is placed by rich Lady Lucre in charge of 'such matters as are ecclesiastical', on the grounds that he is a 'sly fellow' with a 'liberal tongue'. Simplicity's exposure of Simony sets out all the grievances of the Elizabethan Puritan movement against the church establishment, although there are attacks elsewhere on these kill-joy enemies of the stage. Finally, Simplicity, caught trying to survive by a bit of petty theft, is sentenced to be whipped by Diligence the beadle, while the big criminals get away with it. This is contemporary political-cum-moral satire, showing a distinct disaffection with authority. It is eminently political, in the sense of exposing the shortcomings of authority in its defence of the 'little man'. There is a sense that life would be simply better if Simplicity were in charge of things. Such satire could indeed be termed 'subversive' (which of us does not enjoy seeing our oppressors mocked?) and 'Authority' had every reason to be alarmed. Another surviving Robert Wilson play, *The Cobbler's Prophecy* (c. 1590, printed 1594), a patriotic entertainment in honour of the Armada victory, is remarkable for the way it represents a national disunity that almost allows foreign invasion to succeed.

By the time of the English history plays of the 1590s, the validity of alternative positions being allowed to appear on the Elizabethan stage seems to be a fully developed concept. [63]The history plays were, of course, purposely didactic in some respects, and formed an important part of popular education, since they made the past accessible for thousands who would never read the bulky chronicles of Holinshed, Stowe or Foxe.[64]

---

63   See G. K. Hunter, 'Seneca and the Elizabethans: A Case of *"Influence"*,' *Shakespeare Survey* **20** (1967).

64   These Histories were school staples: Raphael Holinshed (d. ?1580) Chronicler. *The First Volume of the Chronicles of England, Scotland and Ireland... Containing the Description and Chronicles of England from the First Inhabiting unto the Conquest.*

John Stowe (1525?–1605) *Chronicles of England* (1580) reprinted with the title *The Annals of England* (1592): an English history from the legendary Brut to Elizabethan times.

John Foxe (1516–1587). *The Book of Martyrs: Acts and Monuments* was

They appealed not only to the audience's intense interest in history as such, but also to people's anxieties, resentments and grievances about current politics. As well as providing a wealth of exciting and stageable stories, containing battle-scenes, sieges, military heroes, and pageantry – all of which helped to sustain patriotic feeling in time of war – the past could offer significant political lessons to the present, with dangers and disasters from earlier times analogous to contemporary troubles which, given the censorship, could not have been presented directly. The selection and adaptation the dramatists made from the often shapeless chronicle material aimed both to give an impression of the past and its conflicts as they actually happened, and served, inevitably, to place the audience in the position of weighing and judging the action. So few of the earlier plays of the first commercial theatres in the 1570s and 1580s survive that it is difficult to generalize, but those which do represented both controversial political issues and the common people's grievances in a way that seems surprisingly bold and direct. Nationalism, monarchism, anticlericalism, fear of Catholic invasion and plotting – all topical and immediate for the popular audience – are appealed to in these earlier 'Chronicle Plays', such as Peele's *Edward I* (?1591) or the anonymous *Edmund Ironside*, each with a warrior king as hero, threatened by the treachery of a demonic Spanish queen or Pope-serving archbishop. The same sense of national pride and foreign menace permeates many of the 'Medleys', a mixture of the older forms: part pageant, part morality play, part clowning and political cabaret, some starring the famous comics, Richard Tarlton and Will Kemp. (Tarlton not only seems to have been very much a political comic, but he is arguably the forefather of one species of the stage Malcontent.

---

begun in 1554 and four editions of the work appeared during his lifetime. The work, violently anti-Catholic in tone, contains horrific descriptions and illustrations of various tortures, burnings, and crucifixions of Marian Martyrs, and is notable for the emphasis on the stoicism and joy with which these martyrs met their deaths.

He kept up the Vice tradition of direct address to the audience, and of 'clowns thrust in to play a part in majestical matters' – a thing which offended arch-conservative royalist Sir Philip Sidney – and adopted the confiding style which gives late-Elizabethan political drama, as Margot Heinemann has it, its 'two-eyed, cross-class, stereoscopic quality...').[65]

As the Armada period came to an end, and as the rulers' fear of popular disorder and religious radicalism intensified in the economic crises of the 1590s, censorship – largely at this point directed from the Archbishop's office – against obvious advocations of misrule from the stage became fiercer.[66] The Chronicle Plays were more or less tolerated, but for dramatic reasons were going out of fashion, and a more complex drama was taking their place in the form of a more subtle history play. Rather amazingly, for these tended to present a highly ambiguous view of England generally and of the order that maintained her, many of these seem to have escaped the censor.

A number of satirical pamphlets did likewise, and at their best, these were erudite, scurrilous and above all, amusing. While Anticlericalism was the supposed purpose of Martin Marprelate's tracts, the satirical tone hits home far more readily than more serious works devoted to the Presbyterian cause might have done. 'Martin' was sometimes prompted by theatre

---

65   See Margot Heinemann's essay, 'Political Drama', in *The Cambridge Companion to English Renaissance Drama*, ed. A. R. Braunmuller & Michael Hattaway (Cambridge: CUP, 1990).

66   Imposed by royal proclamation as part of the royal prerogative, censorship and control were exercised through the Master of the Revels, a court official who arranged court entertainments, licensed companies and playhouses, and to read and approve all plays before they were staged, sometimes refusing to pass them unless changes were made. Printed plays came under the separate censorship of printed books, controlled by the Archbishop of Canterbury and the ecclesiastical authorities and enforced through the Stationers' Company.

business, the 'Martin' authors often responding immediately to stage satires.[67] As 'Mar-Martin' complains:

> These tinkers' terms and barbers' jests, first Tarlton on the stage,
> Then Martin in his book of lies hath put on every page.

The 'Martin Marprelate' tracts (c. 1588–90/1) excited a considerable anxiety. While at first the anonymous, syndicated 'Martin Marprelate' attacked the authority of the Anglican bishops (and Archbishop Whitgift most especially) and argued, ostensibly, for a Presbyterian form of Church discipline and government, these spikily witty pamphlets became more associated with a protest against the muzzling of the presses than with their theological profundity. Prompted by Archbishop John Whitgift's efforts to silence Puritan opposition when, in 1586, backed by the Queen, Whitgift persuaded a reluctant Parliament to make himself and the Bishop of London exclusively authorized to censor books and printing presses, they were among the most vivid political prose satires of the Elizabethan period. So scurrilous were they that the mistrust of them was by no means confined to those in sympathy with the episcopacy; and as 'Martin's' repertoire and notoriety grew, more and more would-be Presbyterian sympathisers chose to distance themselves, publicly withdrawing their support.

The first of the Marprelate tracts, *The Epistle* (which consists not only of anecdotes ridiculing the works of Bishop Bridges,

---

67 'Martin Marprelate' was the pseudonym of the author(s) of seven prose satires printed on a secret press in 1588–89. They were probably the work of Robert Waldegrave, a Puritan printer excluded from work by Whitgift's licensing law; a preacher named John Field who, although dead by 1588, supplied notes later used in the pamphlets; John Penry, a Welshman; John Udall, a dissident priest at Kingston-upon-Thames; and Job Throckmorton. Waldegrave's press was confiscated; all were imprisoned after trial by the Star Chamber in 1590. Penry was later executed. 'Mar-Martin' was a dialogue published in 1589 in counter-attack, written by a literary mercenary (probably John Lyly, and possibly with the collaboration of Thomas Nashe) supposedly at the instigation of Bishop Cooper.

but also vituperative attacks on the private lives of Archbishop Whitgift, and Bishops Aylmer and Cooper in a terse, witty and thoroughly irreverent style) was roundly attacked by Richard Greenham, a celebrated Puritan, who preached a sermon (delivered at St Mary's in Cambridge) saying: 'The tendency of this book is to make sin ridiculous, when it ought to be made odious...' From one who might otherwise have been counted on to support a serious attack on the behaviour of the episcopacy, this was perhaps an unexpected *volte face*, but it was also fair comment: the presentation of sin (whatever it is perceived to be) as ridiculous is, inevitably, a powerfully political manoeuvre. To make sin laughable in the teeth of its power to terrify with guilt and eternal damnation, is to rob it of its power of control, and throws down a gauntlet to the controllers – who, after all, came from both sides of the Episcopal-Presbyterian divide. 'Martin's' response to Bishop Cooper's humourless and pedantic protest, *Admonition to the People of England*, was to provide (in the third tract, *Mineral Conclusions*) thirty-seven ludicrous theological opinions (many of them twisted hilariously out of context from Cooper's *Admonition*) which 'Martin' mockingly attributes to the prelates. The 'Marprelate' tracts succeeded in making the old bishops seem ridiculous, and were symptomatic of a growing mood of daring to challenge, anarchic way beyond the confines of the Presbyterian protest. It is perhaps significant that all of the 'Martin Marprelate' writers still living were eventually arrested and tried, their printing press confiscated, and only one (who was probably as complicit as the rest) was exonerated.

Control and suppression of plays, which were after all never overtly directed or addressed to any specific person, was erratic and unpredictable. In quiet times the Censor might let a good deal pass, but in times of political tension, such as the late 1590s and the first years of James I's reign, government and censors would be much more touchy and severe. The history plays were perhaps a little less vulnerable, having some degree of authenticity, and could so get away with rather more. At the climax of Shakespeare's *Richard II* (c. 1595) when the King is about to be deposed, the Bishop of Carlisle, a Divine-right absolutist, appeals to Parliament:

> What subject can give sentence on his King?
> And who sits here that is not Richard's subject?   (IV, i, 121)

Who indeed? The dramatic question is posed not only to the stage 'audience' of the assembled Parliament, but to the three thousand-odd spectators in the theatre, themselves subjects of a monarch, asked to judge the deposing of a king.[68] The audience is forced to think about the political ideas involved and, potentially, it is not the answer but the *question* that subverts when the questioning is current as well as 'historic'. The bridge between the present and the past is even more apparent in the opening line of *Richard III* (c. 1591) 'Now is the winter of our discontent...' a *now* which fully involves the audience from the outset in the idea that what they are about to see has an immediate and contemporary relevance, as well as serving the purpose of taking them back through an historical time-warp.

The fashion for the more modern history play as it developed away from the staple Chronicles was partly a result of this convenient 'displacement' device. History plays are ostensibly constructed so as to imply a continuation, one which has a relevance for a society viewing its own past, reaffirming a positive belief in its present and future. There is a very important sense in which the Histories and Tragedies differ: whereas the History play portrays the fortunes of many characters as they play out their roles in a nation's continuing life, a Tragedy is devoted chiefly to the struggles of one character. By the same token, the death of a tragic hero conveys the sense of an ending, whereas the impression created by a history play is that the life

---

68 The scene of the abdication at Westminster Hall from the quarto text of *Richard II* is missing, and its absence is usually explained as censorship on the part of Lambeth Palace. See William Shakespeare, *Richard II*, ed. Nicholas Brooke, Introduction, (London: Macmillan, 1973).

of a nation has neither beginning nor end, but will continue and (we can infer from Richard III's deposition) in altogether better and more worthy hands. One could go so far as to say that History permits no hero. The true 'hero' of a history play is the nation: in *Richard III* the only hero is the Tudor regime.

Shakespeare's *Richard III* is apparently uncontentious: it presents us with a view of a ghastly moment in recent history when a mad tyrant threatened all decency and justice, and was duly vanquished by a good 'order' that was destined to triumph. Richard is vile, and his villainy is insupportable in one who holds the sacred office of King. The play, ostensibly, re-affirms the order of the body-politic by setting a new and proper order in place, this re-centralisation of 'good' order the play's essential purpose. And Richard is undoubtedly *bad*. His pride in his superiority derives from his capacity for evil. As a monarch, he stands at the centre of his universe, yet his villainy and malevolence place him at its furthest edges. He denies his bestiality, yet he is described variously as England's 'bottled spider', 'mad dog' and 'ravaging boar'. A grotesque cripple, he plays the role of the virile courtly lover to seduce Lady Anne. A bogus king, his power is not inherited by Divine Right but achieved by murder and sheer force of will (itself ironically the instrument Divine Will in a pertinent echo of Calvin's teaching that God actually provides evil for good to conquer); thus dramatised, his evil is the means by which order may reassert itself, strengthened by the act of conquering. But the 'order' – the ascendancy of the Tudors – can be seen in itself as abhorrent, one in which there is no place for the will of the people, 'formal and terrible' as Nicholas Brooke commented, one which produces, through the series of plays which culminates in *Richard III*, its own antidote: Richard himself. Given all that we have been asked to share with Richard as a dramatic experience – slyly complicit, insinuatingly if grotesquely human, he has exposed for us the sheer nastiness of dictatorship. Richard, crucially, has exposed a deep national flaw, and his 'history' contains the seeds of what Brooke called a 'civil tragedy'.[69]

Roman plays, which to some extent replaced the more politically sensitive, closer-to-home English Histories, retained this vision of a troubled, politically maladjusted society, but had an impact precisely because of their links to the English zeitgeist – representing political situations and activities which were obviously applicable to contemporary situations. While these Roman plays by Shakespeare, Jonson and Chapman among others were frequently based on 'real' ancient history, evincing a genuine scholarship on the part of the dramatists in Roman governmental history, their relevance lay less in history lessons than in the mirror held up to contemporary England. Where scholarship really mattered to these plays was in the presentation of alternative forms of government. *Julius Caesar* (c. 1599), *Sejanus His Fall* (1603), and *Coriolanus* (c. 1605-8) all portray, in one form or another, republicanism as a serious proposition, and all were staged at a point in English politics when a disaffection with tyrannical monarchy was prevalent, and when republicanism was, however covertly, hinted as an alternative. Indeed, the concern in *Julius Caesar* with a democracy denying monarchy is so potentially inflammatory as to make one wonder that it was passed by the censor at all. These plays dispense with 'heroes' as such or, like *Julius Caesar*, leave the hero-question notably and perennially ambiguous (something that has intrigued modern directors ever since) and present for a contemporary Jacobean audience a bleak picture of politics, of politicians' right or ability to govern adequately, let alone humanely. For all that their location is set at a comfortable chronological distance in Ancient Rome, the audience could scarcely have failed to see beyond this to a much more general proposition concerning both government and the governed: civilization changes remarkably little over time; power-politics

69   Nicholas Brooke, *Shakespeare's Early Tragedies* (London, 1968).

are recognizably fraught with treachery at any point in the history of mankind.

The popular conception of the glory of Ancient Rome comes under fire, also. The myth of a glorious Classical past which might inspire a modern civilization is patently wrecked in *Coriolanus,* in which everyone, from the eponymous hero tied to the apron-strings of a power-crazed and doting mother, to the discontented rabble that deposes him, is exposed as childish, credulous and fickle. Even *Julius Caesar,* where Shakespeare's story is superficially faithful to Plutarch's chronicle, Caesar is hardly the virile superman of popular imagination: hard-of-hearing, subject to fits, pompous, superstitious and vain, there is little left of the credible military genius. That *Julius Caesar* is an 'heroic play without heroes' is nowadays a commonplace, and we are constantly led to a point where an heroic figure, an heroic action, could triumph, yet it never does. Rather, it is a play which plays with the idea of 'hero-types', while allowing none of the four central figures to sustain hero-status for long, although each of them potentially could: Caesar himself represents the general-hero of the old guard; Antony the glamorous world-beater with a sense of loyalty; Cassius the eminently intelligent, ambitious politician; and Brutus the morally-aware idealist. Each proceeds to manifest a 'flaw', a flaw that is 'real' and human: prohibitive in practical terms of 'heroism' – and thus impossible not to conclude that 'heroism' is itself unrealistic. Caesar has an epileptic fit in public, which wrecks his credibility; Antony, victor of the civil war is exposed as a mere rhetorician, whose loyalty counts for little; Cassius's ambition and envy lead him to abandon diplomacy and quarrel bitterly with Brutus, rather than persuade him to eliminate Antony; and Brutus' s staunch belief in Stoical virtue proves his eventual undoing: he is simply too naive to compete successfully. From a political point of view, the play exposes the essential fallacy of supreme government. From a dramatic one, Shakespeare's reduction of Caesar's stature permits a greater focus upon Brutus's moral torments. Heroism in the sense of superior wisdom is constantly juggled in this play, and characteristically, Brutus confuses 'virtue', regarded as his own cherished possession, with the right to rule. The argument would appear to be one of cynical adjustment to 'real-politik': Brutus is so insulated by his own self-righteousness that he cannot imagine how Antony, a frivolous and glamorous night-reveller so different from himself, can possibly win approval – yet the great funeral speeches in the Forum (*JC*, III, ii) dramatize this contrast between the idealistic Brutus and the realistic Antony, whose talent for rhetorical persuasion takes precedence over truth. Antony knows far better than Brutus does the fallible recesses of human nature, how to manipulate the publicity machine, and is sufficiently ruthless a politician not to be distracted by mere moral considerations.[70]

ii

Some critical opinion asserts that Brutus is Shakespeare's most complex characterization before Hamlet; that Brutus's intellectual speculations, ambivalences and agonizing hesitations anticipate the later dilemmas with which Hamlet wrangles. In the fictional and mythical plays the problem of 'Order' persisted, more or less as an obsession. Some notional 'good government', smiled upon by a good God – or good gods – is a subtext of such

---

70   See John Wilders, *The Lost Garden: A View of Shakespeare's English and Roman History Plays* (London, 1978).

  Also see Vivian Thomas, *Julius Caesar,* Harvester New Critical Introductions to Shakespeare, (London, 1992).

  Nowadays there seems to be an agreement among scholars that there is strong evidence that *Julius Caesar* was written before *Hamlet. Julius Caesar* was being acted in the summer of 1599. *Hamlet,* just before the play-within-the-play, has the exchange between Hamlet and Polonius which refers directly to Polonius having acted the part of Caesar (Hamlet, III, ii, 87–93). See also E. A. J. Honigmann, 'The date of Hamlet', *Shakespeare Survey* **9** (1956), 27–9, who postulates that John Heminges probably acted both the old-man parts, Caesar in the first play and Polonius in the second, and that Richard Burbage, who certainly played Hamlet, may also have acted Brutus.

plays as *Hamlet* and *The Revenger's Tragedy* among many others, otherwise the opposite portrayal of corruption could have no meaning. In the fictional worlds of Hamlet and Vindice, political order and thus a guiding moral order represented by the courts is sick, defiled, polluted by rotten government, and the justice-machine is seen to be in desperate need of a hero to 'set it right'. Thus, both Hamlet and Vindice occupy places on the 'outside' of the Court to begin with, because, as morally righteous characters, they must exist at a remove from the Courts' dealings. Nevertheless, their roles as revengers will demand forms of infiltration and espionage. Leaving aside for a moment the questionable morality of revenge per se, it is to another, morally wholesome world, represented by such significantly minor roles as Horatio and Antonio, that they are seen to belong initially. But while the 'two wrongs do not make a right' morality inherent in the revenge play will in due course redound on these revenging heroes, it is not this particular trajectory of moral and spiritual descent which constitutes the most disturbing aspect of either hero, or indeed of either play, but rather the quality of Malcontent, of alienation, which seems to come from within rather than to owe its cause purely to external influences, and by which the 'heroic' quality is increasingly compromised.

From the outset, Hamlet's first soliloquy (I, ii), in the all-encompassing 'How weary, stale, flat and unprofitable | Seem to me all the uses of this world!', we might see that even his outraged sensibilities (at the too-hasty re-marriage of his mother to a detested uncle at the height of his grief for his father) cannot quite account for '*all* the uses....'. Similarly, while Vindice's opening speech concentrates on the evils of the Duke's court and the murder of his beloved, the relish in the words 'Faith, give Revenge her due... be merry, merry | Advance thee, O thou terror to fat folks, | To have their costly three-pil'd flesh worn off | As bare as this' – he is holding her skull in his hands as he speaks – makes an instant irony of his requiring much disguise in order to pose at the Court as 'some strange-digested fellow... | Of ill-contented nature.'(I, i) In the course of both plays, an ever-widening chasm develops between the two malcontented heroes and the representatives of the ordinary, imperfect, but morally striving world inhabited by such as Polonius and Laertes, and by Gratiana and Castiza, in which 'good' and 'evil' have a meaning in terms of simple moral choices. As their malcontented qualities are increasingly revealed to the audience, Hamlet and Vindice become less and less reliable as representatives of sane, ordinary virtue, and thus their 'heroism' becomes more and more questionable. Thus, the much debated problem of Hamlet's sanity – where Hamlet's antic madness ends and his true soul-sickness begins – is manifest but unanswerable: a seamless ambiguity in the play, just as Vindice's several disguises, as cynical pandar and melancholic hired assassin, seem barely disguises at all.

These plays rely on the tension between villainy and an existence, implied or represented, of virtue, to which an ordered, reasonable society must aspire. The revengers' task at the outset is to punish the wicked for their deeds, avenge the wronged and thus restore order in a virtuously disinterested spirit. Yet two problems are immediately apparent. The moral position is complicated by the dramatic one: both revengers come to be identified with their quests which, on completion, render them redundant. The moral proposition of righting wrong with wrong – 'Per scelera semper sceleribus tutum est iter': 'the way through crimes is always by crimes', a quintessentially Stoical dictum much quoted by Renaissance playwrights from Seneca's *Agamemnon* – is a tragic one because it implies the revenger's inevitable moral downfall along with the impossibility of any other option. In the Jacobean version, the revenger has his task, but is inevitably corrupted by it: once the task has been achieved, he has no option but to die on its account. As Vindice puts it at the end of the play, 'Tis time to die when we ourselves are foes' (V, iii). This is 'good Stoicism' at its harshest – the acknowledgement of the true nature of things: what happens is not just the only possible result of pre-existing conditions, but the best possible result of those conditions, and to reason otherwise would be to suppose that Reason, the logos, or God, or Providence, does not aim at the 'good'.

But a second problem presented by the Jacobeans – that of what constitutes the 'Good' – is more difficult to reconcile. For into the equation of villainy, virtue and the virtuous revenger – the man who fights wickedness with wickedness for virtuous ends – comes the Malcontent. Both Hamlet and Vindice are, without doubt, Malcontents: Hamlet, the philosophy graduate from Wittenberg, tortured by distrust of virtually all existence including his own; Vindice, the clever, ambitious, bereaved minor courtier, comforting himself with the relish of revenge on a powerful, evil, and essentially stupid Duke. By making Malcontents of these heroes, the playwrights offer a distinctly slanted view of the fundamental good-evil binaries which might otherwise form the bedrock of their plays. The malcontented natures of Hamlet and Vindice force us to look, not upon a neatly restored order but upon the chaotic, untidy, not to say dubiously moral means by which it has been achieved. The hero-Malcontent, on the outside of society – not just a corrupted court, but on the outside of all of us – causes a radical refocus of our view, too. We have been forced to witness, not merely the pitting of good against evil, with virtue triumphing by means which justify ends, but the shaking of an entire belief, whatever the outcome, for even goodness itself is seen as flawed. Despite an inevitable dilution of the Malcontent's potential *political* impact, simply on account of his status (just as the extremities voiced by the Vice and the Fool are rendered at least partially innocuous on the grounds of theirs) dramatically the Malcontent as agent of 'right' is invested with a significant potency, the nub of which is the revelation that 'order' is often far from 'good', and hinted at being thoroughly undesirable. Ultimately, the inheritance of Denmark by such as Fortinbras, and the bleak outlook for a court ruled by the costive Antonio present the bleakest of pictures. Or rather, the neat picture that existed is visibly coming apart.

iii

This picture was the one of the World. The world-picture, with Man's place in the Universe unquestioned, everything connecting at every point, with Man, God's creation, dwelling on Earth at the centre, was becoming skewed. For one thing, emergent physical sciences were beginning to demonstrate something quite different. The analogue of the body of the individual, with the head (symbolically equating to reason) ruling the rest, was seen as a paradigm of civilized society: the 'body politic', with God's anointed ruler, the monarch, in charge. In another famous image, the so-called 'great chain of being', Man was joined to the whole of creation by a continuous linkage, the highest creation reaching from God's celestial throne and, after various orders of angels, to Man's own structured society, from king to peasant, and then down to animal and vegetable life, scrupulously ranked, to the final insensate condition of stones: all of these were part of a nebulous but powerfully pictorial scheme that, by the early seventeenth century, had long been challenged by intellectuals. But its image was persistent, predominant and almost – only almost – unshakeable. The original questionings of these visual constructs came from the early Humanists and Neo-Platonists, who criticized such models as narrow, pedantic and deadening, or too materialistic in terms of practical applications in government, but who nevertheless had no imaginative replacements to offer. Although some serious doubt had been cast upon these geocentric, socially restrictive models by scientists and philosophers, doctrinal authority reinforced them, and popular imagination had simply accepted them - and why should it not? – as true. Political practice relied on them. Any serious questioning was tantamount to heresy.[71] Science presented

---

71   See E. M. W. Tillyard's *The Elizabethan World Picture* (1943) and Arthur O. Lovejoy's *The Great Chain of Being* (Camb. Mass, 1936). The overall framework of the 'great chain of being' survived into the eighteenth century, albeit in a somewhat modified form. In 1651, Thomas Hobbes – who was familiar with Galileo's work on gravity – exposed the evasive circularity of the Schools' explanation, 'out of Aristotle' of the phenomenon. See *Leviathan*,

something of a problem. One weakness, increasingly apparent, lay in the traditional dependence upon empirical observation and common sense to explain the workings of the universe, and the consequent failure to allow for those invisible forces such as magnetism or gravity. The movements of projected bodies posed comparable difficulties. Because the military, then as now, had a professional interest in ballistics, there was widespread speculation on the subject until Galileo solved various difficulties with his theory of inertial movement: that an object naturally continues unless it is positively interrupted. Here as elsewhere, Aristotle's common-sense view that all movement presupposes a mover was beginning to be revealed as inadequate to account for more complex physical laws. The most serious attack on the Aristotelian system, with its unchanging heavens and its earth-centred universe came, not surprisingly, from advances in astronomy. While observation had previously suggested that the Sun circled the Earth – an image repeated in myth and poetry again and again – a process of deduction had led Copernicus to conclude by 1543 that the reverse was true. Ocular proof was not supplied, however, until Galileo Galilei used a telescope to observe the phases of Venus in 1610. In fact, the heliocentric view of the heavens was introduced to English readers by Thomas Digges as early as 1576 in a relatively popular book mainly concerned with astrology, yet although the Copernican system was adopted into some Jacobean almanacs, general acceptance remained elusive for many decades.

Astrology was at this time synonymous with, and indivisible from, astronomy. The branch of such a study which purported to predict human outcomes from movements of stars ante-dated Christianity for hundreds of years, and had of course been the subject of much ambivalence, especially problematic for the Church since the early Christian era, for reasons that are fairly obvious: religion and astrology frequently offered conflicting explanations for the same phenomena. Whereas the Christian

Part 4, ch. 46.

was taught to regard storms, famines and earthquakes as the manifestations of God's secret purposes, the Astrologer made them subject to the movement of celestial bodies and therefore, by his art, predictable. This attribution of good or bad luck to the stars was a direct threat to Christian dogma: as Calvin said, it 'put clouds before our eyes to drive us away from the providence of God'.[72] Bishop Hooper similarly warned that 'it is neither Sun, neither Moon, Jupiter nor Mars, that is the occasion of wealth or woe, plenty or scarcity, of war or peace' but God himself.[73] Naturally enough, for Hooper and his episcopal confreres, long life and prosperity was the reward of godliness, not the legacy of the planets. However, the Church, although officially discouraging Judicial Astrology – the casting of horoscopes to predict an individual's future – seems often to have turned a blind eye to the fact that it was widely practised, sometimes by the clergy themselves, and certainly among kings and queens. Astrology was yet to undergo the process of divide from scientific advances in astronomical observation, and for the sixteenth century, astrological doctrines were part of the educated man's picture of the universe and its workings. Astronomy and astrology were, effectively, virtually the same thing; for if astronomy is the study of the movements of heavenly bodies, then astrology is the study of the effects of those movements. It is neither odd nor contradictory in sixteenth century terms that perhaps the greatest astronomical theoretician of the day, Johannes Kepler, was employed by his patron, Rudolph II, in the capacity of astrologer making predictions for the royal household.

The detailed relationship of the movements of the heavens to earthly events was just another example of the many links and correspondences which were thought to bind the physical universe together. These would be challenged, along with many others, by the gradual assumption of new scientific discoveries in the century and a half between Copernicus and Newton,

---

72   J. Calvin, *An Admonicion against Astrology Iudicall*, trans. G. Gylby (1561).

73   *Early Writings of John Hooper*, ed. S. Carr (Cambridge, 1943), p. 333.

discoveries which were resisted by Christian dogma, which tended to regard 'scientific' explanation with as much suspicion as it did astrological prediction, but it is important that the ambivalence surrounding astrology be not confused with what a later age regarded as conflict between 'science' on the one hand and 'mysticism' on the other. The sixteenth century intellectual conflict with astrological prediction lay more in its clash with the rationalism present in the Humanist view, a rationalism which arose, not from theoretical science, *per se*, but from the quasi-mystical precept of the Humanists that Man, God's greatest creation, possessed the protean ability to be anything he chose.

In this sense, it is wholly limiting that Man should be at the mercy of the stars. When the bastard Edmund in *King Lear* says it is 'the excellent foppery of the world, that… we make guilty of our disasters the sun, the moon, and stars…' (I, ii, 104–6), he is voicing a long-held Renaissance argument against mystical predestination. Man at the centre of his world, the apex of his creation, was a philosophical commonplace in intellectual circles for the Renaissance, and its finest expression can be found in the Florentine Neoplatonist Pico della Mirandola's oration on *The Diginity of Man* (1486): 'O highest liberality… greatest and most wonderful happiness of Man, to whom is given whatever he chooses to have, to be what he will.' Pico's assumptions as to Man's freedom are inevitably aristocratic (as was his intellectual audience), the system being based on a divinely-ordained hierarchy. But the emphasis on the power and potential of Man to do and be whatever he wished, and to dominate the natural world through the exercise of will and imagination also had an inevitably revolutionary interpretation, liberating in several senses. It is no accident that Shakespeare's *Julius Caesar* has retained an important appeal for nations in conflict down the ages, and Cassius's claim that 'Men at some time are masters of their fates: | The fault, dear Brutus, is not in our stars, | but in ourselves, that we are underlings' (I, ii, 137–9) focuses the responsibility for destiny firmly upon Man himself, and in terms of immediate practical politics. It is no accident, either, that such a view found fresh expression at a time when changes in the existing power-structure encouraged such aspirations.

In this 'brave, new' world, the rigorous pecking-order of hierarchy that had existed at all points between the aristocracy and the peasantry was now being challenged, and successfully. In England during Elizabeth's reign, something we would now term 'social mobility' was much in evidence. Elizabeth's later government was largely composed of able and, to an extent, self-made men, like Walsingham, who rose in rank on account of merit rather than of birth.

A fresh cynicism concerning the 'golden age' of Elizabeth and all that this implied also posed questions and contained an inevitable threat. The Armada victory had been replaced by the more disturbing problem of the Succession, already an issue in 1588, one increasingly urgent as the years passed. A monarch made – or broke – a kingdom: this much was certain; but how much he (or she) retained the right to do so had begun to tantalize – at first a small intellectual fraternity which was not so much dedicated to 'revolution' as to the practice of inquiry, but it could never have been entirely disinterested.

Elizabeth was famously more diplomatic in the matter of 'Divine Right' than her successor, James, but the idea of 'Divine Right' was buttressed by an ineluctably powerful mythology. Now, even this myth was becoming slewed. The ancient view, bolstered by the Classics, had always held a contradictory vision of nobility: on the one hand, Princes ruled by dint of ultimate aristocracy; born to rule, Divinely appointed. Yet they were also required to 'earn' such a right; in other words, to be as noble in spirit and in life as they were in birth. Noble birth automatically invested a Prince with a noble soul but, without the outward evidence of noble behaviour, a Prince's position was open to question, as Marlowe's *Edward II* demonstrates with horrid realism. In this play, the diminishing fitness of Edward to rule is constantly compared with that of Mortimer. Mortimer (and therefore, Isabella) is the more deserving ruler, despite Edward's crown. On the other hand, Mortimer's rebellion and his sexual relationship with the Queen is treasonable, crimes for which he dies, but not before we have had time to fully consider the problem of weak subordination in a king. It is of course hugely significant that Marlowe should attract such dramatic sympathy for Edward the man, both in his terrible infatuation with Gaveston and in his appalling death; yet the play also makes an important feature of this very delicate point of the position of kingship. This play is, theoretically, a 'history', but its relevance for the current age was acute, even paramount.

The small pockets of intellectuals who circulated such potentially inflammatory opinions with increasing boldness were 'contained' from an Establishment point of view. Inevitably, however, they came to be regarded as dangerous to a shaky state machine, increasingly exposed by spies, and responded to with violent suppression: for while the revolutionary potential was probably wildly exaggerated, and its counter-blasts the product of fear, it must be remembered that in both Elizabeth's and James's reigns, 'opinion' was in itself regarded as potentially seditious, let alone the charge of atheism, and men died in its cause. It was from a relatively small fraternity that such diverse minds as Christopher Marlowe, Sir Walter Raleigh, and Francis Bacon sprang, all in their various ways rogue forces who would be expelled one way or another: Christopher Marlowe's violent death in 1593 – apparently in a tavern brawl – has ever after provoked questions of deliberate assassination; Walter Raleigh was imprisoned, released, re-imprisoned, and eventually executed in 1618 under James I; Francis Bacon, after an illustrious political career, was forced to retire from Court on several charges of corruption, and died ignominiously in 1626.

Yet this flow of opinion and information was, quite simply, unstoppable, gaining ground in all directions. Throughout the later part of the sixteenth century, political pamphlets, extremist and moderate, flew to and fro with increasing rapidity and constituted a vital if erratic life-source to a widening stratum of society increasingly concerned not only with the acquisition of knowledge, but in debating questions which had come to have a pressing and personal relevance. As John Stachniewski puts it, 'Self-awareness as an individual was often identical with the pain of exclusion... When human beings do not fill or feel able to accept an allotted social niche or when the niches society offers are themselves unstable they are forced to consider both their uniqueness and the nature of the forces controlling their destinies.'[74]

For while the Establishment might have cause for concern with seditious ideas promulgated among an intellectual (but increasingly cosmopolitan, increasingly vocal) minority, the real problem lay in a significant shift in the policy of education, something which the Reformers had vigorously supported, and the result was increasing literacy among the general population. The Roman Catholic hegemony had been successfully challenged in England and toppled, but the new Establishment was very far from stable. One of the chief tasks facing early Reformers of the Church had been in challenging the entrenched dependence on the passive participation in the Latin mass, and the use of relics, pardons, signs and prayers as if they were charms to ward off evil and which had (in the view of the reformers) reduced faith to little more than superstition. Thus, Protestantism had promulgated translations of the Bible into English, and the spread of literacy and the basic education that made it accessible. This inevitably unleashed something of a demon, as it did not lead, as some of the more vigorous reformers had hoped, to people to recognizing a single, Protestant truth. 'Ideas', once exclusively the province of the educated minority, stopped being 'exclusive' once there was a demand for an education which facilitated the reading of them, and although the translation of the basic Christian precepts from the Latin into the English had been, in itself, liberal and

---

74   John Stachniewski, *The Persecutory Imagination: English Puritanism and the Literature of Religious Despair* (Oxford, 1991), p. 70.

liberating, it inevitably ensured the matters being read became common property, up for discussion. This 'problem' eventually necessitated some draconian legislature. The Reformed Church, which had urged its own free spiritual existence, ironically soon found itself demanding that a state machinery be put in place to support its cause, which led, inevitably, to the papists and sectarians being forcibly deterred from their 'heresies', and an elaborate spy-network dedicated to the suppression of Catholic activities sprang into vigorous being. In the wry words of Julia Briggs, 'The religion of a zealous minority operates very differently when it becomes the establishment.'[75]

This zealous minority moreover differed essentially from the humanist reformers. Martin Luther insisted that the individual had forfeited his free will through the fall of Adam, and that salvation was not therefore a matter of personal choice but depended entirely on God's grace. Calvin took this a stage further, believing that the recipients of God's grace, the so-called 'elect', had already been chosen before time began. Leading a good and virtuous life could only be 'evidence' of grace; by itself, it could not secure a place in the Kingdom of Heaven. Therefore radical Protestantism, with its emphasis on reading and inquiry and which had appeared to be founded on a new sense of self-determination and independence, contained at its core this fundamental paradox: that however much Man might negotiate his position in the world, he was quite unable to make covenant with a God whose ultimate justice was pre-ordained. As the (relatively moderate) Puritan theologian William Perkins put it, 'for men are not to imagine that thing must first be just, and then afterward that God doth will it: but contrariwise, first God wills a thing and thereupon it becomes just.'[76]

This denial of self-determination, juxtaposed with the opposite view, the Humanists' long insistence on mankind's central-

---

75   See Julia Briggs's discussion in *This Stage-Play World*, (Oxford, 1983), 66 ff.

76   William Perkins, *The Works*, ed. C. Legge (Cambridge, 1605) p. 496.

ity to his own fortune and welfare, together with the increasing accessibility of the intellectually moderate, rationalist arguments of such as Francis Bacon and Michel de Montaigne to an ever-widening readership, was bound to cause a deepening frustration and impatience with political (and therefore religious) constraints of all kinds, and can have done no other than create a sense of dislocation for many, and outraged defiance for some.

iv

Much of this defiance found its way onto the stage, where not surprisingly a distinctly malcontented flavour began to dominate. Renaissance Humanism had introduced something very different to what had gone before. There had been no 'alternatives' in the mediaeval orthodoxy: Man was subordinate to a jealous God and an entirely jealous Church, which demanded blind faith and unquestioning obedience. However, it is equally significant that the Renaissance Humanists were somewhat at odds with their Classical exemplars, on the grounds that the dominant tradition of pagan antiquity had spoken against the desirability of reward in public life. The Stoics, the Epicureans, Plato and Aristotle had all asserted that there was little hope that those engaged in the public domain could remain so and not compromise the highest philosophical and ethical standards. Power, to borrow a modern maxim, tends to corrupt. Thus, the life of the truly wise man – the Sage – was by definition one which renounced politics, and Christianity reinforced this Classical precedent by making the monastic life the highest vocation for Christians.

The position is therefore inevitably ambiguous; at its worst, in its flattering of princes and worship of power, the Renaissance Humanist emphasis on attainment encouraged the very hypocrisy denounced by ancient philosophers and medieval Christians alike. At its very best, however, what we have here is a serious 'reformation' of the view of Man's place in the world, central and temporal, as well as one which fitted reasonably comfortably with theological notions that Man, as God's finest creation, should attain the pinnacles of achievement by God's will. This could not help but produce a sense of instability. In other words, what one is in the habit of thinking of as a 'given' of nature may in fact be a product of culture. And what belongs to culture, not nature, is within human power to change. Obviously, such a (brave, new) world of cultural possibilities was potentially empowering for many. For some, such as the 'alienated intellectuals' who largely made up the real-life Malcontent tribe, the opposite was true. These had received an education and learning which did not result in the fulfilment of ambitions, and although they possessed the ability and proclivity to question, this could not and did not produce satisfactory answers.

On the stage, Malcontents are frequently portrayed as failures within the parameters of Humanist striving for temporal power and satisfaction, and given to uttering dark portents about the failure of mankind to amount to anything much, let alone the nobility of purpose so dear to the Renaissance Humanists. Frequently, this is attributable to the characters' own sense of personal injury; so while confirmed Humanists like *King Lear's* Edmund will certainly take the position that submitting to fate and fortune is folly, and that a seizing of control is the only answer to resolving one's personal ambition, the apparent presence of a higher earthly justice which eventually foils the Malcontent's plan (in this case, the birth-blight of Edmund's bastardy) becomes another, much more immediate target for railing and abuse.

The stage Malcontent has apparently perceived a truth to which optimists and idealists are wilfully or naturally blind, and political reform – something that might amount to 'good order' – which can amount to little in a dog-eat-dog world where superiority is a matter of power, for power will always be corrupt. The Malcontent enters the corruption with an enthusiasm born of intelligence. But this does not deny the existence of a greater Power, and is not necessarily atheistic. If, like Bosola, the

Malcontent eventually admits to the greater power of God, it is with a knowledge that he has been one of Hell's creatures on earth, and that Hell is his destination in the after-life. But God's earthly representatives have been exposed as sham. Mostly, like Flamineo, the Malcontent goes down railing.

This throws up two rather opposite propositions. The first is that the Malcontent is surely the ultimate revolutionary – the one who stands, literally, for the overturning of everything, the embracer of Chaos as the only law. But this is a paradox, and it could therefore be argued that in embracing Chaos, he is acting in accordance with his 'nature' in doing so, and acting, therefore, in accordance with an Order, of sorts, and one which accords with the Stoical. The likes of Richard III, Vindice, Flamineo, De Flores (and Beatrice–Joanna) and Barabas all utter apparently bravely Stoical sentiments at the very end, sentiments which acknowledge the rulership of Fate. Richard declares: 'Slave, I have set my life upon a cast, | And I will stand the hazard of the die.' (*R III*, V, iv, 310–1) with a resonant pun on the portentous word 'die'. This final acknowledgement of Fate's victory is, importantly, of a piece with a play which offers the idea of Richard's being the chaotic instrument by which Order, in the shape of the Tudors, is gloriously re-established. Richard's villainy has been necessary; without it, the Tudors could not have happened. The tone of Vindice's ''Tis time to die, when we ourselves are foes.' (RT V, iii, 110) is almost cheerful, entirely acquiescent with his sudden fall in fortunes. The 'we ourselves' is particularly pertinent to an ending which has made the visual point of the confusion of identity of the two sets of masquers. Flamineo's tone is infinitely more contemptuous - he sees Fate as a yapping dog at his heels which he cannot shake off: '... Fate's a spaniel, | We cannot beat it from us. What remains now? | Let all that do ill take this precedent: | Man may his fate foresee, but not prevent.' (*WD*, V ,vi, 176–9) – but accepts powerlessness on behalf of Man.

There is in all of these endings more than a suggestion of the embrace of death, if not literally of suicide. Both Flamineo and

[158]

Bosola seem glad to be finally rid of life. Flamineo embraces the appeal of an untroubled oblivion, as if the noise of his own thoughts is finally too much:

I am i'th'way to study a long silence,
To prate were idle; I remember nothing.
There's nothing of so infinite vexation
As man's own thoughts.'   (*WD*, V, vi, 202–5).

Hamlet's punning 'The rest is silence' (V, ii, 337) is a relieved greeting of the cessation of the sheer noise of living, of his own thoughts, as much as a simple observation that, with his death, he can say no more. Nothing of an after-life beyond perfect oblivion seems to enter Flamineo's mind at the point of death; however, it does Bosola's, and there is an inevitable suggestion in this play of redemption, both through the re-asserted justice in his killing of the Duke and the Cardinal and in his claim that this retribution is partly for '… myself, | That was an actor in the main of all | Much 'gainst mine own good nature…' (*DM*, V, v ,83–5). He acknowledges a fundamental 'good nature' as well as the possession of a 'weary soul', and claims a form of nobility in death 'in so good a quarrel'. We see, in the invert-ed imagery of Bosola's dying speech, the temporal world made to appear hellish: 'In what a shadow, or deep pit of darkness, | Doth… mankind live!', while death itself is both welcome and, seemingly, forward-looking: ' Let worthy minds ne'er stagger in distrust | To suffer death, or shame for what is just: | Mine is another voyage' (95 ff.). Bosola, as has already been noted, is an unusual Malcontent in that he is imbued with a focus on human feeling; however, his embrace of his end is similar to others in its final acceptance of the impossibility of human existence. The second proposition, therefore, is that the Malcontent is, in effect, the ultimate reconstructed Stoic: accepting 'nature', but accept-ing that this includes possessing a vileness that most of us (and therefore most of the other representations on the stage) cannot countenance.

Bosola's despair and partial redemption (at least in terms of our sympathy, if not in any absolute sense) comes to engage the idea of the possibility of spiritual redemption. Often, however, there is no sense of heavenly reward in such a surrendering to fate. Instead, the despairing element in these malcontent deaths implies a sense of personal and religious perdition which is certainly bleak, and which reminds us uncomfortably of a human failure of faith. Given that this human failure is almost certainly the result of the equally human ability to reason (faith is bound, in some sense, to be blind; clear reason on the other hand could lead dangerously to atheism) it is based on an old Humanist paradox: God gave reason to Man; but Man might reason God out of existence.

The problem is partly enshrined in the theological and social paradox presented by the Humanists of the fifteenth century who articulated a new and lay view of Christian society that fused traditional Christian values with the civic values of the pagan world, one which had the effect of a general re-orientation of Christian culture with respect to its Classical past. In this, they were at odds with their medieval predecessors, who tended to espouse the idea of the highest virtue as lying in the contemplative life. As James Hankins observes of the Renaissance Humanists,

> it was the very definition of a Humanist to advocate the restoration of classical cultural values... the failings of modern Christendom could be traced to the loss of classical heritage: the wisdom, virtue, military power and practical knowledge of ancient Italy. But to celebrate the Past was inevitably to criticize the Present.[77]

---

77 See James Hankins, 'Humanism and the Origins of Modern Political Thought' in Jill Kraye, ed. *The Cambridge Companion to Renaissance Humanism* (Cambridge, 1996), pp. 118–42.

In other words, while the Renaissance Humanists were not hostile to Christianity as such, they were certainly hostile to many of the cultural values of medieval Christianity. For example, as Hankins goes on to say,

> The condemnation of pride and vainglory... had been a basic part of Christian teaching since its beginnings, but Humanists ... saw that reviving ancient traditions of public virtue would be impossible without also reviving the ancient prizes of fame and glory. *So the rewards of virtue were transposed from the next life to this one.*
> [My italics]

This last point is of exceptional importance, because it emphasises not only the intellectual problem with a type of religious faith which eschewed worldly reward in the certainty of a heavenly one, but also the likely cultural and political impact of such a view. Given this, much of what Humanism stood for in the Renaissance had the effect of undermining the political claims of the late medieval Church. Although often hiding behind the personae of interlocutors in their dialogues, Renaissance Humanists called into question the ideological bases of clericalism, hierarchy, monasticism and the subordination of the political to religious ends. The point really lies in the possibility of alternatives for a society that had been denying such possibilities for hundreds of years.

v

This engagement with the temporal dilemmas presented by Renaissance Humanism provides a precondition for the Malcontent on the late Elizabethan and Jacobean stage, as does another, perhaps more pressing, socio-theological reason why the Malcontent, as destroyer of himself and others, should have had such powerful impact. The theology of the Elizabethan Church managed as it was, in the beginning, by clergymen who had spent the five years of 'Bloody' Mary's reign in Geneva, Zurich or Strasbourg, was basically Calvinist, and therefore predestinarian. That is, they accepted the notion that God has decided who will go to Heaven and who will go to Hell, and Man is powerless to alter this state of spiritual affairs by any act of will of his own. If the Calvinist system is taken to its logical extreme, one encounters a kind of blueprint for malcontentedness. If Man is helpless to influence God's decision to grant grace to the sinner (according to Calvin, this Divine decision is irrevocable) he might also be helplessly reprobate: a total outcast, literally without hope of redemption. If the thing has been decided already, what the Hell? While the majority of believers probably saw themselves as sheep rather than goats – the Elect rather than the Damned – and saw in the misbehaviour around them evidence of their own superiority ('works' being valueless in themselves as spiritual 'insurance', but nevertheless evincing grace in their performance) there also lurked behind this a truly dreadful Doubt, which amounted to an inescapable theological cul-de-sac, a nightmare that might well have haunted the Protestant imagination: for one might be Damned after all. This notion was frequently seen to overtly pervade the drama: Antonio sums up Bosola as one who '... would look up to Heaven, but I think | The devil that rules i'th'air, stands in your light.' (II, i, 98–9). The reprobate is denied by circumstance the possibility of doing good that will grant him grace or of repentance ('looking up') and in this play, the devil-role is served amply well by the Duke. We see a similar impenetrability when Claudius (who combines the devil-role also) tries to pray: 'My words fly up; my thoughts remain below' (*Hamlet*, III, iii).Here, to borrow a modern metaphor, the image of a 'glass ceiling' between the Elect and the Damned is especially strong even if, as in this case, we might judge that Claudius has a weak case for a hearing.[78]

I am deeply indebted to John Stachniewski's chapter on Marlowe's *Doctor Faustus* for the clarity of his exploration of how Calvinist doctrine influenced the phenomenon that I have

---

78   John Stachniewski, op.cit. Chapter 7 pp. 292–331. Stachniewski stresses that he uses the A-Text of Marlowe's *Dr.Faustus* in the main.

termed 'the blueprint for malcontentedness' in its relation to Marlowe's play. It would be redundant to cover the same ground, but a short digest is relevant. Basically it is this: according to Calvin, God first determined what would happen. Then the Devil would for his own malignant purposes set about effecting what God had decreed. Finally, human will would concur with what had been determined twice over by these greater powers. Calvin explains:

> Where it is said that the will of a naturall man is subject to the rule of the Devell, to be stirred by him, it is not meant thereby that man as it were striving agaynst it, and resistyng it is compelled to obeye, as we compell bondeslaves against their wil, by reason of obeying their lordes, to do our commaundementes: but that bey-ing bewitched with the deceites of Satan, it of necessitie yeldeth it selfe obedient to every leadyng of him. For whom the Lorde vouchsaveth not to rule with his spirite, them by just judgement he sendeth away to be moved of Satan.[79]

In other words, the Devil operates on the non-elect – the damned – in effect by the will of God; their will and destiny is to be seduced by Satan. Stachniewski makes a very strong case indeed for this reading of the Prologue to *Doctor Faustus*, so that the 'apparent contradictions between the idea of God conspir-ing Faustus's overthrow and Faustus preferring magic to heaven would, to a Calvinist, make perfect sense.'[80] In these terms, it is difficult to contest the veracity of the logic of:

The reward of sin is death. That's hard... If we say that we have no

---

79   *Institutes of the Christian Religion*, 2. 4. 1.

80   I am deeply grateful to the late Rupert Hodson for his discussion of the presence in the Pater Noster of the plea to the Almighty to 'lead us not into temptation'. Logically, this ought to be a plea to the Tempter, and the Albigen-sians apparently argued it thus; post-Calvin, however, this line in the prayer acquires a particularly mordant emphasis along the Calvinist superstitions outlined: God can 'lead' us into temptation if the question of election or dam-nation has already been predetermined.

sin we deceive ourselves, and there is no truth in us. Why then,
belike we must sin, and so consequently die. Ay, we must die an
everlasting death. What doctrine do you call this? Che sera, sera,
What will be, shall be. Divinity, adieu!   (I, i, 40–6)

What doctrine indeed? It is ironic that, in view of Faustus's dis-
missal of such a passive status, the whole play could be read
as a Calvinist thesis within which the reprobate scholar is not
permitted repentance. Dramatically, in practice, each of the moments where he is urged to do so is tense with the possibility of
saving himself. This play and others balance themselves on such
moral rockers: the human will perceived, as Stachniewski puts
it, as a 'causal wheel within wheels' – ultimately meaningless.
Thus we are back with the portrayal of Bosola's spiritual dilemma, in which redemption is desired and willed, yet not possible
(for some) because God has elected it so.

That God's will is mysteriously behind this election is, in one
sense, elaborately cruel. Why, given a rather more traditional
orthodoxy, should Man, in a covenant with God, not be able to
'negotiate' repentance and salvation? One can see that, to those
dogged by the pressure and corruption of the abuse of pardons,
intentions and similar 'insurances', Calvin's doctrines must have
seemed a liberating breath of clean air; but the creeping suspicion of damnation would have spelt utter despair to some, and
fired yet others with a sense of an altogether other, negative freedom. Damnation grasped and waved aside, Faustus-fashion, is
bound to result in a moral and spiritual perdition that damages
before it finishes. Theology aside, this makes for very powerful
theatre, not least because of a potential tragic dimension.

If we compare the ideas (however tortuous to us now) of the
Calvinistic slant on predestination and the Stoical one of acceptance, it seems that they share much in common. In other words,
the acceptance not only of fate, but of an individual's own personal contribution to it as predetermined and inexorable was
the arena in which the modern Protestant Christian met the

orthodox Classical, and perhaps the reason why, from a theological point of view, Stoicism tended to sit so comfortably with
Christianity, and why, given that the sixteenth century's favourite Classical Stoic was also its favourite Classical dramatist, so
much of the Jacobean drama was shot through with neo-Stoical
ideas, to be challenged or accepted.

CHAPTER SIX

THE STOIC AND THE HUMANIST REVISION

i

Lucius Annaeus Seneca (c. 4 BC–AD 45) was the sixteenth century's most influential Classical dramatist. This fact presents modern scholars with several problems, the least of which is the probability that Seneca the Stoic philosopher and Seneca the writer of tragic plays were not one and the same. However, since the dramatists of the English Renaissance considered both the prose and the dramatic writing attributed to 'Seneca' as having been penned by the same hand, it would be pointless to insist on authorial distinction. Nevertheless, for the sixteenth century Seneca was an ambiguous figure, whose two media did present problems of reconciliation, if not directly of authorship. The dignified, measured humanity of the prose writings present a marked contrast to the violent extravagance of the tragedies and, while much of the Stoic philosophy informs the tragedies, this is offset by the action (or, more usually, reported action) and is diminished, even apparently contradicted by the subject matter. Yet another problem lay in what was then known of Seneca's personal history, which was known to have had its turbulent episodes and which was, in any case, inextricably linked with the Emperor Nero, whose reputation for tyrannical villainy was legend.

Perhaps I should make it clear that by speaking of 'Classical' drama here, we tend to mean Roman, not Greek. Latin was the *lingua franca* of the educated European, and therefore was much more readily read and, significantly for an even wider audience, translated into English. Some Greek tragedy became available (in Latin) in Italy only in the quattrocento; Seneca's plays, on the other hand, had had a fair circulation from the mid-thirteenth century, and Seneca was the chief, if not the only, tragedian. This, moreover, has to be seen in the context of a model which we would recognize more readily as rhetorical epic rather than as 'drama'. This distinction is evinced by the Players, in their rendition of Virgil's *Aeneid* and their poorer attempt at epic tragedy ('The Murder of Gonzago') in *Hamlet*. For the early Renaissance, 'tragedy' was supremely important; but drama as such, as it came to be experienced, was something yet to be explored and experimented with. The Greeks were known to have had a powerful dramatic tradition, but they were awesome and shadowy, and the medium through which they passed to Elizabethans was at second hand, mostly through the translations of the critical writings of Aristotle.

As with the Greeks, very little was known of what Seneca actually did on the stage. Seneca, while very present in terms of text, little was known of him *qua* dramatist, despite some very lofty claims. Julius Scaliger, in his *Poetices Libri Septem* (1561) wrote: 'Seneca, whom I judge inferior to none of the Greeks in majesty: in ornamentation and splendour greater even than Euripides. The plots are indeed theirs, but the majesty of the poetry, the sound, the spirit, his very own.' But Scaliger is referring to poetry: it is the sound and the spirit of Seneca's verse that is important to him. Jasper Heywood prefaced his translation of *Thyestes* (1560) with a dream vision, in which he salutes the ghost of Seneca, praising his 'woondrous wit and regall stile', while Nashe objected to the predatory 'poetasters' who plundered Seneca's works, but still it is Seneca's poetry which is lauded.[81] Later, the

---

81 Twentieth-century criticism has been scarcely more straightforward than that of the sixteenth century. Seneca has, without doubt, been taken for granted in modern studies of sixteenth and seventeenth-century drama as part and parcel of the way that Renaissance dramaturgical invention supposedly ran, and it is here that one runs into danger of not distinguishing enough between the text and the drama. The confident cataloguing of paral-

great English dramatists were compared, inevitably, with Seneca; partly because of a need to dignify the new English drama (as with English literature generally) by direct comparison with the Classics, and a significant lack of other Latin tragedians available for comparison. Michael Drayton praises Ben Jonson as 'strong Seneca or Plautus', and Francis Meres honours Shakespeare with a similar compliment: 'As Plautus and Seneca are accounted the best for Comedy and Tragedy among the Latins, so Shakespeare among the English is the most excellent in both kinds for the stage.' Nevertheless, despite the assumptions implied in 'for the stage', there seems to have been a considerable leap between what was known of Seneca's practical dramaturgy and what was assumed to have had a direct influence on the dramaturgy of Shakespeare, Jonson and others.

The so-called 'Senecan' features which characterize some of the early Elizabethan tragedies: *stichomythia* – that is, dialogue in alternate lines, often in verse, giving a sense of rapid, controlled argument; ghosts; the five-act structure, each act beginning with a 'dumb show' and ending with choruses; messengers, who report violence occurring off-stage; rhetorical speeches couched in formally structured clauses; an apparent fixation on revenge and described horrors; a stress on the ineluctable qual-

---

lel passages and of formal, structural and thematic 'debts' to Seneca propounded by scholarship of the earlier part of the twentieth century seem indeed to have been part of this 'dignifying' process, by which Shakespeare in particular was seen to deserve the appellation of 'classic' dramatist. This critical acceptance gave way, in the nineteen fifties and sixties, to a more cautious but, in its own way, radical, approach, in the course of which almost every other source but the (classical) Senecan has come under review. Still later, this reversion, which some still call sceptical, has given way to a revision of the precise nature of the influence of the classical drama upon the Renaissance. *Mirrour for Magistrates*, a collection of tragic monologues written by William Baldwin, George Ferrers and five others, were first published in 1559, but running into many subsequent editions throughout the 1570s, and two others in 1587 and 1610, these last containing significant additions. It was inspired by John Lydgate's *The Fall of Princes* (1494) which in turn was based on Boccaccio's gloomy recital of tragic lives, *De casibus virorum illustrium*.

ity of fate, are features available in sources other than Seneca, both ancient and more modern. The comedies of Terence, Ovid, Boccaccio's *De Casibus* narratives; *The Decameron* (Boccaccio was available in translation, and highly popular); the English vernacular verse monologues, *Mirrour for Magistrates* and of course, the Miracle Plays, the Moralities and the Chronicles, all provided 'strainers' for these 'Senecan' elements, which included, of course, Seneca's plays themselves in translation and in the original Latin, with which Shakespeare and his contemporaries display clear familiarity.

However, there is no one 'straightforward' Senecan play: Seneca's plays are sufficiently different from one another as to provide a far from homogenous model. From the doom-laden family histories of the *Pelopidae* (the *Thyestes* and the *Agamemnon*) to tales of passionate and sorrowful womanhood (*Phaedra* and *Medea*); from catalogues of bloody and undeserved suffering in the impersonal toils of war (the *Troades*) to the terrible vengeance wreaked upon the hero in *Oedipus*, Seneca's plays offer a great diversity, and the English Renaissance dramatists themselves drew on this diversity in frequently complex and creative ways, often more ambiguously and indirectly than their French and Italian neo-classical counterparts, whose 'debt' is more obviously imitative. Seneca's plays are far too diverse in their subject matter and handling to provide a single pattern, and although there are certain typically Senecan features which crop up again and again, which would have appealed to audiences similarly educated, the English Renaissance dramatists used Seneca fairly freely to suit their own experimentation.

Renaissance dramatists appear to have learned little from Seneca about play-making. Seneca is not even the source of the three Unities (of time, place and space) which for all their arbitrariness were useful in forcing a playwright to think his play through as an organized whole. Most of the finesse of plotting and characterization, including the usefulness of the five-act structure, came from Classical comedy – from Plautus and Ter-

ence. Much more was picked up from popular and religious drama, from prose fiction, and from street-theatre, while tragedy
as an artistic concept was regarded, perhaps fitly, as supremely grand and therefore a little untouchable. Yet Seneca was, for
Shakespeare and his contemporaries, both a text and a tradition, a staple ingredient of a good grammar-school education.
Together with Cato and Cicero, Seneca was considered essential reading on what we would now call the school curriculum,
but Seneca, along with Terence and Plautus, could not help but
constitute a Classical grounding in the perception, however
hazy, of performance. This doubtless had very little to do with
'entertainment', (although, doubtless, it afforded the sort of 'serious fun' that educationalists down the ages have regarded as
valuable pedagogic tools in the classroom) and it was a far cry
from these same scholars' experiences of theatre out-of-school,
which was doubtless regarded by their teachers as vulgar and,
from the educational point of view, valueless. Educated English
Renaissance audiences, like the Roman aristocracy of the Impe-
rial period, were the product of a system with a strong emphasis
on training in Classical rhetoric, and the result was a culture,
among an educated and sophisticated few, for whom – a bit like
ancient Rome – 'truth' was descried as a function of disputation,
In other words, the premium was placed upon the quality of argument, with the 'best' argument winning out as 'true' and the
'drama' lay in rhetoric.

Indeed, where direct attempts to imitate Seneca were concerned, the result was a fairly static collection of formal speeches. This can be seen in the earliest known Senecan imitation:
Albertino Mussato's *Ecerinis*, written for his fellow Paduans in
1315.[82] As a play, its very early date alone makes it significant:
Ecerinis is innovative and experimental, an attempt to revive, in
the drama, the ancient genre of tragedy associated with a level of

---

82   Albertino Mussato, *Ecerinis*, c.1315, ed. and trans. Joseph R. Berrigan
(Munich, 1975). The play was not printed until.1636, despite manuscript circulation.

Classical authorial dignity yet set in the thick of Paduan politics. Yet, while Mussato is the first Renaissance writer, as far as we know, to restore the idea of tragedy to something like theatrical form, nevertheless his play is strong only where Seneca is strong, in bursts of combative dialogue, and interrupted by what appear to be versified stage-directions. Mussato, despite the dramatic mode, is 'thinking epic'. There is some confusion of terms, therefore. Mussato's contemporary, Dante, referred to his own major poetic work as his *Commedia,* and had Vergil call the *Aeneid* his Tragedy (*Inferno* 20.133). Whatever begins with Mussato's *Ecerinis,* it is not the story of Renaissance dramaturgical discovery. The earlier sixteenth-century English dramatists began to push out the boundaries of rhetoric, and experimented with ways of making forcible 'argument' work out from the drama itself, rather than relying on grand declamatory speeches.[83]

The result of English experiments, at first, therefore, is Seneca somewhat undigested, in such landmark works as Sackville and Norton's *Gorboduc* (written and first performed 1561, and first printed in an undated edition c. 1571), which appeased such conservative commentators as Sidney, for whom such 'fidelity' to the classical model meant much, and for whom 'experiment' equalled a virtually heretical deviation. In the portions of *The Defence of Poesie* (1580) where Sir Philip Sidney defines the ideal lineaments of tragedy, he praises Sackville and Norton's *Gorboduc:* 'as it is full of stately speeches and well-sounding phrases, climbing to the height of Seneca's style, and as full of notable morality, which it doth most delightfully teach...' But Sidney's appraisal is ambivalent: while he acknowledges Gorboduc's 'notable morality', he is far more exacting of the style, holding up Seneca as providing the ideal from which he clearly regards the

---

83   See Robert S. Miola, *Shakespeare and Classical Tragedy* (Oxford, 1992) and A. J. Boyle, *Tragic Seneca – An Essay in the Theatrical Tradition* (London, 1997).

playwrights of his own day as having deviated. He goes on to complain:

> ... it is very defectious in the circumstances [the Unities]... For it is faulty both in place and time, the two necessary companions of all corporeal actions. For where the stage should always represent but one place, and the uttermost time pre-supposed in it should be, both by Aristotle's precept and common reason, but one day, there is both many days and places, inartificially [unskilfully] imagined.[84]

Sidney notoriously poured scorn on virtually all tragedies except for *Gorboduc* and still more on the so-called tragicomedies, which he appears to have regarded as a sort of mongrel deviation; but we have to remember that no 'great' English plays existed at the time of Sidney's death in 1586, and the Senecan model must have seemed poorly imitated.

Later dramas are marked by the redeployment of Senecan features – and indeed Seneca's lines – in the works of several important English dramatists, but now the transition from ancient to modern is much more complete, and an artistically experimental movement established. In Kyd's *The Spanish Tragedy*, Shakespeare's *Titus Andronicus* and *Richard III*, Marlowe's *Edward II*, Chapman's *Bussy D'Ambois*, Middleton's *The Revenger's Tragedy*[85] and several plays by Marston, Seneca makes a significant

---

84   In his *Poetics* (4th Century BC) Aristotle made certain observations about Greek tragedies: they concentrated on one complete action , or events which took place within a single day and night, and in a single place. These descriptions became known as the 'dramatic unities' of Action, Time and Space. It is clear that the English (as opposed to the French) dramatists of the sixteenth and seventeenth centuries tended to treat these 'Unities' as only occasional guidelines. The fathering of the strict adherence to the 'Unities' onto Aristotle is, in any case, almost certainly misplaced.

85   *The Revenger's Tragedy or The Loyal Brother* (first printed anonymously in 1607 as having been performed by the King's Men). No source is known, and the authorship was formerly attributed to Cyril Tourneur. Nowadays the play is generally accepted has having been devised by Thomas Middleton.

re-appearance, but now it is transfigured from the original, and placed in a new context. With a popular audience, Seneca had been 'placed'; he was valuable, even venerated, as source-material, and his presence undoubtedly conferred and confirmed the plays' intellectual status, but by now, the popular entertainment had married the scholarly, and had issue. In a parallel, the pagan had married the Christian.

Manner and matter probably require clarification. Seneca's manner was frequently imitated but in the increasingly confident context of a newer model which was much more spectacular and active than merely rhetorical and declamatory; in short, it was much more designed for the stage than anything which could have been known of Roman theatre. Seneca's matter, on the other hand, continued to provide a source, historically as well as morally, but the history is frequently updated and the morality is given a contemporary thrust, in accordance with a culturally Christian society. In Hieronimo's soliloquy in *The Spanish Tragedy* (III, xii), in which he proclaims his intention to avenge the death of his son, we can clearly see this admixture of the classic-pagan and the Christian. Hieronimo enters with a book in his hand:

> Vindicta mihi!
> Ay, heaven will be reveng'd of every ill
> Nor will they suffer murder unrepaid.
> Then stay, Hieronimo, attend their will,
> For mortal men may not appoint their time.
> [Reading] 'Per scelus semper tutm est sceleribus iter.'
> Strike and strike home, where wrong is offer'd thee,
> For evils unto ills conductors be,
> And death's the worst of resolution:
> For he that thinks with patience to contend
> To quiet life, his life shall easily end.
> [Reading again] 'Fata si miseros juvant, habes salutem;
> Fata si vitam negant, habe sepulchram.'
> If destinies thy miseries do ease,
> Then hast thou health, and happy shalt thou be:

If destiny deny thee life, Hieronimo,
Yet shalt thou be assured of a tomb:
If neither, yet let this thy comfort be;
Heaven covereth him that hath no burial.
And to conclude, I will revenge his death! (III, xii, 1–20)

Lines 6 and 12 are direct quotations from Seneca's *Agamemnon* and *Troades* respectively. The tone of the speech is declamatory, typically Senecan. What is striking about this passage is not only the familiarity with the Senecan Latin text which Kyd expects of his audience (a thing surely highly significant in itself) but the way the text is used dramatically, to convey a transition between the Christian view of vengeance, represented by the opening allusion to Romans 12: 19 ('Vengeance is mine; I will repay, saith the Lord'), to a non-Christian code of 'justice', the private execution of revenge, underscored by the copy of (presumably) Seneca's tragedies in Heironimo's hand.

ii

It is common to forget that Seneca was much better known to the Elizabethans as a Stoic philosopher, and that from a moral philosophical standpoint, this adoption of the pagan Classical into Christian moral education appears to have been a relatively seamless process, for the obvious reason that a priming in Christian doctrine made so many of the Stoical precepts entirely acceptable and familiar. They were, in so many ways, essentially the same. Thomas James, the curator at the Bodleian at the end of the sixteenth century and the translator of Guillaume du Vair's *The Moral Philosophie of the Stoicks* (1598), wrote: 'No kind of philosophie is more profitable and nearer approaching unto Christianitie… than the philosophie of the Stoicks.' The fundamental principles of Stoicism: passive resistance (apathaea) to the vicissitudes of personal fortune was much in tune with the Christian idea of 'turning the other cheek'; and victory through reason and philosophy over natural desire fitted with an ideal

Christian behaviour that eschewed pride and looked to the af-
terlife for reward. These ideals encompassed and transcended
doctrinal differences between Catholic and Protestant, and thus
Seneca found considerable favour with reformists of all colours.
The Lutheran humanist Philip Melanchthon quoted from the
Thyestes:

> O how much evil does ambition breed? We present this to the
> spectators therefore as a useful model; for you will be justified in
> finding from its tragedy that there is nothing worse than ambition,
> which commonly overturns all things human and divine, both hu-
> man law and Divine law.[86]

Even Erasmus, whose sympathies with the Protestant reformers were strongly mitigated by his horror of violence, praised
Seneca, citing him as having 'a zeal for honest action, carrying
the mind of the reader into the heights, far above the base concerns of men, especially where he is warning against tyranny'[87]
and Erasmus's prefatory letter to the Bishop of Cracow in 1519
explains why St Jerome included Seneca in his Catalogus sanc-
torum: 'not because of proven sanctity… [but] on account of his
love of religion': an acceptance which was not without its ambiguity, for in the same letter Erasmus adds: 'if you read him
thinking of him as a pagan, then he appears to have written like
a Christian; but if you read him as a Christian, then he appears
to have written like a pagan.' This double vision is essential to the
English Renaissance 'reading' of the new drama, and it posed, as
ever, a paradox.

---

86   Philip Melanchthon, *Corpus Reformatorum* (?1521) ed. by Halle, vol. xix,
p. 787. Melanchthon (1497–1560) was professor of Greek at Wittenburg University and succeeded Luther as the leader of the Reformation movement in
Germany in 1521.

87   Erasmus, *Institutio Christiani Principis* [The Education of a Christian
Prince] (?1516). He edited the works of St Jerome in 1519, and attracted notoriety after his attacks on Luther in *De Libero Arbitrio* (1523).

The English Renaissance dramatists' ethic was of course Christian (by culture, if not necessarily devout) and this made for a new drama that was quite distinct from Seneca's. Fulke Greville, something of a 'Senecan' dramatist himself, noted the incompatibility of the two different sets of ethics in terms of the effect upon the drama. In his *Life of Sir Philip Sidney*, published in 1625, Greville speaks first of ancient tragedies which

> exemplify the disastrous miseries of man's life, where Order, Laws, Doctrine and Authority are unable to protect Innocency from the exorbitant wickedness of power, and so out of that melancholic vision sit horror, or murmur against Divine Providence.

Conversely, according to Greville, these modern tragedies 'point out God's revenging aspect upon every particular sin, to the despair or confusion of mortality.' The central distinction is, as Greville sees it, that the ancient (and he means Senecan) world was, because its gods were unjust, a world of total injustice, an injustice inevitably central to ancient drama. The drama of an 'enlightened' Christian world, however, shows mankind unable to face up to the justice of an essentially just God in terms of particular sins, but not overall corruption.

In Jacobean tragedy, innocents perish – Lavinia, Cordelia, Lady Macduff and her children, etc. are sacrificed as surely as Hippolytus and the children of Thyestes and Medea – but the massacre of these innocents eventually proves or at least asserts a Christian moral, whereas Seneca's dramas frequently leave the 'evil' happily in possession of what their wickedness has achieved: Atreus gloating in his power over his brother and nephews, Nero disposing of his relatives, Medea borne off in her magic carriage, Aegisthus and Clytemnestra in possession of Argos, and an impotent chorus which can only rail and rant and (as Greville says) 'murmur against Divine Providence'. But Greville is perhaps defending a too-comfortable polarity between the ancient and the modern which quite simply does not exist in many of the so-called 'enlightened, Christian' plays. While such plays as *Macbeth* and *King Lear* appear to affirm an eventual moral order, on closer examination they probably do not after all. The theodicy evinced in *King Lear* is a rather special case to which I shall be returning, but certainly I would suggest that even *Macbeth* is not wholly secure in this respect: Malcolm's retraction is troubling because it is unconvincing, not so much because we cannot believe in his essential unworldliness, but rather because we *can*. His pose-striking, his adolescent naïvety, makes for unconvincing order-re-establishment material, and his deliberate disingenuity in that crucial scene with Macduff is surely not intended to encourage confidence. Perhaps in a more subtle sense, in its affirmation of 'a world of total injustice', Senecan drama *per se* has far more in common with the flawed world-order portrayed in so many Elizabethan and Jacobean plays than Greville allowed.

Not all contemporary critics took the 'notable morality' of Seneca's plays as much for granted as had Sidney, and some went to trouble to justify the virtuous intent of the Tragedies in Christian terms. In 1563, at a point in time when the English concern with the drama was undergoing some of its severest criticism on moral rather than aesthetic grounds, Robert Neville, in his preface to his translation of *Oedipus* exhorts:

> Wonder not at the grosseness of style… mark thou rather what is meant by the whole course of History; and frame thy lyfe free from such mischiefes, wherewith the World at this present is universally overwhelmed… in such sort that I abhorre to write: and even at the thought thereof I tremble and quake for very inward grief and fear of mind: assuredly perswading myselfe that the right high and imortall God will never leave such horrible and detestable crimes unpunished… For the which cause… have I suffered this my base translated Tragedy to be published… Myne only intent was to exhort men to embrace Vertue and shun Vyce…

This anticipates the stand taken by Thomas Newton who, in his troubled preface to his edition of *The Tenne Tragedies* (1581), wrote:

> And where it is by some squaymish Areopagites surmyzed that...
> these tragedies... with many phrases literally tending... sometimes
> to the prayse of Ambition, sometime to the mayntenaunce of Cru-
> elty, now and then to the ratification of Tyranny, cannot be digest-
> ed without great danger of infection;... .if it might please them...
> to mark and consider the circumstances... the direct meaning of
> Seneca himselfe, whose whole writinges... are so farre from coun-
> tenauncing Vyce, that I doubt whether there be among all the Cat-
> alogue of Heathen wryters, that with more gravity of philosophi-
> call sentences, more waightyness of sappy words... beateth down
> sinne, loose lyfe, dissolute dealinge and unbrydled sensuality...

The degree of protestation in both of these earnest assevera-
tions, that the treatment of vice serves the cause of virtue, suggests that neither Neville nor Newton was entirely convinced of
the matter. Nevertheless, it should be noted that these apologies
appear almost twenty years apart, and by the time of Newton's
edition, the anti-theatrical debate had reached a rather different point, and was concerned much more with the effect of the
theatre upon public morals. By the 1580s, the 'squaymish', who,
as has been noted already, included professional journalists as
well as zealots, were directing their fire not against Seneca but
against the theatre as a whole. Newton was entering, at one of
its more ferocious periods, the long-running ethical and critical
debate concerning the theatre, one which had splintered into a
bewildering range, subtle and crude, informed and fanatical, of
attacks and defences of the dramatic form itself: tragedy, comedy, tragedy versus comedy, tragedy with comic elements, classical and contemporary, as well as of the theatre itself as the venue
of vice. The most vitriolic criticism tended to be reserved for the
modern play-makers who were accused of perverting the Classics and all the moral and aesthetic values they stood for.

By the turn of the century, the attitude to Seneca as presented on the stage was one of ambivalence to say the least, and in
1604 John Marston is voicing an almost commonplace detrac-
tion in *The Malcontent*, when he has Pietro respond to Bilioso's
sycophantic mention of Seneca with: 'Out upon him! He writ of
Temperance and Fortitude, yet lived like a voluptuous Epicure
and died like an effeminate coward.' (III, i, 25–27).

iii

English Renaissance drama can be considered as characterized
by situations in which, as G. K. Hunter has it, 'person is set against
person and group against group, so that the *validity of alternative
positions* is allowed to appear' (my italics).[88] First and foremost,
this must involve the audience's judgement of moral and political dilemmas presented on the stage, and secondly poses them
the further uncomfortable dilemma that there may well be no
simple, unequivocal judgement to make. In this sense, it would
seem that while Seneca's plays may have affirmed for their original audiences the monstrous-seeming injustice of the gods, to
which Stoical indifference was the only valid spiritual response,
the Seneca-influenced drama of the Renaissance opened up a
range of possible responses, only one of which was Stoical 'fortitude' – that is, the serene and resigned response to matters beyond one's control. Rather, they tended to demonstrate that this
is no answer at all. However, there is another essential difference
between Senecan tragedy and the major 'Senecan' tragedies of
the English Renaissance: one which is essentially political. In
the two Roman plays of Ben Jonson, *Sejanus His Fall* (1603) and
Catiline His Conspiracy (first performed 1611) the Senecan influence is particularly strong, but the pagan injustice is allowed its
own especial irony by the dramatist. Both the Classical and the
Christian systems of belief propounded submission to higher
powers, but in Jonson's plays it is exposed as a powerful tool of
social control. Classical Stoicism, of course, resists 'alternatives',

---

88   See G. K. Hunter, '*Seneca and the Elizabethans*', op. cit.

and rests solidly on the premise that existence is governed by a rational design. The highest and the best life for human beings – creatures uniquely endowed with a rational faculty – is a life in accordance with that design, in accordance with a 'nature' that 'designed' the 'rational faculty'. This concept of the best life was variously understood and interpreted by the earliest formulators of the philosophy – Zeno, Cleanthes, and Chrysippus, as well as by later Stoics, but in general it meant a life directed by right reason, a life reconciled to the end of all life. Grief, fear, desire, and ambition were human, but 'wrong', and, given the nature of things, beside the point. Right reason, the old philosophers held, could be taught or cultivated, and would amount to 'wisdom'. The progress towards wisdom manifests itself in the individual's ability to discriminate between those matters that affect the virtuous life, for good or bad, and those which are irrelevant to it (*adiaphora*). This capacity to distinguish and, subsequently, to choose, consists in recognizing first that the rational creature can operate rationally only in those matters over which he has control. War, famine, death in the family, treachery in others: these are matters over which the philosopher, or sage, has no control and toward which he must cultivate a humane indifference (*apathaea*). But when choice can frustrate or contribute to the perfection of the individual as rational creature, here the philosopher must discipline himself in desire and aversion, acceptance and rejection. The sign of perfection is the rational control that can be rationally achieved, and begins with the ability to receive impressions (*phantasiae*) rightly, to order the external world in terms of its relevance to perfection. It ends in the triumph of private serenity.

Stoicism did not and could not hold all the answers for a Christian world in great religious and political flux, especially when one considers the particular problems that attended the Calvinist ethos. For the Humanist Neo-stoics, still inclined to Classical authority, there had long been much philosophical discrediting of certain Stoical ideals (notably by Erasmus) and later by such intellectual libertinists as Michel de Montaigne, Walter Raleigh and Francis Bacon, for whom the whole debate of truth – of what truth is and how it can be known – was re-opened and variously resolved. Their Humanist philosophical revision is partly responsible for a profound change of outlook in the drama. One effect of the Renaissance concern with Humanism was the contention that the possessor of *humanitas* could not be merely a sedentary and isolated philosopher or man of letters. On the contrary, he must be of necessity a participant in active life, and to a certain extent the author of his own destiny, a thing which brought him into direct conflict with the Stoical ideal of detachment from the world. Erasmus acerbically criticizes that 'double-strength Stoic, Seneca', who strips his wise man of every emotion...[and] 'leaves him no man at all but rather a new kind of god, or *demiurgos*, who never existed and will never emerge. Nay, to speak more plainly, he creates a marble simulacrum of a man, a senseless block, completely alien to every human feeling.'[89] Thomas More's *Utopia* eschews the rigorous cultivation of virtue for virtue's sake and urges the enjoyment of moderate pleasures, believing that 'Nature herself prescribes a life of joy' – that is, pleasure – apparently seeing no contradiction between earthly enjoyment and religious piety.[90] Michel de Montaigne's *Essays* refute the notion that knowledge of the intellectual arts alone could teach the sovereign art of life.[91]

These criticisms (which through our own lens surely appear staggeringly modern) seem to characterize the main distinction between Classical Stoicism and Neo-Stoicism in the time of the Renaissance, are reflected variously in the drama and with

---

89 Erasmus, *The Praise of Folly* (1509).

90 Sir Thomas More, statesman, scholar, martyr. The standard edition of More's writings is the Yale edition of *The Complete Works*, ed. Edward Surtz, J. H. Hexter, et al., 5 vols (1963–69).

91 Michel de Montaigne, French philosopher and essayist. John Florio translated his *Essays* into English in 1603. See *The Complete Essays*, trans. by M. A. Screech (London, 1993).

varying degrees of centrality. Sometimes the argument dodges uncomfortably between acceptance and repudiation of ancient Stoical ideals; and sometimes, where there is apparent acceptance of some of these, the sheer force of emotional realism can propel the Stoical view into eclipse. Macilente in Ben Jonson's *Every Man out of his Humour* (1599), a character who, when we first see him, epitomises the well-travelled, well-adjusted man who is anything but 'malcontented' but who, by the end of the play, has descended into a frustrated rage and asks, rather desperately, 'but, Stoique, where (in the vast world) | Doth that man breathe, that can so much command | His bloud, and his affection?' (I, i, 2–4). 'Blood and affection' are essentially human characteristics, vital needs which Macilente recognizes as impossible to suppress if one is to acknowledge one's humanity. Edgar's speech at the beginning of Act IV of *King Lear* begins, confidently enough:

> Yet better thus, and known to be condemned,
> Than still condemned and flattered. To be worst,
> The low'st and most dejected thing of fortune,
> Stands still in esperance, lives not in fear...
>
> (IV, i, 1–4)

But the Stoical tone is sustained only until the appearance of Edgar's father, Gloucester, however: a hideous and pitiful sight with his eye-sockets still bleeding from his recent torture. Edgar's stoical comforting of himself gives way to an immediate lament:

> ... World, world, O world!
> But that thy strange mutations make us hate thee,
> Life would not yield to age.   (IV, i, 10–12)

and thus the reflection that one would not contemplate age (and therefore death) if life on earth were not so dreadful as to make the end welcome.

This is at once a glance at the inadequacies of Stoical fortitude in the presence of terrible emotional shock and grief, as well as a rejection of the comforting model of the Wheel of Fortune, where one may be at the bottom of the cycle but, since cycle it is, one is borne up again.

> Oh gods! Who is't can say 'I am at the worst'?
> I am worse than ere I was...
> And worse I may be yet. The worst is not
> So long as we can say 'This is the worst.' (IV, i, 25–28)

Not only is Stoical fortitude rejected as eminently complacent and inadequate, but the model that provokes such a stance – in this case, Fortune's wheel – is seen as inadequate also. Far from being able to rely on being borne up again, as Edgar admits in the shock of emotion, one is in the unimaginable position of one who has an infinite way to fall. There is no model adequate; there is simply the hysterical panic of one who recognizes a 'worst' *beyond* 'the worst'.

Edgar's disguise is doubly problematic, since it serves the function of allowing him to affect the action *incognito,* as we see in his leading his father to a bogus Dover Cliff in order to perpetrate some sort of illusion of 'miracle', as well as in his correspondence with those who are fully informed about the French invasion/rescue, at the same time as placing him at the extreme of human low-life, unable to affect anything. Yet this is a disguise, one moreover born of aristocratic ingenuity, for Edgar is the legitimate heir to an earldom. So how much of his Stoical stance is a disguise (and thus bogus) also? 'Poor Tom', if this role-within-a-role is to have any veracity, must be sustained by fortitude and a belief in its purpose, that is, of a person who is deliberately living his disguise, like a veteran under-cover agent, to the point of alter-ego. But 'Poor Tom' is an anomaly, in that most disguises require dressing up – 'robes and furred gowns hide all' – yet Edgar's is pared down to a literally bare minimum:

his disguise involves virtual nakedness. Secondly, and even more problematic, is the inevitable frustration with the plot: because we do know that 'Poor Tom' is a disguise, then why does he not put his poor father out of his misery and reveal his true identity, when it is obvious that such a knowledge would probably be the best possible antidote to suicide? He later admits in Act V – 'O fault!' – that his pretence has gone too far. Edgar's Stoicism is, therefore, arguably fake, because 'Tom o'Bedlam' is essentially an act; but, since it is also the last resort of a hunted man who accepts his fate, the faux-stoicism becomes a reality for the fugitive naked soul which Edgar has come to be. I would argue that where Edgar's Stoicism is seen to break down, the breakdown is valid; that is, we are not witnessing the son of an Earl suddenly prompted into the breaking out of a fancy-dress that he can no longer sustain (although it is that too) but, from the point of a dramatic, as well as a moral overview, we are seeing the breakdown of Stoicism as untenable when it is confronted with the irrepressibly moving.

iv

Dramatically, we see the chorus leaving the ranks of ineffectual commentators and bursting into action. Effectively taking the place of Lear's Fool, whom Edgar eventually renders redundant after the end of Act III, Edgar as 'Poor Tom' functions on the periphery of the action, and can serve only as a commenting voice which observes, judges but does not affect, until he steps out of this role and into his true 'Edgar' role, in which, of course, he affects a great deal, culminating in the climactic fight with Edmund in Act V.

The *choros* is a legacy of the Classical drama, the commenting voice of impotence, powerless to affect decisions or actions; the voice of bystanders. In the drama of the Ancient Greeks, it was a loud, often wailing voice, subtle only in language. Yet it was a powerful dramatic and narrative tool: the popular judge, powerless to bring judgement; the medium through which the audience connects, identifies with it as bystanders too. It is not difficult to see how this chorus-voice becomes the voice of 'the people'. Wise before, during and after the event, and whether it takes the form of the popular judgement of servants on their betters or of supernatural forces at work, foreseeing but unable to avert disaster, the chorus element appealed to many Renaissance dramatists, and we can see it subsumed into the experimental drama in various guises. So we have the Weird Sisters in *Macbeth,* most obviously, and the King of Denmark's Ghost, but also the many servants' and minor roles in other plays where underlings are given a serious voice in judgement upon their superiors.

In some plays, the 'chorus'-commentary takes a distinctively malcontented turn: in other words, it takes the idea of 'wisdom', marries it to the idea of 'futility', and ironises it. We can see this in overtly 'choric' Malcontent figures, such as Thersites, Jaques and Feste, and in the choric elements invested in Bosola and Flamineo who, in spite of their degeneracy, are allowed to pose as 'frustrated moralists, desperately suppressing the 'knowledge' that would stifle action.'[92] Thus it is that the Malcontent in his position on the margins of the microcosmic play-world supplies an 'analogue' of the play itself, in his function as cynical commentator on the real world, and the drama, in its status as a mere stage play, is licensed to make such comments, and the old classical device, thus used, makes a modern irony of the precepts of Stoical wisdom, ironically making use of the old classical device. Other representations of the Malcontent figure – Richard III, for instance, and Bosola, and Flamineo – make far more potent figures, more damaging, more engaged with the 'action', whose moral complexity possibly elevates them into tragic figures, but these too view the action from the distance of a ghastly wisdom, and fulfil the same choric function in this respect: to empha-

---

92   Lee Bliss, *The World's Perspective: John Webster and the Jacobean Drama* (Brighton, 1983).

sise the political and moral, as well as emotional, problem of in-volvement in an imperfect world by dramatizing, negatively, its opposite. Thus the Malcontent point is made, and not so much by a malcontented figure as by the play itself.

Yet other plays of this period do not rely upon one single fig-ure to make the malcontented point; instead, the shortcomings of detachment are presented by characters who are shown not as malcontents born, but as made: that is, being in the process of disaffection and dissent. In John Marston's *Antonio's Revenge* (1600/1601) Antonio at one point reads a key passage from Seneca arguing the value of Stoic indifference (II, ii, 45), only to dismiss it passionately as inadequate for a person actually steeped in heartbreak. In the same play, Pandulpho, who up to a point plays the ideal Stoic in adversity, finally breaks down, admits he has been deceiving himself, and joins Antonio's plot, motivated by passionate grief. This play unmistakably approves of the action of the kind that Andrugio takes in *Antonio & Mel-lida* (1599/1600), its predecessor, where here, too, the Stoical ap-plication of the ideal of rational control is repudiated, as is the whole notion of a 'wise' natural law in which all is designed for the best:

> Philosophy maintains that nature's wise
> And forms no useless or imperfect thing.
> Did nature make the earth, or the earth nature?
> For earthly dirt makes all things, makes the man.
> Moulds me up in honour; and like a cunning Dutchman
> Paints me a puppet even with seeming breath
> And gives a sot appearance of a soul.
> Go to, go to; thou liest, philosophy!   (*Ant. & Mel.*, III, i, 31–38)

The argument concerns what, in truth, is 'nature'. The random, imperfect nature of 'earthly dirt' is what Andrugio perceives as human truth, in which his embracing of his own individual will and inclination to the depths of grief allows him essential, if vile, humanity. When his old friend and counsellor Lucio, fearful of 'more louring fate', urges him to abandon his railing passion and accept – 'clip' – all fortune, he utterly rejects the notion:

> There's nothing left
> Unto Andrugio, but Andrugio;
> And that nor mischief, force, distress nor hell can take.
> Fortune my fortunes, not my mind, shall shake.' (III, i, 62–5)

And follows with: 'Myself, myself, will dare all opposites'(77). Several points are immediately striking. Andrugio's self-reliance of course epitomizes the Humanist rationalization perfectly in its rejection of Fortune as an inevitability to be merely accepted, and he endorses it by his refusal to bow to 'force' or 'mischief' visited upon him by others, insisting instead on his own self-belief, a strength that 'will dare all opposites'. This becomes, in turn, proof against 'distress', ambiguously meaning both reduced circumstances and emotional anguish. Andrugio's utter rejection of 'philosophy' as 'liar' is conspicuously outraged: it would seem he has been sold a pup. 'Philosophy', (and by this is implied Stoic philosophy specifically) is indeed a 'liar', mendaciously promising a comfort and dignity that fails to deliver. Much depends upon stresses. 'Not my mind' can be read at once to mean 'not *my* mind', that is that Andrugio himself will be proof against such superstitious indoctrination as will force him simply to accept his fate; on the other hand, 'not my *mind*' implies an independent will apart from the soul, apart from the threat of 'hell', and one which insists upon its own judgement regardless. Either way, Marston makes the point; and whereas once, in Seneca's plays and in the earlier 'Senecan' dramas produced by the mid-century Elizabethans, this type of combative dialogue would have served to 'prove' the point about tyranny one way or the other (between justice and injustice in rulership), here, the tyranny is seen to lie in the Stoical philosophy itself. In this play, Andrugio is seen to be justified in his self-belief; overcoming his initial reluctance, he proceeds to mastermind the plan to outwit Piero which, in this first part of the Antonio story, succeeds.

In George Chapman's *Bussy D'Ambois* (c. 1604), the Stoical position is reversed, as it were, with the eponymous hero shown first as seizing individual control, only to surrender stoically to his fate at the end. Bussy's condition at the opening of the play is accurately diagnosed by Monsieur: 'A man of spirit beyond the reach of fear, | Who (discontent with his neglected worth) | Neglects the light, and loves obscure abodes' (I, i, 46–7). In other words, Bussy is a Malcontent, entirely recognizable, and apparently easily accessible to bribery: '... apt to take fire at advancement' (I, i, 50). 'None loathes the world so much, nor loves to scoff it, | But gold and grace will make him surfeit of it.' (I, i, 52–3). This evaluation is cynical, but apparently accurate, and Bussy proceeds to behave exactly as predicted. His analysis of the hypocrisy of the French Court has all the Malcontent's extravagance of language, but although he scoffs, he does take the gold, accepting Monsieur's notion that Fortune's gifts must be swiftly taken. However, he proceeds then to disrupt the order of the Court, but in an increasingly heroic, rather than malcontented, spirit, in what Nicholas Brooke identifies in his Introduction to the play as 'a brilliant amalgam of self-deception and positive values'.[93] Bussy is a social upstart and an adventurer, one anxious to exchange his 'threadbare suit' for 'gloss enough' to show himself to advantage, an ambition worked on by Monsieur, who alludes to Bussy's 'long smother'd spirit'. This 'spirit' would appear at first merely venal, yet when he kills three newly-made enemies in a duel, deaths regarded at first by Henry as 'wilful murders... past my pardon', Bussy begs, not for his life but for acknowledgement of his human right to live:

> That I may so make good what God and Nature
> Have given me for my good: since I am free
> (Offending no just law), let no law make
> By any wrong it does, my life her slave...   (II, i, 193–6)

---

93 George Chapman, *Bussy D'Ambois*, ed. Nicholas Brooke, The Revels Plays (Manchester, 1963), Introduction, xxxvii ff.

Let me be King myself (as man was made)...   (II, i, 198)

The stress is on the heroic freedom of which man is capable; the appeal is to the ancient (and Renaissance) concept of an original Golden World from which the present is a decline. Bussy has no idea of challenging the King's authority as such; the final assertion is that there is no conflict:

Who to himself is law, no law doth need,
Offends no King, and is a King indeed.   (II, i, 203)

Yet the assertion 'to himself is law' is a seriously radical one, and of a piece with Bussy's claiming a sort of heroic-defiant entitlement of freedom and parity of Virtue, both in terms of the political order at Court, and in a wider moral framework. This potentially anarchic existence terrifies Bussy's mistress, Tamyra: 'So confident a spotless conscience is; | So weak a guilty...'(III, i, 8–9), yet Bussy finds it exhilarating: 'Sin is a coward Madam, and insults | But on our weakness...'(III, i, 18–19).

Bussy's extraordinary, solipsistic rise is countered by Fortune, however. Act III marks the height of Bussy's ascendance: he has claimed his adulterous Countess; he is established at the King's elbow as his Eagle, the champion of Truth; but from this moment the descent begins with the reassertion of power by those with juster claims to it, and Bussy's downfall is plotted between Guise and Monsieur and the cuckolded and furiously jealous Montsurry. This in itself is perhaps unsurprising, since it has been obvious for some time that Bussy's ascendance is unstable, based at least partly on a view of himself and the world that is naively untrue. But just as our perceptions of Bussy have been caused to swerve uneasily between villain and hero, assassin and defiant liberator, that he should regain a partial dignity at the end by dying a Stoical death is probably all of a piece with everything being potentially reversed and reversible in this play. Thus nothing, such as the Montsurrys' marriage, and the priest–pandar who conjurs devils, is as it first appears, but undergoes further revolutions, so that at the end of the play, we see a sad reconciliation between Tamyra and Montsurry who part, but in mutual forgiveness, and Comolet's ghost sounding like a Christian friar. We have already witnessed the impotence of Behemoth: 'This is your slackness, not t'invoke our powers | When first your acts set forth to their effects' (IV, ii, 76–7), thus firmly placing (or replacing) the responsibility for action with Man. Bussy's dying speeches are quite literally echoes of Seneca: lines 147–55 of V, iii are almost literally translated from Hercules' speeches on his pyre. But Bussy is not finally allowed to present himself as the emblem of the dying hero, forgiving his enemies and ordaining reconciliation between Tamyra and Montsurry. His fortitude is shocked into ultimate despair by another visible emblem, that of Tamyra wounded and bleeding as Adultery punished, and he responds emotionally and with regret, and in a manner that is wholly unlike Hercules' contempt for Dejanira. Ultimately, in this play, Man is the essentially shabby hero, who finds no ultimate heroic peace in 'philosophy'.

Thus these plays appear, at least in part, to be directly engaged in the discrediting of Stoic detachment as essentially inapplicable to a modern view of Man, yet the philosophical position is by no means straightforward. It could be objected, for instance, that the Stoical position, valid in itself, was misappropriated in the case of Bussy – and certainly one can see that the individualist position is equally discredited. Order is reasserted; those left alive and intact at the end of *Bussy D'Ambois* are those who had power at the start.

Thus it would be mistaken to regard the Stoic position as being treated with complete cynicism in these plays. Far from it: Marston clearly values the Stoic fortitude in Feliche and Pandulpho-Feliche, both of whom are intended to be taken seriously as characters. Feliche's praise of Stoic content:

I envy none, but hate or pity all;

For when I view with an intentive thought
That creature fair, but proud; him rich, but sot;
Th'other witty, but unmeasured arrogant.
Him great, yet boundless in ambition;
Him highborn, but of base life; t'other feared;
Yet feared fears, and fears most to be loved;
Him wise, but made a fool for public use;
Th'other learned, but self-opinionate -
When I discourse all these, and see myself
Nor fair nor rich nor witty, great, nor fear'd,
Yet amply suited with all full content,
Lord, how I clap my hands and smooth my brow
Rubbing my quiet bosom, tossing up
A grateful spirit to omnipotence.　　(*Ant. & Mel.*, III, ii, 42–60)

is, as G. K. Hunter observes, both morally exalted and poetically beautiful.[94] Yet his paean more than smacks of the complacency of one who lives at a remove from real life. On the other hand, there is almost a wistfulness, not only in this speech and what follows it *per se,* but in plays in general which as it were 'try on' the Stoical position only to scout it; an inescapable sense of inherent tragedy in a human condition that has grown too sadly wise, too aware, for Stoical disengagement and contentment to apply. Marston immediately follows this speech by a scene in which Feliche's sentiments are undercut by his patent inability to support them. What seems to concern Marston here is not the way one attitude forms out of another to form a coherent and psychologically credible plot, but how one attitude tends to collapse to reveal the unexpected co-existence of something else. Stoical values and behaviour are mitigated, even annulled by human passion. The 'smooth brow' is permitted only to those who do not or cannot really live.

John Marston strongly attacked the notion of Stoic apathy in his verse satires: 'Preach not the Stoic's patience to me' (*Scourge*

94　John Marston, *Antonio & Mellida*, ed. G. K. Hunter, Regents Renaissance Drama Series, (London, 1965), Introduction, p. xiv.

of Villainy, II, 6, 1598) Stoical patience being something which
he seems to have regarded as far too close to lethargy. This general impatience with an unsatisfactory philosophy as applied to
real life might partially account for the emergence onto the Elizabethan stage of the 'representative' man driven to virtual insanity by frustration and a desire for retribution, revenge. At almost
all points the 'human alternative' would seem to be essentially
at war with the so-called Christian–Stoic ethics. Certainly Marston seems to have perceived it this way, both in the collapse
of Feliche's self-congratulatory detachment, and in Andrugio's
anguished claim to selfhood.

The stage Malcontent, of course, is not a 'representative' man,
but one whose bitter, cynical, clever perceptions have led him
into a hatred of the ordered world and all it stands for. This would
be his personal, even tragic eccentricity, were it not for the fact
that the external world is now perceived as wholly unordera-
ble, and the notion of 'order' itself so flawed as to render private
serenity in such a world as wilfully disengaged, ingenuous. The
Malcontent is frequently given to utterances which are entirely
in keeping with Stoical precepts (often because they merely suit
his purpose) but which cannot, given his alienated, sometimes
reprobate, condition amount to anything other than a kind of
dramatic inversion of Stoicism and all it might stand for.

Iago's persuasion of Roderigo into tool-villainy consists partly of urging him to 'be a man', and in convincing him that his
despairing 'love' for Desdemona is 'merely a lust of the blood,
and a permission of the will' (*Othello* I,iii). He knows what he is
about: the success of Iago's own villainy rests squarely in his capacity for self-control: 'Though I do hate him as I do hell pains,
| Yet, for necessity of present life, | I must show out a flag, and
sign of love...' (I, i).

v

The role of the discredited wise man, a faux-sage given to Stoical
utterances, one who is quickly perceived either to have become

entirely disenchanted with this striving for serenity, or to have distorted the old philosophy for his own ends forms , perhaps, a vital part of what might be considered 'malcontented' drama. Such a character evinces a notion that all strivings are demonstrably worthless. It does not take an individual Malcontent to show us. Indeed, there is a considerable paradox at work, since the Malcontent is known and seen to be just that: malcontented, and as such we can mistrust, from the comfortable ranks of the audience, his rancid view of the world.. From him, we can expect exaggerated statements of the loathsomeness of things which we need not necessarily take to be the product of anything but his warped humour, and thus he contains in his own aspect his own dramatic dilution.

Thus, Thersites can reduce the Trojan War to 'All the argument is a whore and a cuckold' (*Troilus and Cressida* II, iii, 77–8) and human love and suffering to 'Lechery, lechery, still wars and lechery' (V, ii, 194/5); can describe the hero Ajax (not unjustifiably) as 'beef-witted', all in what seems a gross over-simplification and one which owes more, we might feel, to his state of mind, to his humour, than any reasonable observation.   But paradoxically, the play, far from offering a positive view of war, love or heroism to offset such an infected view, demonstrates the utter futility of all of these things. Thersites' curses and jaded evaluation of man are of course no more efficacious in diagnosing and treating the sickness of the world than is the professional-soldier approach of Hector, the death-before-dishonour approach of Troilus, or the philosopher-statesman approach of Ulysses, yet heroism, professionalism and statesmanship *ought* to be effective. They are not, either in terms of the ultimate Order almost teased at in this play, nor in the abilities of the human agencies in charge of re-ordering. Thersites the satirist seems to have grasped an essential truth, however exaggeratedly voiced.[95] Dignity, courage and honour are present as ideas on the margins, as it were, but exposed as spurious. Cressida's declaration

95   See A. P. Rossiter, *Angel With Horns*, op.cit.

of constancy may be genuine enough – her passion is quite real, as is her grief at her separation from Troilus, but she is essentially shallow. Achilles fights, not because order and integrity have been established, but prompted by personal rage. Ulysses' disingenuousness is exposed when he turns his back on all the absolute values implicit in his much quoted 'Degree' oration (I, iii) and in his attempt to prompt Achilles to action in III,iii, telling Achilles in effect that there *are* no absolute values, that honour is the pay-off in the ceaseless business of self-advertisement.

Ulysses articulates, in his two major speeches, two contrary (and seemingly irreconcilable) philosophical positions: the Neo-Platonic and the Humanist-sceptical. Both are insulted by being merely 'used' for a pragmatic purpose. (Achilles proceeds to win the war with perfect cynicism: so much for reputation.) But it is not merely that Ulysses has revealed his own, pragmatic, Machiavellian nature in the context of the plot, but that the play itself has revealed a considerable gap between the system of values set out in the 'degree' speech and its application. This particular manipulation of a standard set of Elizabethan values surely accords far more closely with A. P. Rossiter's evaluation of *Troilus & Cressida* as a 'comedy of ideas' than any notion of the play as reinforcing absolutes, especially when one considers his proposition that: 'There is no such thing as true honour... on either side, Trojan or Greek. All the high thinking comes to nothing: ceases to apply the moment men have to act...'[96] In short, *Troilus & Cressida* is a play which follows directly and endorses the malcontented humour of Thersites; it is utterly cynical about love, honour and heroism, utterly disbelieving in ultimate order and the virtue of men and women.

The Thersites role is necessarily a kind of double-bluff: it cannot be as bad as he says, and nor is it, if we take what he says literally. We react instinctively against such vile and noisome pictures as he presents, we want to believe in the constancy of the lovers, in the principled statesmanship of Ulysses, the hon-

---

96   A. P. Rossiter, *Angel With Horns*, op.cit., p. 148.

our and integrity of Achilles. Yet very quickly we learn that these are illusions; that we, like Thersites, and to an extent with him, will be disappointed. His moral criticisms hide an avid curiosity about life which brings him only raging misery at its meanness and meaninglessness, disillusions we are forced to share. This is 'malcontented' drama, inasmuch as it evinces disillusion with all the apparent affirmations of order and worth, one of those 'modern experiments in moral anarchy.'

Hamlet is another modern moral experiment. Much of the discourse turns directly on Stoical ideals, which Hamlet both embraces and repudiates. Any discussion of Hamlet as Malcontent (and indeed *Hamlet* as malcontent drama) must surely be predicated on the play's concern with the dramatized working-out of this Renaissance problem, through Hamlet's internal conflict between the traditional Stoical precepts and 'modern' Renaissance ones, and his inability to adhere to either. His self-disgust at being the possessor of the all too human emotions of grief and fury, at once too weak and too strong to permit him to commit the revenge-regicide urged on him by his father's Ghost, constitutes an impotence with which we see him wrestle for much of the play.

The Stoical attitude to revenge is not straightforward. Stoic and Neo-Stoic treatises were mostly insistent that revenge was not permissible and, sitting comfortably with Christian ideals, they counselled forgiveness. Guillaume du Vair wrote: 'Let us thinke, that the greater the injurie is, the better it deserveth to bee pardoned, and that the more just our revenge is, the more our gentlenes is to bee praised,'[97] echoing Marcus Aurelius who recommended that the injured should always practise love and meekness, thereby preserving equanimity and serving as an example to the malicious.[98] Justus Lipsius classified anger, wrath

---

97 Guillaume du Vair, *The Moral Philosophie of the Stoicks* (tr. 1598).

98 Méric Casaubon, (transl.) *Marcus Aurelius Antoninus the Roman Emperor, his Meditations Concerning Himself* or *The Golden Book of Marcus Aurelius* (1634).

and revenge as affections proceeding from 'natural frailty and weakness... incident only to weaklings', a point dilated upon by French theologian and philosopher Pierre Charron, who observed that desire for revenge often victimizes the revenger, engulfing him in boiling self-destructive passion, something we see again and again in the revenge plays of the English Renaissance.[99] Seneca however, in the Stoical prose, does allow for the possibility of retribution, but only if achieved through calm, dispassionate performance of duty:

> Officia sua vir bonus exequetur inconfusus, intrepidus; et sic bono viro digna faciet, ut nihil faciat viro indignum. Pater caedetur: defendam; caesus est: exequar, quia oportet, non quia dolet.
>
> *De Ira*, 1.12.2–3

> [The good man will perform his duties undismayed and unafraid; and he will perform things worthy of a good man such that he will do nothing unworthy of a man. If my father is attacked, I shall defend; if he is murdered, I shall seek vengeance, because it is proper, not because I grieve.]

'Not because I grieve...' If Hamlet were a good Stoic then, at least after the lights of Seneca, righteous retribution for a foully murdered father would be not only 'proper', but possible and, since there is the insistence on emotional detachment, unproblematic in all but the practical sense of how to do the deed. But Hamlet is not a 'good' Stoic, certainly not a consistent one, and he does grieve: and the 'deed' is endlessly put off. He first attempts the murder in the heat of outrage and kills the wrong man; when it finally occurs, it is done almost on impulse, the seized climax of a rapid concatenation of events. For Hamlet neither true indifference nor such rigid self-control is possible. Yet tapping the well-springs of human emotion in any positive way also presents

---

99   Pierre Charron, *De la Sagesse*, (1601) translated as *Of Wisdome*, by Samson Lennard (1612), pp. 92–3, 529–30.

him with a terrible problem: Hamlet's emotions tend to produce words, not actions. The two murders we see him commit on the stage are sudden and impulsive, done almost without thought (and of course the murder of Polonius is an accident, a bodged attempt to kill Claudius) and he is appalled by his mistake. His 'successful' murder of Rosencrantz and Gildenstern (the one we do not see) is, by his own report both planned and opportune, and his emotional involvement is minimal, as his sense of the fitness of the action is paramount. In this, and this alone, he seems to be fulfilling Seneca's prescription for the proper spirit in which to undertake retribution. As he tells Horatio, '... they did make love to this employment. |They are not near my conscience.' (V, ii, 57–8).

But the word 'conscience' in this play is highly ambiguous throughout. A straightforward reading of this line would give us 'I am not morally troubled by having killed them'; in other words, 'conscience' means simply an awareness of the difference between right and wrong. But elsewhere, 'conscience' has already acquired double, if not triple, meanings. Many commentators have claimed that 'conscience', where it appears towards the end of the famous soliloquy in III, i, means introspection: that is, the consciousness of the possibility of a nightmarish life after death which makes us too afraid to commit suicide. However, Philip Edwards is emphatic that introspection is not the meaning of 'conscience' in this speech, and that the inner knowledge of right and wrong is.[100] Nicholas Brooke cites Bradley's argument that 'conscience' here means 'consciousness': that is, the process of thinking and not the moral faculty, but he goes on to elucidate his own belief that 'conscience' means the moral faculty as well. I suggest that 'conscience' adumbrates yet a third association: that of an emotional, as well as a simply moral, response. There

---

100   See William Shakespeare, *Hamlet, Prince of Denmark* ed. Philip Edwards, The New Cambridge Shakespeare series (Cambridge, 1985),Introduction, pp. 40–61 and Nicholas Brooke, *Shakespeare's Early Tragedies*, op. cit., pp. 194–7.

is an emotional crescendo reached in the 'To be or not to be' soliloquy that marks a considerable emotional 'distance' from the measured debating tone of the beginning. This is an essentially dramatic speech, spoken with mounting passion, by a man who knows and feels 'the whips and scorns of time', 'th'opressor's wrong' and 'the pangs of disprized love'. These are surely not merely debating points in a moral argument, but full of an almost tangible emotional language designed to have a dramatic impact on its hearers. We, the audience, might respond to Hamlet's speech as Hamlet has already responded to the First Player's 'Hecuba' speech, and thus I would argue that if 'conscience' has acquired an emotional charge, so an emotional element might be permitted into a reading of 'they are not near my conscience'. As well as 'I am not morally troubled by having killed them', and 'I do not think about them', Hamlet is also admitting that he simply does not *care* about Rosencrantz and Gildenstern as people – the young men who briefly have been his friends. This is important, because where Hamlet does 'care', or has cared (for his father, for Gertrude, for Ophelia and even, in a perverse way, for Claudius) the caring gets hopelessly in the way of action.

The only person for whom Hamlet appears to 'care' uncomplicatedly is Horatio, and it is in the scenes with Horatio that we see a quite different Hamlet. Of his delighted recognition of Horatio in I,ii, there is a sudden shift in tone from the hopeless melancholy of the preceding soliloquy, and we are allowed a vital glimpse of what Hamlet would be like if he were not melancholy, of what life could be like if it were not 'rank' and 'gross'. But then Horatio is, in Hamlet's estimation, a good Stoic, capable of rising above the vicissitudes of Fortune: a quality which he admires profoundly but cannot imitate:

> ... for thou hast been
> As one in suffering all that suffers nothing
> A man that Fortune's buffets and rewards
> Hast ta'en with equal thanks. And blest are those
> Whose blood and judgement are so well commeddled

That they are not a pipe for Fortune's finger
To sound what stop she please. Give me that man
That is not passion's slave, and I will wear him
In my heart's core, ay in my heart of heart,
As I do thee.   (III, ii 57–64)

This speech, admiring one 'that is not passion's slave', is paradoxically a passionate one (at the same time as providing a reasoned
argument for Horatio's credentials as witness) and Hamlet pulls
away from the emotion of his declaration with a manly and very
English 'Something too much of this'. Hamlet has in any case already been established as far removed from Horatio, much as is
Malevole from Celso in Marston's *The Malcontent*. Hamlet was
'born to set it right'; Horatio need never trouble because he was
born to do nothing of the kind.

Celso, like Horatio, is the hero-malcontent's boon-companion
and confidant; but unlike Horatio, he is all for action at the beginning, but only in a strictly Stoical sense: '… let's mutiny and
die' (I, iv, 25). Celso accepts Fate on behalf of both of them: that
is, that it is necessary to fight righteously and to die for the cause,
which suggestion Malevole instantly rejects, in pseudo-Stoi-
cal terms: 'Oh, no, climb not a falling tower, Celso; | 'Tis well
held desperation, no zeal; | Hopeless to strive with fate'(28–30).
Malevole's implication that it is his fate, to be borne stoically, to
'live, and lurk in this disguise!'(30) and is soon contested by his
evident relish in the Malcontent role.

Hamlet's archetypal Stoic struggle with 'passion' throughout
the play sees him pronouncing on the need for temperance and
moderation in his admonition to the Players to 'use all gently,
for in the very torrent, tempest and, as I may say, whirlwind of
your passion, you must acquire and beget a temperance…' (III,
ii, 4–8), in an echo of fundamental Stoic principles, resembling
similar admonitions of Seneca, Epictetus, Marcus Aurelius and
their descendants. Yet this is a stage-direction to a group of actors, and the Players have already prompted Hamlet's anguished
realisation that he has far more cause for passion than a mere

actor reciting an impassioned speech. He perceives that his lack of sufficient passion inhibits his necessary action – of killing Claudius – but instead he must '… like a whore unpack my heart with words…' (II, ii, 538), in other words, rail like a Malcontent. Similarly, his articulation of the cardinal Stoical dictum: 'there is | nothing either good or bad, but thinking makes it so' (II, ii 249–50) is a powerful echo of Guillaume du Vair: 'Wherefore, let all these things remaine indifferent, as being made good or evil, by the minde of man.'[101] But it is Hamlet's sense of both good and evil co-existing externally – he has after all both seen and heard the Ghost – that conflicts so radically with an equal and opposite (Stoical) conviction that they must not. Stoical detachment offers very little of the comfort to Hamlet that it might; he construes it frequently as inhibiting action, because of his conviction that action requires sufficient passion, passion that will raise him to the heights of heroic action, not to none at all. There is a terrible irony in the play's exposure of Stoical detachment as the expedient way of murder, at the same time as exposing its opposite – passion – as insufficient or, as Hamlet so frequently regards it, overwhelming, chaotic, and impotent.

Hamlet's attempts to apply Stoical ideals of both behaviour and thought redound on him as if he were fundamentally unfit for them. As an essentially 'modern' Elizabethan (for he is certainly this as well as being a seventh-century Dane) unfit he might well be. His continual self-inquiry is far more reminiscent of the reconstructed Humanism set out in Montaigne's *Essays*, in which Montaigne perceived in human events a multiplicity so overwhelming as to defy theoretical analysis. The Stoics' interpretation of the Pythian oracle 'Know thyself' is simply not enough. This Stoical strategy of contemplation aims to free the mind from perturbation and *contumelia* – the outrages of Fortune – but Hamlet's mind is never free, and knowing himself is always mitigated by his perceptions of others. This play ex-

---

101 Guillaume du Vair, op. cit. He was referring here specifically to riches and poverty.

poses the inadequacies of all kinds of resonant platitudes (and not merely Stoical ones) in a manner that invites the audience to be judge of their worth and effectiveness. As Philip Edwards points out, while 'Claudius knows the proper response to death, Laertes to sex, Polonius to everything... with each person we see the insufficiency of their moralising.'[102] We learn what dark deed Claudius is hiding in I, v (though it is not confirmed until III, i, 50), and see that he is hiding it even from his new wife, who in turn tried to hide her adultery from her late husband. Laertes, for all his complacent sententiousness on the matter of sexual continence, is suspected, albeit in a fairly light-hearted manner, by both his sister and his father of an inclination to the 'primrose path' of dalliance. Polonius advocates reticence, truth and straight-dealing, but is garrulous and devious and, for all his obsequious humility before Claudius, we quickly perceive his overweening ambition. Poor Ophelia is, of course, merely going crazy, but without Hamlet's intellectual power of articulation. Hamlet's malcontentedness becomes far more explicable when viewed in contrast with these others, and can be seen at least in part as the response of one who suffers a sense of betrayal not only by other people, but by his whole perception of meaning. (This play gives more actual words to a hero than any other Shakespearean text; and *Hamlet*, in terms of sheer wordiness, and word-play, constantly begs to be perceived at one and the same time as a text: the kin/kind pun, for instance, assumes reading, as well as hearing.) The hypocrisy of the ever-ready platitudes is exposed by the conduct of those who utter them, and dismissed by Hamlet as mere 'saws of books'; but the 'saws of books' themselves, that is the measured and serene reasoning of both the Classics and of Christian doctrine – everything to which the noble man with a noble conscience might aspire – are exposed, along with the society in which he lives and was

---

102 William Shakespeare, *Hamlet, Prince of Denmark* ed. Philip Edwards, op. cit. Introduction, p. 46.

destined to rule, as shabby, even meaningless in terms of actual human experience.

It is not, therefore, a simple matter of Hamlet's being unfitted for an existence in accordance with Stoic principles (or indeed Christian ones) but those principles themselves which are revealed as unrealistic when applied to life as constructed by the play. Living in harmony with nature is impossible, since, apparently, nature itself is inharmonious, and Hamlet is unable to see beyond its apparent chaos. Instead, Hamlet's contemplations of nature: human, societal, familial, environmental – reveal only mystifying contradictions, producing 'things rank and gross' (I, ii, 136). Hamlet's nausea at the thought of living and breeding things, everything would seem to point to death, yet even the clean bare bones of death at the graveyard scene (V, i) offer only the proposition of the pointlessness of endeavour and ambition in life, in a series of contemplations which swing and shift in tone from the worldly and cynical, to the merely bewildered. The bones of the parochial lawyer prompt Hamlet to a reflection on the pointlessness of property and the ultimate powerlessness of the law; the subsequent reflection on what became of the mortal remains of Alexander and Caesar in a reduction of the 'noble dust' to 'a bung for a barrel' is not only a cynical tilt at nobility and heroism (the flippant dilation on 'how a king may go a progress through the guts of a beggar' in IV, iii, 28–29) but hints, in an equally flippant echo of the Nicene Creed, at the impossibility of resurrection. Yorick's skull prompts Hamlet's happy childhood memories of the man in life, but confronted with the synecdochic man in death, these are 'abhorred' in his imagination, and Yorick is now 'quite chop-fallen' as if in eternal dismay at his condition. Here, 'nature', in terms of the cycle of life and death, permits of no afterlife either: man's spiritual nature is left out of count. Elsewhere in the play, the afterlife is viewed paradoxically, as the undeserved peace to which Hamlet might consign the praying Claudius, and as exemplified by the presence of the Ghost, a traveller who has returned, but whose authenticity is constantly questioned.

vi

In *Hamlet,* the dramatic 'nature' of the Senecan ghost-figure – Seneca's own, and Elizabethan versions of it – is also called into question, partly because as a present figure on the stage, it can be, literally, questioned. Its enigmatic presence in *Hamlet,* unlike its counterparts in Seneca and Kyd, where the usual Senecan inventory of Hades' torments provides the Ghost with an unquestionable veracity, invites the sort of disbelieving bewilderment uttered by Hamlet so frequently. Its silence at first, then its refusal to speak of its hellish prison-house, and at the same time its insistence on being a part of the dramatic action – 'Taint not thy mind, nor let thy soul contrive | Against thy mother aught...' (I, v, 85–6), and its injunction: 'Leave her to heaven,' counterbalanced by its regret at missing the Christian sacraments before death, raise it beyond the mere function of a dramatic device, beyond a mere prologue to revenge, and, of course, beyond the pagan. Shakespeare's Ghost is a hybrid being, Senecan and Christian. But what might constitute a reassurance of eternal ordering for Hamlet instead serves to confuse him further, adds to his sense of universal betrayal, and pitches him ever back onto his own fragmentary judgement unaided by any authentic sense of ultimate order.

I have suggested that a Malcontent, in one of his aspects, is a negative image of the Stoic sage. In *Hamlet,* this negative image is split. Hamlet is both philosopher and prince-hero; he is a thinker trapped in a dilemma which can only be resolved by a man of action. Sage-hood is therefore denied him because of the pressing need for action, action which he finds impossible to undertake in the necessary detached spirit of Stoicism. His self-examination constantly exposes not only his failure in action but results in a tortured self-disgust at the inadequacies of the human condition of which he is not only an inextricable part, being a man, but, as a noble prince, a paragon. Ophelia's delineation of the ideal Renaissance prince, culminating in: 'Th'expectancy and rose of the fair state' (III, i. 146) elevates Hamlet above his fellow Danes and of humanity, but rings especially hollow when 'the fair state' – and this is not Denmark merely – is shown to be thoroughly corrupted, and reveals the 'rose' as blighted. No sooner does Hamlet perceive external evil – in Claudius, in the corrupting 'frailty' of women – than he perceives his own irredeemable part in it: 'it were better my mother had not borne me' (II, ii, 290–1); and 'Man delights not me' (III, i, 121) which inevitably must include himself. Hamlet's 'wisdom' permits him only monstrous and maddening recognitions of the vileness of a world of which he himself is a vile part. Although, as Robert S. Miola observes, 'Hamlet for the most part presents Stoicism as an ideal that is admirable but difficult to imitate in the shadowy world of Elsinore', it can be seen that this 'difficulty' is nevertheless an honest one. The role of the Stoic sage, on the other hand, is accorded to the villain Claudius, and is essentially sham.[103]

Claudius first appears in I, ii as the calm purveyor of Stoic consolation, claiming to have achieved moderation in grief, 'wisest sorrow'; thus, in taking the death of his father so much to heart, Hamlet commits 'a fault to nature, | To reason most absurd'. Claudius's speech is a pastiche of common Stoic precepts, derived from the standard and much-imitated consolatory models of Cicero, Plutarch and Seneca. In good Stoical fashion, Claudius instructs Hamlet to follow nature, which ordains that all living things must die, and to control his passions. Later, Claudius again strikes the Stoic pose to Laertes: 'You cannot speak of reason to the Dane |And lose your voice' (I, ii, 44–5). The scenes which follow, in which we learn that Claudius is none other than Hamlet's father's murderer, expose Claudius's hypocrisy and radically undercut his Stoical advice. As he admits in an

---

103   Robert S. Miola, *Shakespeare and Classical Tragedy: The Influence of Seneca* (Oxford, 1992), 58 ff.

aside, the 'painted word' hides an ugly deed (III, i, 50–2). Claudi-us, a very wily villain if nothing else, contrives 'accidental evils', planning misfortunes for others while urging detachment upon the victims. He sets up Hamlet's meeting with Ophelia, 'as 'twere by accident' (III, i, 30); when he assumes the Stoic role to com-fort Laertes after the death of Polonius, again he appeals to the son's reason and 'judgement' in his grief (IV, v, 152), preaching 'patience' (211). Then he fixes the duel so that even Gertrude will 'uncharge the practice, |And call it accident' (IV, vii, 67–8). The Stoic watchwords: 'reason', 'thinking', and 'judgement' echo in various forms in Claudius's speeches, but by now, our awareness is importantly altered. We can see that philosophical rhetoric has been monstrously perverted: that Claudius is using Stoic language and precept for manipulation, treachery and murder.

Claudius is essentially a 'competent' ruler in the Machiavelli-an fashion; thus, when it suits him, he is a counterfeit Stoic, but he is far from being a Malcontent, at least when we see him. It is a little tempting to speculate on a back-story: that, before the murder of his brother, Claudius was malcontented in the man-ner of Cain, whose image recurs many times. But dramatical-ly, the Claudius role is a device, in counterpoise to the device offered by the Hamlet role, by which a morally and politically questioning play can examine and expose the potential for abuse and oppression inherent in such doctrine, when manipulated by one who is not a true sage, but merely cleverly ambitious, untroubled by his conscience. Of course, in this most complex of plays, Claudius is not merely this. We do see evidence that he has a moral conscience which is capable of being 'lashed' (III, i, 50); we see him badly shaken by the 'Mousetrap', and his pan-icked call for 'light' (III, ii, 243), and while threat of exposure alone might explain his reaction, this is considerably affected by the subsequent scene in which he tries, unsuccessfully, to pray. Here, more than anywhere, we have a glimpse of a falli-ble *man*, not merely a two-dimensional villain; here, Claudius's own tragedy is manifest in the profound moral and theological dilemma in which he is caught, and our sympathies, I suggest, cannot possibly be straightforward. Instead, he offers further proof of Hamlet's - and *Hamlet's* - tragic view of humankind as infinitely corruptible. By witnessing Claudius's flawed humanity, which we see again, in his semi-candid confession to Laertes of his total attachment to Gertrude (IV, viii, 11–16), we are not permitted any more straightforward separation between good and evil, order and chaos, light and darkness, than Hamlet is. We have been forced to view the world as a thing perplexed with no absolute answers.

CHAPTER SEVEN

ENDINGS: CONSIDERING
KING LEAR

i

The Malcontent figure began to dwindle from the stage during the 1620s, perhaps inevitably, given fashion. 'Sophisticated'
public theatre before its abrupt closure at the Interregnum had
turned to narrower social portrayals, or to embrace European
trends which were much more inclined to portraying shallower
villains, under-developed as characters. The great dramatists of
the era were either dead – Thomas Kyd and Christopher Marlowe had died in the previous century, and Shakespeare died
in 1616 – or had moved on. Jonson had turned his attention to
London comedies, and although the famously brilliant 'city' satires are certainly cynical in their view of mankind in general as
hopelessly greedy, vain and guileless, witlessly deserving of its
fate, or else criminally intended, sly and clever, and deserving
only ill-gotten gains as far as can be got away with, their proponents are scarcely malcontented in any profound sense. These
plays 'play' on our sympathies, allowing us an unwonted delight
in witnessing criminal improvisation which takes advantage of
human frailty, but they destroy little or nothing of an audience's
belief in an ultimate order of Good and Evil; there is no ultimate
voice of hopelessness, only of temporal despair at plans gone
awry, and although harsh punishments await the criminals in
the end (*Volpone* is especially savage) there is no true voice of
conscience.

From about 1620 onwards, malcontentedness portrayed in the
theatre became a shadow of the shocking thing it had been, and

although some characters, notably in plays by Philip Massing-
er and various colleagues, continued to echo the malcontented features of Webster's Flamineo and Bosola, and Middleton's
Vindice, they are faded by comparison with their earlier counterparts. Even John Ford's 'Tis Pity She's A Whore (c. 1630), in its
portrayal of a malcontented world, is something of a shadow in
its debt to earlier, more obviously Jacobean dramas. Its themes:
incest, plotting and murder are familiar, perhaps by now rou-
tinely passé for an audience well-versed in such things on the
stage; and its handling is not truly monstrous, despite the irresistible and – by now – tritely old-fashioned heaping of corpses
on the stage in the last act. Contrasted against the background
of society's cruelty and banal corruption, the solemn and idealistic union between the lovers, Giovanni and Annabella, is
portrayed compassionately, even poetically, and its morality is
mostly unambiguous. The world, through the shallow, vindic-
tive hypocrisy of the other characters, is shown as vile, while
the lovers are given a tragic dimension, again in debt to Romeo
& Juliet. Only Vasques, its Malcontent, is given some obscurity
of motive, something along the lines of Iago, but at the end he
is simply the leader of a murderous gang. This is, given its main
theme, a bravely 'modern' treatment of incestuous love, but it is,
ultimately, about Love: it is not about Malcontent.

In this book, I have attempted to address two main points:
first, that the Malcontent was for a brief time, chiefly between
the mid 1580s to the 1620s, a recognizable figure on the stage
which, though it drew many of its features and demeanour from
a real-life exemplar was nevertheless a vital part of an innovative theatrical development; secondly that this figure was part
of, and predicated upon, a drama which was in itself inclined
to 'prove' the Malcontent view in the larger picture. This malcontented quality tended not only to expose and mock social,
moral and political fallacies in the manner of good satire, but
to go further, not always satirically, to shatter the play-world's
portrayal of the real world's ideals and aspirations. In this lay its

brief power. These ideals combine typically into religious and humanist concerns; man's willed achievements, in accordance with a Classical precedent, and blessed by a Christian God's grace. A 'malcontented' play, I have argued, permits neither of these tines of English Renaissance thought ultimately to stick or stay. Human achievement in love, war or politics, or indeed in any sphere of human intercourse, is shown to be shallow and without real substance; while faith either fails, or God is noticeably absent from the faithful. In such plays, the picture of human existence is a bleak one in which a pervading purposelessness gains ascendancy. In both the predominantly tragic or comic mood, audiences are not permitted, either in tears or laughter, any lasting or comforting sense of a wider purpose derived from the message of the play. It is therefore a very short distance, as with irony everywhere, from this perception to one in which this is applicable to their own world and to themselves.

Obviously, the idea of the *play* as 'malcontented' applies to some plays of the period more than to others, but the distinction is by no means straightforward. Some 'Malcontent' plays apparently turn full-circle, leaving at least the suggestion of moral and political order to re-emerge after a reign of chaos. *The Malcontent* achieves this relatively uncomplicatedly as part of its comic *coup de grace*; *Richard III* sees at its close the re-establishment of order under strong Tudor rule; the ending of *Hamlet* almost reconstitutes the idea of the 'hero' in Fortinbras and leaves us with the good Horatio as the 'recorder', the truthful witness; *The Revenger's Tragedy* leaves a devastated Duchy in the virtuous if draconian hands of Antonio. However, although these endings suggest the cessation of the chaotic nightmare, they cannot negate the fact that, for most of the play, not only have we been witnessing disorder, disunity and spiritual chaos, but we have been actively invited to question the merits of order, unity and serenity, *and to enjoy it* – by means of what Nicholas Brooke called 'horrid' laughter.[104] Other plays, notably *Timon of Athens*,

---

104   Nicholas Brooke, *Horrid Laughter in Jacobean Tragedy* op. cit.

Troilus & Cressida, The White Devil, The Changeling leave behind a much more total sense of destruction, hopelessness and
annihilation, and can perhaps be more specifically regarded as
'malcontented', since they have delved deep enough into the human morass of moral questioning and still offer no promise of
salvation, morally or politically, personally or socially. Regardless of endings, however, is the underpinning idea that, in the
words of Travis Bogard, 'Life… is a moral chaos. Ultimately, no
clarifying philosophy is possible…'[105] an idea which is bleakly
persistent throughout many such works, plays which are symptomatic, not merely of an ever more politically-aware society,
but of what J. W. Lever describes as 'the broken humanity of
Renaissance Europe'.[106]

We see this in a highly complex form in *Hamlet*. Hamlet himself is undoubtedly a Malcontent, and *Hamlet* is undoubtedly a
'malcontented' drama; yet nevertheless the play does offer some
small restitution of the idea, and the ideal, of virtuous heroism
at its end, albeit one that that remains rooted in the dead Hamlet rather than in the characters of either Horatio or Fortinbras
who remain alive to carry on. That Hamlet is central to the play
as its Malcontent as well as its hero is a significant factor in the
way the play is received by the audience. However, it is argua-
ble that *Hamlet* contains, at least within Hamlet's dying regard
of Fortinbras as his successor – the 'delicate prince' (however
unlikely this delicacy may seem) of a former speech – and of
Horatio as the witness of the truth, dissuaded from his Stoical
suicide, the seeds of some justice and of a little hope. With a new
ruling class, a fresh cast of characters, it is implied, the wheel
turns once more, taking with it the new aspirants to power and
glory, possibly to a new and more truthful order now that the
arch-deceiver Claudius is finally dead. At least the Ghost can
rest, now that Hamlet has at last fulfilled its wishes. Hamlet has

105   Travis Bogard, *The Tragic Satire of John Webster* (London, 1955), p. 31.
106   J. W. Lever, *The Tragedy of State: A Study in Jacobean Drama* (London, 1971).

had, and has taken, the opportunity to make his peace with the dying Laertes; and Gertrude's death has an ironic symmetry: for she will be judged 'by heaven,' as the Ghost intended. But all these things imply a just heaven which does exist after all, and while the sublunary world beneath it might be flawed and full of imperfections, a relative justice may triumph on earth too, and this despite the overt villainy, the frequent failure of love and loyalty, the corruption at the heart of state and the centrality of malcontentedness in Hamlet himself.

ii

King Lear, on the other hand, despite the sense of disorder, madness and social disruption which pervades the play from the beginning, is full of portrayals of human constancy, forgiveness and loyalty; its Malcontent, Edmund, though vital in a 'pro-active' sense to the plot, is never central, and the audience is never deeply concerned with his individual fate. Yet this play ultimately would seem to offer far less hope than *Hamlet*. I would go so far as to assert that *Lear* is arguably the most completely nihilistic of all the malcontented dramas of the period, precisely because it sets up such positive moral values only to shatter them. The play indicates the insolubility of what we might call the human condition at all levels; and both the Stoical and the Christian responses to the human problems in the play are revealed as utterly futile, a futility confirmed by the play's almost unbearably harrowing – and controversial – ending. It is as if the Stoical response (of acceptance) and the Christian one (of belief in, and appeal to, salvation) are themselves presented as mutually cancelling. Edgar's disguise as Tom O'Bedlam is quintessentially an embrace of the Stoical attitude to Fortune, for having brought himself to the lowest point of human existence, he claims, he can go no lower. Yet this claim, by the time of the entrance speech at the beginning of Act IV has acquired a complacence which, for dramatic reasons if nothing else, must surely soon be broken. Therefore:

Yet better thus, and known to be condemned,
Than still condemned and flattered. To be worst,
The low'st and most dejected thing of fortune,
Stands still in esperance, lives not in fear.
The lamentable change is from the best;
The worst returns to laughter. Welcome, then,
Thou insubstantial air that I embrace:
The wretch that thou hast blown unto the worst
Owes nothing to thy blasts...   (IV, i, 1–9)

gives way to

O gods! Who is't can say 'I am at the worst'?
I am worse than e'er I was... and worse I may be yet.
                    ... The worst is not
So long as we can say 'This is the worst'.   (IV, i, 26–8)

once he sees Gloucester's bleeding and blinded misery. In the same scene, Gloucester's utterances are accepting of fate in a way that we now recognize as typical of him: 'As flies to wanton boys are we to th' gods; | They kill us for their sport.' (IV,i, 36/7) despite the apparent control-taking humanism of the gift of his purse to Poor Tom and the apparent wish to involve himself personally in the reversal of Tom's fortunes: 'So distribution should undo excess, |And each man have enough.' (IV, i, 65–6).

Aid for the poor is, of course, a Christian duty, and Gloucester, though misguided, is essentially representative of the fallible Christian. Yet Gloucester falls into the Christian sin of despair in his suicide bid at Dover and, when 'saved' by a seeming miracle, regrets the escape that was offered in the Stoic doctrine:

Is wretchedness deprived that benefit
To end itself by death?
'Twas yet some comfort
When misery could beguile the tyrant's rage
And frustrate his proud will...   (IV, v, 61–4).

His ultimate resolve to 'bear affliction till it do cry out itself,' however, is itself undercut by Lear's mad entrance, the scene having a dramatic symmetry with Gloucester's own blinded and stricken entrance at the climax of Tom/Edgar's Stoical exposition at the beginning of IV, i. Following on so immediately, the implication is that the bearing out of affliction can and does go a stage further: into madness and, perhaps, into a kind of 'reverse perception,' one in which crazy Lear regards himself as 'every inch a king' (IV, v, 103) and is still convinced that 'Gloucester's bastard son | Was kinder to his father than my daughters | Got 'tween the lawful sheets,' (110-2). Lear turns both Christian and Stoical perceptions upside-down, as of course does the play.

Lear's madness is the 'sane' mirror of the spurious 'sanity' of other characters. His daughters dole out their generosity in terms of an allowance of followers and foot-soldiers, just as he quantifies their filial love in the same measure. On the one hand there is the mean-seeming but perfectly valid and sane recognition of Lear's inability to retain an army; on the other, there is Lear's mad-sane judgement of their trust and love for him that could and should not require him to give his army up. This is no real measure of 'love', of course; love is something which has been established by Cordelia already as unquantifiable. That Goneril and Regan have neither love nor trust is apparent to the audience, and half-apparent to Lear himself: therefore, audience and Lear are more 'truthful' than are Goneril and Regan. But if Cordelia represents truthfulness and love (which Lear cannot see) his other daughters represent untruthfulness and greed, which Lear also cannot see. Lear, in his increasing madness, bridges truth and lies, because his madness continually (and maddeningly) reveals the truth. On the other hand, Edgar, however much he comes to involve himself in the role of Tom O'Bedlam, is playing a role, and we are constantly thrown against this knowledge when we are asked to believe in his stoical *sententiae*. The image of perfect Stoical detachment comes towards the end of the play when, to Cordelia's 'Shall we not see these daughters and these sisters?' Lear retorts with 'No, no, no, no! Come let's away to prison; | We two alone will sing like birds i' th' cage,' (V, iii, 7–9). This is worlds away from Edgar's own stoic endurance – singing, with nothing to sing for – but somehow it is far more believable than anything that Edgar can utter.

It has been argued that there remains an important and discernible distinction between the utterly evil and the thoroughly good in this play, even if Cordelia (as the thoroughly good) and Lear (good, reconstructed out of madness) do not thrive. This would be conveniently unambiguous if it were not for the fact that all of this play's representations of the good are shown as so very much weaker, morally or physically, than the seemingly invincible evil of their opponents. The least equivocally righteous characters must hide, and have either to be in disguise (Kent and Edgar) or banished (Cordelia): by implication, righteousness must go in disguise or fail. But once the disguises are abandoned or penetrated, there is no heroic triumph of virtue. Cordelia is killed, and although Edgar and Kent are survivors, they are not saviours. Albany's 'conversion' leads him to succeed only to a virtually dead kingdom. Edgar's fallibility is crucial to a play which increasingly refuses to allow any of the characters (and therefore, to allow us) any spiritual comfort from either Christianity or Stoicism, nor indeed any hope in the great institutions of humankind.

The play opens like the Histories, with the King's abdication and the division of the kingdom. It also ends like the Histories, with the proclamation of a new king. Between the prologue and the epilogue there is a civil war. But unlike in the Histories, as Jan Kott pointed out, the world is not healed again.

> In *King Lear*, there is no young and resolute Fortinbras to ascend the throne... no cool-headed Octavius to become Augustus Caesar; no noble Malcolm to 'give to our tables meat, sleep to our nights'.[107]

---

107   Jan Kott, *Shakespeare Our Contemporary* (London & New York,

The History plays frequently concluded with the new monarch inviting those present to his coronation. In *King Lear*, there will be no grand coronation ceremony, for there is no one whom Edgar can invite. In Gloucester's words, 'This great world shall so wear out to nought.' Those who survive – Edgar, Albany and Kent – are, as Lear has been, just 'ruin'd pieces of nature.'

This sense of the play's comfortlessness is more or less universally accepted by many later-twentieth-century critics and commentators. Before the 1960s, however, many critics argued quite the opposite, and pointed specifically to *Lear*'s affirmative Christianity, or if not quite this, then at least to an assumption that the play gives the lie to any truly despairing view of man's inhumanity to man. The sheer contradiction in the various interpretations of the play by earlier critics and those who came later is startling in itself. For a play to be open to such a wide moral, as opposed to political, interpretation (as in the case of *Julius Caesar*, for example, where later ages variously emphasized or adapted the roles of the central quartet to accord with the political timbre of the time) is surely in itself odd, even disturbing. That A. C. Bradley in 1904 should declaim: 'Should we not [call] this poem *The Redemption of King Lear*, and [declare] that the business of 'the gods' with [Lear] was… to lead him to attain… the very end and aim of life?'[108] but that Jan Kott in 1965 should assert that 'In *King Lear*… orders of established values disintegrate. All that remains at the end of this gigantic pantomime is the earth, empty and bleeding,'[109] is enough to press into nagging doubt not the vagaries of criticism merely, but the very troubling aspects of this particular play which could possibly have made such diametric impressions upon not only critical thought but also the dramatic interpretations which were influenced by it. For contained in such diversity of interpretation, there is an inevitable directorial dilemma, since it is possible (and without

1964, 1974).

108   A. C. Bradley, *Shakespearean Tragedy* (London, 1904).

109   Jan Kott, op. cit.

rewriting the ending, as had the Restoration dramaturgs) to present at the end a Lear who is deluded and who momentarily fools the audience; a Lear who is deluded and fools nobody; and an altogether more ironical and desperate Lear who indulges the illusion of Cordelia's survival but knows that it is the product of a desperate and hopeless wish.

King Lear is of course set in a pagan, pre-Christian Britain, but there is inevitably much to suggest a Christian perception of God, just as the play's politics are pre-eminently Elizabethan. Virtually all the post-Bradleian 'New' Critics read the play in this ultimately redemptive Christian way, citing the loyalty and truth of Cordelia, Kent, Edgar and the Fool, Lear's magnificent spirit and, of course, the retributional deaths of Edmund, Goneril and Regan. In 1959, L. C. Knights was definite that the play evinces 'fundamentally Christian values… For what takes place in *King Lear* we can find no other word than renewal,' in an argument which runs that Shakespeare was writing at an historical moment in which such 'established assumptions about Nature' were being eroded, and that 'to some minds Nature was ceasing to appear as a divinely ordained order and was beginning to appear as an amoral collection of forces,' but makes a distinction between 'some minds' and Shakespeare's own.[110]

Shakespeare almost certainly did share this amoral view, however. His principal source, the anonymous *The True Chronicle History of King Leir and his Three Daughters* of c. 1590, ends with a scene in which Leir and his youngest daughter, Cordella, are alive and reconciled, presumably set to live happily ever after. This would have afforded an obvious, comforting conclusion had Shakespeare wished it, but he appears to have chosen an old story with a happy ending and proceeded to shatter it deliberately with an ending that is seemingly without any hope at all. The older play gives us a far more stupid and criminal King, and, besides, Shakespeare's other sources for the play – the *Mirrour for Magistrates*, Holinshed's *Chronicles* and Spenser's *Faerie Queene*

---

110   L. C. Knights, *Some Shakespearean Themes* (London, 1959).

– all retain the amoral savagery of folk-tale, ending with Lear's death and Cordelia's suicide. Thus Shakespeare's version of an ending appears to have been, if anything more, rather than less, faithful to older, non-dramatic sources. Shakespeare's Cordelia does not, of course, commit suicide: she is killed, but her death is a merciless, even, gratuitous, retribution.[111]

The Restoration and the eighteenth century had perceived Shakespeare's treatment with indignant scepticism. His authorial decision to kill Cordelia and leave Lear to die of a broken heart was seen as a dramatic and moral flaw by Samuel Johnson, who was the first major critical voice in the centuries of controversy which have followed. For Dr Johnson, it is Cordelia's death especially (rather than Lear's or Gloucester's) that seems contrary to all notions of moral justice, especially given the reconciliation scenes in Act IV. With the deaths of the wicked children (Regan, Goneril and Edmund) it seemed to Johnson that the play was moving towards a comfortable moral conclusion in which good was eventually to triumph over evil, a triumph accentuated by Edmund's deathbed repentance. But this is dashed by that terrible stage direction: 'Re-enter LEAR with CORDELIA [dead] in his arms.' Johnson much preferred Nahum Tate's production in the Restoration theatre in which the play is reconstructed to end with Cordelia alive and reunited with Lear and about to marry Edgar, a union blessed by both of their fathers, for Gloucester, too, has survived. The eighteenth century altogether seems to have been in consensus regarding the ending of *Lear*; for from the first performance of Tate's version in 1681 to Edmund Kean's presentation in 1823, the play was performed with a symmet-

---

111   *The True Chronicle History* was first published in 1605, but written much earlier. Two additional sources include John Florio's translation of Montaigne's essays (1603) and Samuel Harsnett's *A Declaration of Egregious Popish Impostures* (1603). The story of Lear and his daughters was first told in Geoffrey of Monmouth's *Historia Regum Britanniae* (1137), from which Raphael Holinshed derived his account in his *Chronicles* (1587 edn). Shakespeare also read Edmund Spenser's version of the tale in *The Faerie Queene* (Book 2, canto xi).

rically happy ending. Thus it might be tempting to dismiss the eighteenth century, both its critical attitude and its audiences, as merely sentimental. However, Johnson was not noted for his sentimentality, nor for his solidarity with the 'publicke', yet it was nevertheless upon such public response to the harrowing nature of the ending of Shakespeare's play that Johnson justified his judgement: 'In the present case the publicke has decided', marvelling that anyone could prefer Shakespeare's ending. He himself, many years before, had been so shocked by Cordelia's death, that it was only the need to revise the last scenes of the play as an editor that forced him to re-read the ending which he found personally painful.[112]

The main thrust of Johnson's objections was the play's apparent denial of Christian salvation or even of common justice in the Shakespearean ending. The German critic, Schlegel, writing in 1811, provided a somewhat different and emphatically down-to-earth angle on this point with his opinion that although the melancholy ending was the 'proper' one, it was essential for audiences to remember that for all they might be moved by Cordelia's 'heavenly beauty of soul', Shakespeare had nevertheless chosen to set his play in a pre-Christian Britain, so that both the good and the wicked must be regarded as heathens, not Christians. The fate of the characters in *King Lear* is commensurate with the darkness of the heathen (that is, unenlightened) world,

---

112   Johnson's comments on the ending of *King Lear*, taken from the Preface and Notes of his edition, 1765, are reprinted in F. Kermode (ed.), *King Lear, Macmillan Casebook* (London, 1969). Dr Johnson was reading Rowe's edition – see below.

Nicholas Rowe, *The Works of Mr. William Shakespeare*, 1st edn, 1709; 2nd edn, 1714, is the first to include the word 'dead' in the stage direction. Many later editors have continued to prejudice readers by following him in this. Both Q and F leave open Cordelia's physical state. The ambiguity of Cordelia's state is crucial: throughout the scene 'the audience continues to alternate between hope and despair'. (See Derek Peat's essay: ' "And that's true too": *King Lear* and the Tension of Uncertainty,' *SS*, 33, 1980. Nahum Tate's adaptation of *King Lear* was produced in 1681.

and therefore the apparently un-Christian ending is literally
that, and justified and justified by historical verisimilitude.

Nowadays, Schlegel's argument has little appeal for critics
who regard it as side-stepping the issue; there is, obviously, a
Christian theodicy that informs *King Lear* simultaneously with
the 'heathen' one: a bi-polar, stereoscopic vision that informed
the Roman plays, too, which could be at one and the same time
historically literal enough to examine a different political culture as well as make mordant comment upon an English Elizabethan one. But *Lear* is not principally about an unenlightened
world as such, and its impact derives partly from its relevance to
the problem of Man's existence universally and, significantly, for
the English Elizabethan/Jacobean one in which it was written:
one in which great orders threaten to collapse, chaos looms, and
nothing that Man believes augurs much salvation, especially if
that salvation, temporal or spiritual, depends upon a belief in
great orders. If Lear is a pagan tyrant, he is one whose monstros-
ity is mitigated in Act I by Cordelia's Christian forgiveness, and
that of the King of France, who believes in her implicit goodness. Cordelia, on the other hand, might be held to represent
a Christ-figure who is sacrificed in Act V, but one without any
promise of resurrection or redemption. The excited energy of
Lear's last lines: 'Look on her, look her lips! | Look there, look
there!' (V, iii, 284–5) have since prompted some critics to attempt to mitigate the irony of this, as A. C. Bradley did in his
argument that Lear should not die in 'agony' with the knowledge of Cordelia's death, but in 'ecstasy' with the 'illusion' that
she lives. All of these commentators seem to have been unable
to countenance the true, and I should say malcontented horror
of the play. Ultimately, surely, Cordelia is 'as dead as earth', and
no heaven is suggested at all; all that survives is Lear's delusion.

A twentieth century shattered by two world wars has prompted criticism of a less sentimental nature, one prepared to acknowledge the play's ultimate nihilism. In 1951, William Empson perhaps most completely anticipated the post-1960s critical

view by his utter rejection of any Christian view of redemption the play might have afforded, and by seeing '[the gods] as … facetious and full of mean jeering tricks. I think this pious acceptance of the gods does a great deal to recall the old picture of them as criminal lunatics.'[113] For Empson, all gods, Christian or pagan, are mean and cruel and petty; for him the play offers no consolatory movement towards redemption or renewal, maintaining merely a somewhat old-fashioned, Senecan picture, of gods whose motivations are obscure, and who are unable and unwilling to intervene in a world in which humanity's good intentions can only ever result in annihilation. On the apparent meaninglessness of the play's final act, Empson remarks: '… the death of Cordelia, and the death of Lear in consequence of it, are different from those of any other Shakespearean tragedy in that they seem wilful… the death is like a last trip-up as the clown leaves the stage…' Barbara Everett scouted her New Crtiticism predecessors roundly: 'Those critics who find [Christian allegory] in the play… are interested in the kind of 'poetic' statements which the play seems to make, *in contradistinction from what actually happens.*' (my italics).[114] W. R. Elton concluded that the play's final moments are indeed ironic, offering not transcendence but the void: 'In this dark world, the last choruses tell us, we find the promised end, or image of that horror, in which man's chief joy is to be removed from the wrack of this tough world and in which man's solace is – ultimate irony! – the illusion that that which he most loves still breathes: No redemption stirs at this world's end; only suffering, tears, pity and loss and illusion.'[115]

There is surely little but bleakness in such a play, in such an ending. A Malcontent play it certainly is, offering little but a vision of moral, spiritual and political chaos, in which the comfort of *apathaea* is again and again seen as either forlorn or impossi-

113   William Empson, 'The Fool in Lear' in *The Structure of Complex Words* (London, 1951), 150 ff.

114   Barbara Everett, 'The New *King Lear*' CQ, 2, (1960).

115   W. R. Elton, *King Lear and the Gods*, (Los Angeles, 1966).

ble; in any case to fail; and the hope in salvation is dashed. It is only possible, therefore, to regard *King Lear* very much in terms of a play of its age; a play which embraces the very worst aspects of the relationship of a thinking but confused mankind with ideals of civilization, order, kingship, religion, classical and biblical authority and a sense of *humanitas*. For while it is obviously not a 'Renaissance play' in the modern idiom, there appears to be, at the heart of *King Lear*, a culmination of all that that Age might perceive as worthless and untrue. And although its Malcontent figure, Edmund, might be relatively undeveloped and perfunctory, its Malcontent message is not.

Yet, looked at from a slightly different point of view, one has to understand the force of Dr Johnson's repudiation of the play's ending before we accept sheer nihilism. It is only reasonable that we should find aspects of this play vile, and disturbing to witness. As Nicholas Brooke pointed out,

> while the play insists on our adjusting to a state of universal disorder, of looking hard at that... , there are values, good as well as evil;... they can have no reference beyond themselves, no ultimate sanction – they are quite superfluous, in fact. It is the very superfluity which alone is encouraging: without superfluity there would be no hope...'[116]

This is surely true: for superfluous though they may be to whatever the opposite is of a 'moral message', we do see Cordelia, Kent, Edgar (however naively) and the King's Fool engaged in a form or forms of love, loyalty and truth; and no, it is not significant to any ideal of order promulgated in the play; it merely exists: it simply is, without a grand design that can or will support it. 'O, reason not the need,' as the man said.

---

116   For a very full discussion of the critical debate surrounding the play's ending, see Nicholas Brooke 'The Ending of King Lear' in *Shakespeare 1564-1964 – A Collection of Modern Essays by Various Hands* ed. Edward A. Bloom, (Brown, R. I., 1964). Compare Kenneth Myrick's 'Christian Pessimism in King Lear' in the same volume, pp. 56–7.

It is the apparent nullity of the ending of *King Lear* that has been the focus of much of the critical controversy. This play's ending and, indeed, endings in general, beg the question of whether the ending of any play can significantly alter its main thrust. In *The Sense of an Ending*, Frank Kermode discusses the differences between myth and fiction as he defines them, and the way that popular stories tend to stick closely to established conventions, while major novels tend to vary them more and more: 'The story that proceeded very simply to its predestined end would be nearer myth than the novel or drama.' The nature and impact of *peripeteia*, or tragic reversal of any story consti-tutes a respect for our sense of reality, yet depends upon our confidence of the end. Of *King Lear*, he notes:

> ... the falsification of an expectation can be terrible, as in the death of Cordelia; it is a way of finding something out that we should, on our more conventional way to the end, have closed our eyes to. Obviously it could not work if there were not a certain rigidity in the set of our expectations.'[117]

The expectations *King Lear* arouses are very strong, and this is presumably because of the tale's mythic quality.

iii

I have been arguing fairly strenuously that even where endings are apparently conclusively 'happy', where order and justice seem to have been restored, the foregoing business on the stage (especially if we have been compelled during the course of the play into perceptions, even alliances, that suggest the viability of opposites or at least alternatives) cannot possibly permit us an unadulterated comfort in a 'happy' conclusion. To use Ker-mode's model, it would seem as if a story that belonged to the

---

117   Frank Kermode, *The Sense of an Ending: Studies in the Theory of Fiction* (Oxford, 1967, rev. 2000)

expectations of reality had suddenly been, in an unlikely manner, contorted back into a myth. Even in relative lightweights such as *Twelfth Night* and *A Winter's Tale*, where the endings seem to be forced and ultimately untenable, reveal a different sort of reality: the reality, perhaps, of myth-making, and the spuriousness of the neatness of their endings is one more vital element in the malcontent-dramatist's trick-bag.

King Lear probably has the makings of a case for an exception, in that the play inverts the moral schema and allows the ending, rather than its main argument, to make the malcontented point. Edgar and Edmund portend this also, for if it is with these two final combatant representatives of Good and Evil that the moral power finally rests, then the good–evil polarity is far from neat. Edgar reveals a capacity for both self-righteousness and cruelty. Very little would appear to excuse Edgar's failure to reveal his identity to his father on seeing Gloucester blind and hearing him acknowledge his mistake. The apparent wish to exact a further punishment seems the most obvious explanation of the withholding of his identity; and, when the most obvious and effective way to cure his father of the desire to commit suicide would be by revealing himself, the elaborate and humiliating hoax of Dover Cliff seems to be vilely gratuitous. Explanations offered by critics in the earlier part of the twentieth century, essentially justifying Edgar's motives in terms of his good intentions seem unsatisfactory. Even when Gloucester pleads:

> O! dear son Edgar,
> The food of thy abused father's wrath;
> Might I but live to see thee in my touch
> I'd say I had eyes again   (IV, i, 21–4)

Edgar refuses to reveal his identity, thus metaphorically depriving Gloucester of his eyes afresh, a 'blinding' that links him to the mutilating cruelty of Regan and Cornwall. This revelation of Edgar's capacity for a cruelty no different in essence from the cruelty of the play's obviously evil characters has to be shock-ing, yet it is Edgar who is to become the ruler at the end, Lear's successor, the man who must, in Albany's charge, 'the gor'd state sustain.' While we could construct 'psychological' explanations for Edgar's behaviour, cite his jealousy of his father's other son, blame a long-held childish wish to teach his father a 'lesson' – I am not sure that psychological explanations have more rele-vance than emblematic ones, or indeed dramatic ones; for me, the most satisfactory accounting for the grotesque walk up no hill to no cliff to no suicide and its subsequent bathos is primari-ly concerned with dramatic effect. Gloucester's 'suicide' becomes 'only a somersault on an empty stage'[118] and, since this is what we see, it seems the most credible explanation, if ultimately enig-matic. The critical search for psychological accounts have largely been attempts to dignify Edgar's position, as well as to dignify the symbolism of this scene. The much bleaker view: that this grotesque walk is neither full of promise for our lives, nor a pic-ture of mankind making his way up through Purgatory is sure-ly far more apt. Edgar, rather than representing the conquering Christian-chivalric hero, is instead Man in his shabby littleness.

This profound flaw at the Christian and heroic centre of this play is one of the two reasons I can see for *King Lear's* qual-ification for 'malcontent drama' of a supreme kind, neither of which has specifically to do with the ending merely, although doubtless it is the ending which alerts us to a profound sense of destruction. The second reason is the role of Edgar's opposition, Edmund. Edgar's is the most Christian sensibility in the play, as Edmund's is the most Machiavellian. If the Machiavellian fails in the end, he very nearly succeeds; and if the Christian succeeds, his success is surely deeply compromised. Just as Edgar repre-sents the (albeit flawed) chivalric Christian hero, Edmund is the flawed representative of the Humanist ideal or, looked at the other way up, Edmund is the ultimate Machiavellian malcon-tent flawed in the end by a belated desire for salvation. Equal-

---

118   Jan Kott, op. cit.

ly and conversely, just as Edgar's cruelty and cowardice can be demonstrated, so can Edmund's ultimately humanitarian, even Christian, sensibility: ('Some good I mean to do, | Despite of mine own nature. Quickly send...' V, iii, 217-8). If a Christian-affirmative redemptive reading of *King Lear* can consider Edgar's cruelty in a forgiving light, so must it consider Edmund's capitulation also. But while there is surely no doubt that at the end, Edmund 'means well', there is also little doubt that this – and Edmund's spiritual fate – means little to us by this point in the play. It soon becomes only too obvious that no intervention of Edmund's will make any difference. By now, it is all far too late: everything has gone wrong.

Edmund, for G. Wilson Knight, represented the 'primitive' in the stages of Man's spiritual evolution.[119] Taken at a Humanist-Christian level, there is plenty of neo-Platonist precedent for this view: for any man to be purely concerned with the temporal world of his own ambition involves Error, and therefore Edmund, wholly concerned with himself, and compared with Lear's concern both with his kingdom and with how he is loved (however erroneously he works these things out) and Cordelia's concern with others, with truth and with love, is after these lights, a spiritual 'primitive'. However, Wilson Knight's construction, that three of the protagonists: Edmund, Lear and Cordelia, respectively 'correspond to three periods in man's (Christian) evolution: the primitive, the civilized and the ideal,' and to three temporal stages, the past, the present and the future, misses a fundamental point: the most powerful *reasoning* in *King Lear* belongs to the Malcontent Edmund, who possesses a reasoning which is anything but primitive. The critical search for psychological accounts have largely been attempts to dignify Edgar's position, as well as to dignify the symbolism of this scene. The much bleaker view: that this grotesque walk is neither full of promise for our lives, nor a picture of mankind making his way up through Purgatory is surely far more apt. Edgar, rather than

119   G.Wilson Knight, *The Wheel of Fire* (London, 1949).

representing the conquering Christian-chivalric hero, is instead Man in his shabby littleness. He sees with a scientific cynicism the futility of a belief in the stars; he sees through the ignorance and prejudice of a strict social and moral code that condemns him to a bastard's lot, and sets out to overturn it. At the end, he appears to accept his ultimate reprobate fate in a cycle of earthly fortune that allows no redemption and probably would not accept it if it did. If his dying speeches bear a little resemblance to Stoic fortitude, this is perceptibly at odds with his demeanour while he thought he had a fighting chance. Similarly, his role as Renaissance Man is dubiously pragmatic, as is his role as lover and, if we consider the matter entirely bathetically, as man of letters. At the end, of course, he is the soldier who claims a noble death at the hands of an equally noble opponent and, despite his final good intention: 'some good I mean to do', we cannot help but see that this is the last attempt of a dying noble to be seen to act nobly at the last, especially, perhaps, in his own eyes.

Since the 1960s, it has become more or less axiomatic with critics that *Lear* is a play which ultimately rejects all the human values it sets up. Nevertheless, these 'values' cannot be taken wholly for granted. 'Malcontent' drama is perhaps best understood as that which reveals, uncompromisingly, the terrifying aspects of Nature, and the Nature of Man, into which category his civil and civilizing nature also falls. A. P. Rossiter, writing in 1961, said:

> We are forced to recognize something germane to our 'sense of Nature' in the [dramatic] art of the sixteenth century, with its revelation of a 'terrible new universe': a world which has, as it were, split open to reveal its core, an under-nature, which invites artistic expression in terms of agony, distortion, clashing paradox, diabolism. We are also made to realise the validity of feeling like that about both external nature… and internal human nature equally.'[120]

---

120   A. P. Rossiter, op. cit.

This is what happens in *King Lear*. The play shudders with natural fear, a fear that gets continually confused with substance.
All is 'so slippery that | The fear's as bad as falling'; Lear fears
madness while he is still sane enough to make the distinction.
Once Order breaks down – broken, moreover, by Order's own
central figure, the King, Rossiter's 'under-nature' breaks out,
surges over the world, making terrible sense of Edmund's claim:
'Thou, Nature, art my goddess.' He, Goneril, Regan, Cornwall
and Oswald represent types of an 'old law of Nature' which has
reasserted itself: and the chaos which results is not only in the
State and the Family, but equally in the physical storm and in
Lear's 'the tempest in my mind', which is madness. The scenes on
the storm-blasted heath show Lear as 'unaccommodated Man',
in a natural universe where all the gods – any God – have failed.

The sixteenth and early seventeenth century had great cause
to be obsessed with breakdown, with disintegration. 'Think,'
says A. P. Rossiter,

> of what the Black Death was… and then of human rage, obsession,
> mass-hysteria; of heartless craft and treachery; of politic lying by
> those who knew their own mendacity and its cheating-value; and
> of the quintessence of the urge to destroy which invades all minds
> behind the 'pride, pomp, and circumstance, of glorious war'. All
> those are part and parcel of Nature: and there is no escape but
> by death or lunacy… unless into… various sorts of fools' paradis-
> es… This terror in Nature is only an element in the whole, but one
> which caught some of the great sixteenth-century artists by the
> throat and bore them away…'

It is perhaps the ultimate irony that we are speaking here of art,
of artists; for this is essentially contrived 'disintegration,' Chaos
in five neat acts. The ending of *King Lear* is not, after all, wave
upon wave of chaotic reality, but a series of symphonic codas.
Kyd, Marlowe, Shakespeare, Jonson, Chapman, Webster, Marston, Middleton were the artists, borne away on the terrors of

their times into sometimes vile and frequently invigorating inspiration.

BIBLIOGRAPHY

Primary Sources

ANTON, ROBERT, *The Philosophers Satyrs* (London, 1616)

ARISTOTLE, *The Works of Aristotle*, ed. W.D.Ross, 8 vols (Oxford, 1908-31).

ASCHAM, ROGER, *The Scholemaster*, ed. Edward Arber (London, 1897).

BACON, FRANCIS, *The Major Works*, ed. Brian Vickers, Oxford World Classics (Oxford, 2008).

— *The Advancement of Learning and New Atlantis*, ed. A. Johnston, (Oxford, 1974).

BALDWIN, WILLIAM, and others, *The Mirrour for Magistrates*, ed. L. B. Campbell (Cambridge, 1938).

BALE, JOHN, *Select Works of John Bale, D. D.*, ed. H. Christmas, Parker Society (Cambridge, 1848).

BEAUMONT, FRANCIS, and FLETCHER, JOHN, *The Works of Francis Beaumont and John Fletcher*, ed. A. Glover and A.R.Waller, 10 vols. (Cambridge 1905-12).

BRIGHT, TIMOTHY *Treatise on Melancholy*, ed Thomas VautroUier, Facsimile Text Society (New York, 1940).

— *The Anatomy of Melancholy*, ed. F. Dell and P. Jordan-Smith (New York, 1948).

— *The Anatomy of Melancholy*, ed. William H, Gass, NYRB Classics (NY, 2001).

CASTIGLIONE, BALDASSARE, *The Book of the Courtier*, tr. Charles S Singleton, ed Daniel Javitch, Norton Critical Editions (NY: 2002).

— *The Book of the Courtier*, tr. Sir T. Hoby, (London, 1928).

CHAPMAN, GEORGE, *Bussy D'Ambois*, ed. Nicholas Brooke, The Revels Plays (Manchester, 1964).

— *The Plays of George Chapman*, vol. 1, The Tragedies, ed. T. M. Parrott (London 1910)

— *The Plays of George Chapman*, vol. 2, The Comedies, ed. T. M. Parrott (London, 1913)

CHETTLE, HENRY, *The Tragedy of Hoffman*, ed. H. Jenkins, Malone Society (Oxford, 1950).

DAVIES, JOHN, OF HEREFORD, *The Complete Works of John Davies of Hereford*, ed. A. B. Grosart (Edinburgh, 1878).

DEKKER, THOMAS, *The Dramatic Works of Thomas Dekker*, ed. F. Bowers, 4 vols. (Cambridge, 1953-61).

DRAYTON, MICHAEL, *The Works of Michal Drayton,* ed. J. W. Hebel, 5 vols., (Oxford 1961).

EARLE, JOHN, *Microcosmographie,* ed. Edward Arber (London, 1895).

ELYOT, SIR THOMAS, *A Book Named The Governour,* ed. H. H. S. Croft, 2 vols. (1880).

ERASMUS, DESIDERIUS, *Praise of Folly,* tr. Hoyt Hopewell Hudson (Princeton, 1941).

FIELD, NATHAN, *The Plays of Nathan Field,* ed. W. Peery (Austin, Texas, 1950).

FOXE, JOHN, *The Acts and Monuments of John Foxe,* 4th edn, ed. J. Pratt, 8 vols. (1877).

GOSSON, STEPHEN, *The School of Abuse,* ed. Edward Arber (1895).

— *Plays Confuted in Five-Actions,* ed. W. C. Hazlitt, *The English Drama and Stage* (London, 1869).

GREENE, ROBERT, *The Life and Complete Works in Prose and Verse of Robert Greene, M.A.,* Cambridge and Oxford, ed. A.B.Grosart, 15 vols, (1881–6).

GREVILLE, FULKE, *Life of Sir Philip Sidney,* ed.Nowell Smith (Oxford, 1907)

— *Poems and Dramas of Fulke Greviile, First Lord Brooke,* ed. G. Bullough, 2 vols. (1938).

HALL, JOSEPH, *Characters of Virtues and Vices* (1608) in A. Davenport and T. E. Kinloch, eds. *The Life and Works of Joseph Hall* (Oxford, 1951).

HEYWOOD, THOMAS, *The Dramatic Works of Thomas Heywood,* ed. R. H. Shepherd, 6 vols. (1874).

HOBBES, THOMAS, *The English Works of Thomas Hobbes of Malmesbury,* ed. Sir William Molesworth, 11 vols. (London 1840).

HOOPER, JOHN, *Early Writings of John Hooper, D.D.,* ed. S.Carr, Parker Society (Cambridge, 1843).

JONSON, BEN, *Ben Jonson,* ed. C. H. Herford, P. and E. Simpson, 11 vols. (Oxford, 1925–52).

— *The Alchemist & Other Plays,* ed. Gordon Campbell, Oxford World's Classics (Oxford, 2008).

KYD, THOMAS, *The Spanish Tragedy,* ed. P. Edwards, The Revels Plays, (Manchester, 1959).

LODGE, THOMAS, *The Works of Thomas Lodge,* ed. Edmund Gosse, 4 vols. (London, 1883).

LYLY, JOHN, *The Complete Works of John Lyly,* ed. R. Warwick Bond, 3 vols. (Oxford, 1902).

MACHIAVELLI, NICCOLÒ, *The Discourses,* tr. L. J. Walker, rev. B. Richardson, ed. B. Crick (Harmondsworth, 1974).

— *The Prince,* tr. G.Bull, rev.edn (Harmondsworth, 1981).

MARKHAM, GERVASE and SAMPSON, WILLIAM, *The True Tragedy of Herod and Antipater,* ed. G. N. Ross (London, 1979).

MARLOWE, CHRISTOPHER, *The Works of Christopher Marlowe*, ed. A. H. Bullen, 3 vols. (London, 1885).
— *Doctor Faustus*, ed. J. D.Jump, The Revels Plays (Manchester, 1962).
— *Doctor Faustus*, ed. Rasmussen, E. and Bevington, D., The Revels Plays (Manchester, 1993).
— *Edward the Second*, ed. Charles R. Forker, The Revels Plays (Manchester, 1994).
— *The Jew of Malta*, ed. N. W. Bawcutt, The Revels Plays (Manchester, 1978).
MARSTON, JOHN, *The Works of John Marston*, ed. A. H. Bullen, 3 vols. (London, 1887).
— *The Selected Plays of John Marston*, ed.MacD.P. Jackson and M.Neill (Cambridge, 1986).
— *Antonio and Mellida*, ed. G.K.Hunter, The Revels Plays (Manchester, 1965).
— *Antonio's Revenge*, ed. G. K. Hunter, The Revels Plays (Manchester, 1966).
— *The Malcontent*, ed. G. K. Hunter; The Revels Plays (Manchester, 1975).
MIDDLETON, THOMAS, *The Works of Thomas Middleton*, ed. A. H. Bullen, 8 vols. (London 1885-6).
— *The Revenger's Tragedy*, ed. R. A. Foakes, The Revels Plays [edition attributes to Tourneur] (Manchester, 1966).
— and ROWLEY, WILLIAM, *The Changeling*, ed. Patricia Thomson, New Mermaids (London, 1964).
MONTAIGNE, MICHEL DE, *The Complete Essays of Michel de Montaigne*, trans, and ed. M. A. Screech (London, 1993).
MORE, THOMAS, *Utopia and A Dialogue of Comfort*, ed. John Warrington (2nd edn. London, 1951).
MUSSARTO, ALBERTINO, *Ecerinis* [with Antonio Loschi, *Achilles*], ed. and trans. Joseph R. Berrigan (Munich, 1975).
NASHE, THOMAS, *The Works of Thomas Nashe*, ed. R. B. McKerrow, 5 vols., 2nd edn rev. F. P. Wilson (Oxford, 1958).
NORTON, THOMAS and SACKVILLE, THOMAS, *Gorboduc, or Ferrex and Porrex*, ed. Irby B. Cauthen, Jr. (RRD, 1970).
OVERBURY, SIR THOMAS, *Miscellaneous Works of Sir Thomas Overbury*, ed. E. E. Rimbault (1890).
PAINTER, WILLIAM, *The Palace of Pleasure*, ed. J. Jacobs, 3 vols. (1890).
Parnassus Plays: *The Pilgrinage to Parnassus, The Return from Parnassus* Pt I, and *The Return from Parnassus* Pt 2 [subtitled *The Scourge of Simony*] ed. J. B. Leishmen (London, 1949).
PRESTON, THOMAS, *Cambises*, in ADAMS, (1924).

SENECA, LUCIUS ANNAEUS, *Moral Essays,* ed. and trans. John W. Basore, 3 vols. (London, 1928-35).
— *Agamemnon,* ed. R. J. Tarrant (Cambridge, 1976).
— *Hercules Furens,* ed. John G. Fitch (Ithaca, 1987).
— *Medea,* ed. C. D. N. Costa, (Oxford, 1973).
— *Phaedra,* ed. Michael Coffey and Roland Mayer (Cambridge, 1990).
— *Thyestes,* ed. R. J. Tarrant (Atlanta, 1985).
— *Troades,* ed. Elaine Fantham (Princeton, 1982).
SHAKESPEARE, WILLIAM *The Complete Works,* gen. eds S. Wells and G. Taylor (Oxford, 1986).
As You Like It, ed. Michael Hattaway, The New Cambridge Shakespeare (Cambridge, 2009).
— *Hamlet, Prince of Denmark,* ed. Philip Edwards, The New Cambridge Shakespeare (Cambridge, 2003).
— *Julius Caesar,* ed. Martin Wiggins, Penguin Shakespeare (London, 2005).
— *Othello,* ed E. A. J. Honigman, Arden Shakespeare (London, 2001).
— *The Tragedy of King Lear,* ed. Jay L. Halio The New Cambridge Shakespeare (Cambridge, 1992).
— *The Tragedy of Macbeth,* ed. Nicholas Brooke, Oxford World's Classics (Oxford, 2008)
— *The Tragedy of King Richard III,* ed. John Jowett, Oxford World's Classics (Oxford, 2008).
— *Timon of Athens,* ed John Jowett, Oxford World's Classics (Oxford, 2008).
— *Troilus & Cressida,* ed Kenneth Muir, Oxford World's Classics (Oxford, 2008).
— *Twelfth Night, of What You Will,* eds Roger Warren and Stanley Wells, Oxford World's Classics (Oxford, 2008).
SIDNEY, SIR PHILIP, *The Complete Works of Sir Philip Sidney,* ed. Albert Feuilerat, 4 vols (Cambridge, 1922–26).
STEVENSON, WILLIAM, *Gammer Gurton's Needle,* in Elizabethan Plays, ed. A. H. Nethercot, C. R. Baskerville and V. B. Heltzel, rev. edn (London, 1971).
UDALL, NICHOLAS, *Ralph Roister-Doister,* ed. Frederick S. Boas (London, 1934).
WEBSTER, JOHN, The Complete Works of John Webster, ed. F. L. Lucas, 4 vols (London, 1927).
— *The Duchess of Malfi,* ed. J.R.Brown, The Revels Plays (Manchester, 1964).
— *The White Devil,* ed. J.R.Brown, The Revels Plays (Manchester, 1960).
WILSON, JOHN, *The Dramatic Works of John Wilson,* ed. J. Maidment and W. H. Logan (London, 1874).

Secondary Sources

AGGELLER, GEOFFREY, 'Nobler in the Mind': the Stoic-Skeptic in English Renaissance Tragedy, (Newark, Delaware, 1998).

ALLEN, M. J. B., Marsilio Ficino and the Phaedran Charioteer (Berkeley, 1981).

ALTMAN, JOEL B., The Tudor Play of Mind: Rhetorical Inquiry and the Development of Elizabethan Drama, (Berkeley, Ca., 1978).

ARMSTRONG, W. A., 'The Elizabethan Conception of the Tyrant' RES 22 (1946), 161–81

— 'The Influence of Seneca and Machiavelli on the Elizabethan Tyrant,' RES 24 (1948), 19–35

AUGUSTIJN, C., Erasmus, His Life, Works, and Influence (Toronto, 1992).

AXTON, MARIE, The Queen's Two Bodies: Drama and the Elizabethan Succession (London 1977).

BABB, LAWRENCE, The Elizabethan Malady, A Study of Melancholia in English Literature from 1580 to 1642 (East Lansing, Mich., 1951).

BALDWIN, T. W., Shakespeare's Five-Act Structure (Urbana, III, 1947).

BATE, JONATHAN, Shakeapeare and Ovid (Oxford, 1993).

BAWCUTT N. W., '"Policy", Machiavellianism, and the Early Tudor Drama,' English Literary Renaissance, 1 (1971), 195–209

BEVINGTON, DAVID M., From 'Mankind' to Marlowe: Growth of Structure in the Popular Drama of Tudor England (Cambridge, Mass., 1962).

— Tudor Drama and Politics: A Critical Approach to Topical Meaning (Cambridge, Mass., 1968).

BLISS, LEE, The World's Persepctive: John Webster and the Jacobean Drama (Brighton, 1983).

BOGARD, TRAVIS, The Tragic Satire of John Webster (London, 1955).

BOWERS, FREDSON, Elizabethan Revenge Tragedy 1587-1642 (Princeton, NJ, 1940).

BOYCE, BENJAMIN, 'The Stoic Consolatio and Shakespeare,' PMLA 64 (1949), 771-80

BOYLE, A. J., (ed.), Seneca Tragicus - An Essay in the Theatrical Tradition (London, 1997).

BOYER, CLARENCE VALENTINE, The Villain as Hero in Elizabethan Tragedy (NewYork, 1914).

BRADBROOK, M. C., Themes and Conventions of Elizabethan Tragedy, 2nd edn (Cambridge, 1952).

— Shakespeare: The Poet in His World (London, 1978).

BRADEN, G., 'Senecan Tragedy and the Renaissance', Illinois Classical Studies 9 (1981), 277-92.

— *Renaissance Tragedy and the Senecan Tradition: Anger's Privilege* (New Haven, Conn. 1985).

BRADLEY, A. C., *Shakespearean Tragedy*, 2nd edn (London, 1905).

— *Feste the Jester'* in *A Book of Homage to Shakespeare*, ed. I Gollancz (Oxford, 1916), pp. 164–69.

BRAUNMULLER, A. R. and HATTAWAY, M. (eds), *The Cambridge Companion to English Renaissance Drama* (Cambridge, 1990).

BRIGGS, JULIA, *This Stage-Play World*, (Oxford, 1983).

BROOKE, NICHOLAS, 'The Moral Tragedy of Doctor Faustus,' *Cambridge Journal* 5, (1952) 662–88

— 'The Ending of King Lear' in *Shakespeare 1564-1964:A Collection of Essays by Various Hands* ed. by Edward A. Bloom (Brown, R I, 1964).

— *Shakespeare's Early Tragedies* (London 1968).

— *Horrid Laughter in Jacobean Tragedy* (London 1979).

— 'Structural Experiments in English Classic Drama' in Michel Bitot, ed. *Divers Toyes Mengled: Essays on Mediaeval and Renaissance Culture* (Tours, 1996).

BUTLER, FRANCELIA, *The Strange Crtitical Fortunes of Shakespeare's Timon of Athens* (Ames, Iowa, 1966).

CAPUTI, ANTONY, *John Marston*, Satirist (New York, 1961).

CAVELL, STANLEY, *Disowning Knowledge in Six Plays of Shakespeare* (London, 1987).

CHAMBERS, E. K., *The Elizabethan Stage*, 4 vols. (Oxford, 1923).

CHARLTON, H. B., *The Senecan Tradition in Renaissance Tragedy* (Manchester, 1946).

COOK, JUDITH, *Shakespeare's Players* (London, 1983).

COSTA, C. D. N., (éd.) *Seneca*, (London, 1974).

CRAIK, T. W., 'Violence in the English Miracle Plays', in M. Bradbury, D. Palmer and N. Denny (eds), *Medieval Drama*, Stratford-upon-Avon Studies 16 (1973), 173–95

CRUTWELL, PATRICK, *The Shakespearean Moment* (London, 1954).

CUNLIFFE, J. W., *The Influence of Seneca on Elizabethan Tragedy* (London, 1893, rept. New York, 1965).

CURTIS, MARK H., 'The Alienated Intellectuals of Early Stuart England', *Past and Present* 23 (1962), 25–43.

D'AMICO, Jack, *Shakespeare and Italy, the City and the Stage* (Gainesville, FL, 2001).

DOLLIMORE, J., *Radical Tragedy*, 2nd edn (London, 1989).

EDWARDS, PHILIP, 'Introduction to William Shakespeare,' *Hamlet, Prince of Denmark* (Cambridge, 1985), 1–71.

ELIOT, T. S., 'Seneca in Elizabethan Translation' in *Selected Essays,* 3rd edn (London, 1951), 65–105.

— 'Shakespeare and the Stoicism of Seneca', in *Selected Essays*, 3rd edn (London 1951), 126–40.

ELTON, W. R., *King Lear and the Gods* (Los Angeles, 1966).

EMPSON, WILLIAM, 'The Fool in Lear' in *The Structure of Complex Words* (London, 1951) 125–187.

EVERETT, BARBARA, 'The New King Lear' CQ 2 (1960) 325–339

FINK, Z. S., 'Jaques and the Malcontent Traveler', *Philological Quarterly* 14 (1935), 237–52.

FINKELPEARL, PHILLIP J., *John Marston of the Middle Temple* (Cambridge, Mass, 1969).

FOAKES, R. A., 'On Marston, *The Malcontent*, and *The Revenger's Tragedy*', *The Elizabethan Theatre* 4 (1978), 59–75

GIBBONS, BRIAN, *Jacobean City Comedy* (London, 1968).

GREENBLATT, STEPHEN, *Renaissance Self-Fashioning: From More to Shakespeare* (Chicago, 1980).

GRIFFIN, MIRIAM, *Seneca: A Philosopher in Politics* (Oxford, 1976).

GURR, ANDREW, *Playgoing in Shakespeare's London* (Cambridge, 1987).

HALIO, JAY L., 'Introduction to William Shakespeare', *The Tragedy of King Lear* (Cambridge, 1992), 1–89.

HANKINS, JAMES, 'Humanism and the Origins of Modern Political Thought' in Jill Kraye, ed. *The Cambridge Companion to Renaissance Humanism* (Cambridge, 1996). 118–141.

HARRISON, G. B., *The Life and Death of Robert Devereux, Earl of Essex* (London, 1933).

— 'An Essay on Elizabethan Melancholy' suffixed to Nicholas Breton, Melancholike Humours, ed. G. B. Harrison, (London, 1929), 49–89.

HEINEMANN MARGOT, *Puritanism and Theatre: Thomas Middleton and Opposition Drama under the Early Stuarts* (Cambridg,e 1980).

— 'Political Drama' in Braunmuller, A. R. and Hattaway, M. (eds) *The Cambridge Companion to English Renaissance Drama* (Cambridge, 1990), 161–206.

HERRICK, M. T., *Italian Tragedy in the Renaissance*, (Urbana, Ill., 1965).

HIJMANS, B. L., JR., 'Drama in Seneca's Stoicism', *Transactions and Proceedings of the American Philological Association* 97, (1966), 237–51.

HUNTER, G. K., 'English Folly and Italian Vice: The Moral Landscape of John Marston, J.R.Brown and B. Harris (eds.) *Jacobean Theatre*, (Stratford-upon-Avon, 1960).

— 'Introduction to John Marston', *Antonio andMellida* (London, 1965), ix–xxi.

— 'Introduction to John Marston', *Antonio's Revenge* (London, 1966), ix–xxi

— 'Seneca and the Elizabethans: a Case-Study in *"Influence"*', *Shakespeare Survey* 20 (1967), 17–26.

— 'Seneca and English Tragedy', in C. D. N.Costa (ed.) *Seneca* (1974). 166–204.

JONES, ROBERT, *Engagement With Knavery: Point of View in Richard III, The Jew of Malta, Volpone and The Revenger's Tragedy* (Durham, Duke, 1986).

KARHL, STANLEY J., *Traditions of Medieval English Drama* (London, 1974).

KENYON, J. P., *The Popish Plot,* (London, 1972).

KERNAN, ALVIN, *The Cankered Muse: Satire of the English Renaissance* (New Haven, Conn, 1959)

Kidnie, Margaret Jane, ' *"Suit the Action to the Word"*: An Early Seventeenth-Century Allusion to Hamlet in Performance', *TN* 44, (1995), 62–5.

KNIGHTS, L. C., 'Seventeenth Century Melancholy', *The Criterion* 13, (1933–4) 105–34.

— *Some Shakespearean Themes* (London, 1959).

Kott Jan, *Shakespeare Our Contemporary* (New York and London, 1964; repr. 1974).

LATHAM, AGNES, 'Intoduction to William Shakespeare', *As You Like It* (London, 1975).

LEVER, J. W., *The Tragedy of State* (London, 1971).

Lucas, F. L., *Seneca and Elizabethan Tragedy* (Cambridge, 1922).

LYONS, BRIDGET GELLERT, *Voices of Melancholy: Studies in Literary Treatments of Melancholy in Renaissance Drama* (London,1971).

McALINDON, T., *English Renaissance Tragedy* (Basingstoke, 1988).

MELCHIORI, GIORGIO, 'Peter, Balthasar, and Shakespeare's Art of Doubling', *MLR* 78(1983), 777–792.

MIOLA, ROBERT S., Shakespeare and Classical Tragedy:: The Influence of Seneca (Oxford, 1992).

MUIR, KENNETH, The Sources of Shakespeare's Plays (New Haven, Conn., 1977).

MULRYNE, J. R., 'The White Devil and The Duchess of Malfi', in J. R. Brown and B. Harris (eds.), *Jacobean Theatre,* Stratford-upon-Avon Studies 1 (1960), 201–25.

MYRICK, KENNETH, 'Christian Pessimism in *King Lear*' in *Shakespeare 1564–1964 – A Collection of Modern essays by Various Hands,* ed. by Edward A. Bloom (Brown, R. I., 1964).65–70.

ORWELL, GEORGE, 'Lear, Tolstoy and the Fool', in *Shooting an Elephant and Other Essays* (London, 1945).

PATTERSON, ANNABEL, *Censorship and Interpretation: The Condition of Writing and reading in Early Modern England* (Madison 1984).

Peat Dereck, ' *"And that's true too"*: King Lear and the Tension of Uncertainty', *SS* 33 (1980)43–53

RINGLER, A., JR., 'Shakespeare and His Actors: Some Remarks on King Lear' in Wendell M. Aycock (ed.), *Shakespeare's Art From A Comparative Perspective* (New York, 1981), 193.

ROSSITER, A. P., *Angel With Horns and Other Shakespeare Lectures*, ed. Graham Storey (London, 1961)

— *English Drama From Early Times to the Elizabethans* (London, 1950).

RUOFF, JAMES E., *Handbook of Elizabethan and Stuart Literature* (NY, 1975).

SAINTSBURY, GEORGE, *History of Elizabethan Literature*, 2 vols (London, 1890).

SALGADO, GAMINI, *The Elizabethan Underworld* (London, 1977).

SALINGAR, L. G., 'The Revenger's Tragedy and the Morality Tradition', *Scrutiny* 6 (1938), 402–423.

SANDBACH, F. H., *The Stoics* (London, 1975).

SHAPIRO, JAMES, *1599 - a Year in the Life of William Shakespeare London*, (London, 2005).

SPENCER, THEODORE, 'The Elizabethan Malcontent', in J. G. McManaway, G. E. Dawson, and E. E. Willoughby (eds.), *Joseph Quincy Adams Memorial Studies* (Washington, DC, 1948), 523–35.

— Death and Elizabethan Tragedy, (Cambridge, Mass, 1936).

SPIVACK, BERNARD, *Shakespeare and the Allegory of Evil: The History of a Metaphor in Relation to His Major Villains* (London, 1958).

STACHNIEWSKI, JOHN, *The Persecutory Imagination: English Puritanism and the Literature of Religious Despair* (Oxford, 1991).

STOLL, ELMER EDGAR, 'Shakespere, Marston, and the Malcontent Type', *Modern Philology* 3 (1905–6), 281–3.

— John Webster (Cambridge, Mass., 1905).

Stone, Lawrence, *The Crisis of the Aristocracy, 1558–1641* (Oxford, 1965).

Sturgess, Keith, *Jacobean Private Theatre* (London, 1987).

— 'Introduction', 'John Marston', *The Malcontent and Other Plays* (Oxford, 1997), vii–xxxii.

THOMAS, KEITH, *Religion and the Decline of Magic* (London, 1971).

THOMAS, VIVIAN, *The Moral Universe of Shakespeare's Problem Plays* (London, 1987).

— *Julius Caesar: New Critical Introductions to Shakespeare* (London, 1992).

VICKERS, BRIAN, *Classical Rhetoric in English Poetry* (London, 1970).

Wells, Stanlley, *Shakespeare & Co.: Christopher Marlowe, Thomas Dekker, Ben Jonson, Thomas Middleton, John Fletcher and Other Players in His Story* (London, 2006).

WELSFORD, ENID, *The Fool: His Social and Literary History* (New York, 1935).

WHARTON, T. F., 'The Malcontent and "Dreams, Visions, Fantasies"', *Essays in Criticism* (1974), 261–274.

— Moral Experiment in Jacobean Drama (Basingstoke, 1988).

WILLEFORD, WILLIAM, *The Fool and His Sceptre: A Study in Clowns and Jesters and Their Audience* (London, 1969).

WIGGINS, MARTIN, *Journeymen in Murder: The Assassin in English Renaissance Drama* (Oxford, 1991).

— (in association with Catherine Richardson), *British Drama, 1533-1642: A Catalogue,* 10 vols [projected] (Oxford, 2012–).

WILDERS, JOHN, *The Lost Garden: A View of Shakespeare's English and Roman History Plays* (London, 1978).

WILSON KNIGHT, G., *The Wheel of Fire* (London, 1949).

YACHNIN, PAUL, 'The Powerless Theater,' *ELR* 21 (1991) 49–74.

YATES, FRANCES A., *Shakespeare's Last Plays: A New Approach* (London, 1975).

INDEX

playwrights 89
fosters malcontentedness 86–94
Urbino 73
Ur-Hamlet 2
Utopia 181

V
Vair, Guillaume du
  echoed in Hamlet's words 200
  Moral Philosophie of the Stoicks
    174, 195
  on forgiveness 195
Vasques ('Tis Pity She's A Whore
    208
Vice 7, 22–23, 64, 114, 115
  antecedent of Malcontent 19, 20
  originally type of clown 20
Vindice (Revenger's Tragedy) xi, 5, 7,
    55–56, 94, 99
  made Malcontent 49–50, 55
Virgil 80
  Aeneid 111, 167
Virtue 21
Volpone 207

W
Wager, Lewis
  Life & Repentance of Marie
    Magdalene
  defends theatre 120
Walsingham, Sir Francis 126, 128
Webster, John
  additions to The Malcontent 25

Duchess of Malfi, The 5, 31, 87, 95,
    98, 101, 104
  underlying despair 105–106
  White Devil 86, 94–95
  despairing ending 210
Weis, René 95
Wells, Stanley 81
Welsford, Enid
  on the Fool 23
What You Will 86
White Devil, The 86, 94–95
  despairing ending 210
Whitehall
  Italian locations stand in for 72
White, Thomas
  denounces theatre 124–125
Wiggins, Martin 3
Winter's Tale, A 223
Wit's Miserie 84
Wittenburg, University of 175
  Hamlet alumnus 95
Wolfe, John
  publishes Machiavelli 80
Women Beware Women 72
World & the Child, The 115
Wycliffite satire 117

Y
Yachnin, Paul 11
Yorick (Hamlet) 202

Z
Zeno 180

www.ingramcontent.com/pod-product-compliance
Lightning Source LLC
Chambersburg PA
CBHW030941150426
42812CB00064B/3091/J